THE BECKHAM EXPERIMENT

THE
BECKHAM
EXPERIMENT

How the World's Most Famous Athlete
Tried to Conquer America

GRANT WAHL

 THREE RIVERS PRESS • NEW YORK

Originally published in hardcover in slightly different form
in the United States by Crown Publishers,
an imprint of the Crown Publishing Group,
a division of Random House, Inc., New York, in 2009.

Cataloging-in-Publication Data is on file with the Library of Congress.

ISBN 978-0-307-40859-4

Printed in the United States of America

1 3 5 7 9 10 8 6 4 2

First Paperback Edition

To Céline, my favorite person in the world . . .

CONTENTS

THE BECKHAM EXPERIMENT

THE BECKHAM EXPERIMENT

In the summer of 2005, on a gorgeous morning in Marina del Rey, California, I bumped into an old acquaintance in the lobby of the Ritz-Carlton Hotel. In almost any other city in any other country, David Beckham would never have dared to tempt the paparazzi and swarming fans who track his every move. But here he was, hands in his pockets, comfortable, unbothered, just like any other bloke. It had been two years since our last meeting, a long and candid interview in New York City just before Beckham's move from Manchester United to Real Madrid—the world's biggest sports story of 2003. Now Real was in town for a preseason exhibition game against the Los Angeles Galaxy. Beckham and I said hello, caught up with each other, and (not for the first time) talked about his desire to play in America someday. He sounded earnest, but I figured that day was six or seven years away, when Beckham would be a spent force on the European scene.

Less than two years later, in May 2007, I found myself sitting across from Beckham in Madrid, just the two of us in a quiet makeup room for an hour. On a rainy day in the Spanish capital, he had arrived at the studio by himself, an entourage of one in an outfit bearing no logos. In his plain white V-neck T-shirt, ordinary blue jeans, and five-year-old brown work boots, he could have passed for a cattle hand in Kalispell. In his only interview with a U.S. sports journalist before he joined the Galaxy that July, Beckham explained why he had shocked the sports world four months earlier by signing at age thirty-one with a team in Major League Soccer, the eleven-year-old U.S. soccer circuit.

"When I'd spoken to you before, the U.S. always interested me on the soccer side more than anything, and at some point I always thought I would play in America," Beckham told me. "But it came earlier maybe than I actually expected. A decision had to be made, and I've always gone on a sort of gut instinct: *Is it the right time?* I believe it's the right time. I've spent four good years in Madrid playing with some of the best players in the world. I've played in Europe for almost fifteen years at the highest level and won just about everything I possibly could. And then this was offered to me: Do I want to be an ambassador for the MLS?"

It's not often that the world's most famous athlete decides to leave the comfort and security of the environment in which he became a global icon and embark on a new and risky adventure in one of the few countries where he isn't a household name. Yet that is exactly what David Beckham was doing by leaving Europe to join the Galaxy on a five-year contract. He certainly didn't need the money after earning an estimated $150 million in the five years before his move to America. Nor did he need the fame after marrying Victoria Adams (aka Posh Spice of the British pop group the Spice Girls), winning seven league championships in England and Spain, serving as captain of England for five years, and establishing himself as an undeniable global marketing force from Europe to Asia. Nor did Beckham need to drop down to MLS's lower standard after proving with Real Madrid and England in the first half of 2007 that he could still thrive at the sport's highest levels.

But to hear Beckham make the case, the decision to relocate his wife and three young sons to Los Angeles was an easy one. "It didn't take me long to think about, to be honest," he said. "Moving the family to the U.S. was probably one of the easier decisions, just because the lifestyle was going to suit the children and me and Victoria. And on the playing side, I had to look at everything. I've always known the level is not as high as it is everywhere else in the world. But if I can make a difference and make people more aware and make kids realize that you can actually go into higher levels and make a great living playing soccer, that's what I'm going over there to do. I'm not silly enough to think I'm going to change the whole culture, because it's not going to happen. But I do have a belief that it can go to a different level, and I'd love to be part of that."

Beckham knew he was bringing a raft of expectations with him, many of which he was already trying to dispel. He was not coming to become a Hollywood actor, not then, not ever. ("Acting is never something I've been interested in," he said.) He was not coming to score three goals a game. ("That's one thing I'm worried about, because people probably do think they're going to see me turn out and we'll win our first game ten-nil.") And he was not coming simply to be a marketing tool (though his signature cologne, Instinct, was available in many fine drugstores). "I'm moving to America because of the soccer," Beckham insisted. "I didn't want to make it into a big sort of hoo-ha where it was more about other things than the soccer. It's not a big brand thing."

Yet the task facing Beckham—to make soccer matter on a regular basis in the U.S.—would be enormous. The greatest player of all time, Pelé, couldn't turn soccer into the daily religion that it is nearly every-where else in the world when he played with the New York Cosmos in the late 1970s. (His league, the NASL, folded a few years after he re-tired.) Nor did the U.S.'s hosting of the 1994 World Cup. Since its incep-tion in 1996, Major League Soccer had gained stability and produced competent young American players, but it was still losing money and had yet to advance beyond niche status. There were plenty of Americans who considered themselves occasional soccer watchers—the U.S. televi-sion audience for the 2006 World Cup final (16.9 million) beat out the average audiences for that year's NBA Finals (12.9 million) and World Series (15.8 million)—but they followed only the sport's biggest events, and the few hard-core American soccer fans preferred the European Champions League and the superior leagues in England, Spain, and Mexico to MLS.

Despite the challenges, the man who created *American Idol* was convinced that Beckham could pull it off. Simon Fuller, Beckham's manager and the chief executive of 19 Entertainment, acknowledged that making soccer really matter in the U.S. would be a "far greater" challenge than his previous successes, which included turning *Idol* into America's most popular television program and conquering the U.S. market with the Spice Girls in the 1990s. But that hadn't stopped this mastermind of the music world from hatching a "grand vision" (Fuller's words) for the next chapter of his most famous sports client's career. "There seems to be a real foundation now for soccer" in America, said Fuller. "David is the most iconic of footballers, and he's achieved pretty much everything you can achieve in Europe, apart from maybe winning a big tournament with England. He's still in his early thirties, still playing remarkably well, and you have to start thinking: What's the next adventure? The States is the last frontier in terms of soccer. Everywhere else on earth, soccer is huge. It's *the* sport. And while many people have tried before, no one has seemed to have cracked America."

The last frontier. A grand vision. An adventure. There was something quintessentially American about what these Brits were trying to achieve. Beckham vowed that he was in this New World Adventure—the Beckham Experiment—for the long haul. Otherwise, why would he have signed a five-year deal? "If you have most things you want in life, you can take it easy, you can retire, you can continue to take money off a team in Europe," Fuller said. "But together with David our ambition is bigger than that. Shoot for the stars, and if you don't hit them, then it was fun trying.

"If you do hit them, then you've made history."

Having covered the U.S. soccer scene for ten years at *Sports Illustrated*, I knew that the Beckham Experiment would be one of the most audacious projects in recent sports history, not least because the chances for failure were so high and the personalities involved were so big.

The next two years would perhaps be the most rollicking stretch of Beckham's storied career. There would be plenty of surprises, good ones and bad ones. There would be lost-in-translation frustrations and unintentional comedy. There would be full stadiums, media hype galore, and the enormous ego clashes that result whenever you mix money, sports, and Hollywood. The most compelling aspect of the Beckham Experiment was this: Nobody knew how it was going to turn out. Even if Beckham and the Galaxy were successful on the field, would mainstream America respond? Would Beckham's undeniable charm win over the Yanks? Or would he be just another Robbie Williams, joining the ranks of Brits whose worldwide appeal failed to translate on these shores?

If there was ever a book about American soccer that demanded to be written, this was the one, in large part because it was about not just the sport but so much more: the engineering of American celebrity, the powerful seeking more power, the clash of cultures and American exceptionalism. For years, too, I had craved the chance to chronicle the ongoing inside story of a team, to do more than just parachute into town for a couple days for a snapshot magazine story. It was one thing to interview Beckham in Madrid on the eve of his American arrival, when optimism reigned and he had as much buzz as any Hollywood blockbuster. But it would be quite another to interview him underneath the stands in Columbus, Ohio, on Buck-a-Brat night after a Galaxy loss in October.

And so, in the summer of 2007, I began a sixteen-month journey following Beckham and the Galaxy across America, a pursuit that continued until the global saga leading up to his scheduled return to the Galaxy from Italian giant AC Milan in July 2009. I went to the games, of course, but I also visited the offices, homes, and hotels of the players, the coaches, the moneymen, and the message shapers. I had meals with them in their houses, in Los Angeles–area diners and dive bars, and in fancy New York City sushi restaurants. Along the way I developed an even greater appreciation for American soccer players, who tend to be smarter and more insightful than their counterparts overseas and in other sports, owing to their college educations, their need to find other jobs during and after their playing days, and the humility that comes with earthbound incomes (as little as $12,900 a year) and soccer's place in the pecking order of American sports.

For years, whenever anyone has learned that I cover soccer for an American sports magazine, I am invariably asked when the sport will "make it" in the United States. My answer is always the same: Hell if I know. I am not a soccer proselytizer, and I don't know if soccer will ever be one of the top three spectator sports in the United States. But I do love this game, and I find it fascinating that so many wealthy investors—wildly successful billionaires, in fact—continue to sink so many dollars into the proposition that soccer can indeed "make it" here as a viable enterprise.

Ultimately, the purpose of the Beckham Experiment was to try to change soccer's position in the hierarchy of U.S. spectator sports. By the time it was over, Beckham's American adventure would be regarded as the moment soccer finally reached a tipping point in the United States—or as the moment the American consumer proved impervious to the machinations of a star-making expert like Simon Fuller. David Beckham may have been desperate to crack America, but so too was soccer itself. Whether or not they succeeded, it was going to be one memorable journey.

CHAPTER 1

WE ♥ BECKHAM

The man at the wheel of the Cadillac Escalade was nervous.

Not nervous about the paparazzi. David Beckham viewed the men with the cameras as a benign nuisance, a presence as constant as the Southern California sun, even though a larger swarm than usual—more than three dozen—was waiting for him this morning outside the iron gate of the Beckham estate on San Ysidro Drive. His new home was a spectacular mansion, even by Beverly Hills standards: an $18.2 million, 13,000-square-foot Xanadu with an Italian-style red tile roof and sprawling views of Los Angeles all the way to the Pacific. His wife, Victoria, had filled the house with orchids, and near the pool outside stood two palm trees, which the Beckhams' three young sons quickly turned into a makeshift soccer goal.

Nor was Beckham nervous about the perilous drive ahead. It was 7:30 A.M. on July 13, 2007, Beckham's first full day living in the United States, the day the Los Angeles Galaxy would introduce him as the newest member of the American sports firmament. When asked if he'd be riding in a helicopter to Galaxy practice, the better to avoid the notorious Los Angeles traffic, Beckham had acted as if his manhood was being challenged. "No, definitely not," he said. "I'll have a car, and I'll be driving." An automobile connoisseur with a taste for hip-hop culture, Beckham had bought a customized black Escalade, a massive SUV with twenty-four-inch alloy rims. His number, 23, was stitched into the leather headrests and cast in a medallion that replaced the Cadillac insignia on the grille. It was perfect for Hollywood, the kind of car you'd see on MTV's *Pimp My Ride*.

Yet Beckham couldn't help but feel butterflies as he drove down

Angelo Road, west on Sunset Boulevard, and south on the San Diego Freeway, past Santa Monica, past Manhattan Beach, past the city's fashionable addresses, until he arrived in Carson, a working-class suburb composed of African-Americans and immigrant neighborhoods of Korean-, Chinese-, and Hispanic-Americans. The main entrance of the Home Depot Center, Beckham's new professional home, was across the street from a KFC. The HDC itself was a lush sporting playground, a $150 million complex that included tennis and track-and-field stadiums, an indoor velodrome, twelve soccer practice fields, the Los Angeles branch of the David Beckham Academy, and the Galaxy's 27,000-seat stadium, the finest soccer facility in the United States. Beckham passed security, parked his Escalade near the bottom of the stadium's supply ramp, and took a deep breath.

You could learn a lot about Beckham from his first drive to work in Los Angeles. He was smitten with fancy cars. He enjoyed having fun with the paparazzi by taking them through drive-thru windows, like the one at Starbucks where Beckham grabbed his usual *venti* java. He was obsessive about punctuality, always arriving early to events, the sort of OCD behavior that drove him to arrange soda-pop cans in identical rows of four in the refrigerator, labels facing forward, and to vacuum perfectly straight lines in the living-room carpet, like the mowed rows of a soccer field. And, not least, he got nervous when it came to public speaking or meeting new people.

Beckham's new Galaxy teammates might have been shocked to know that Beckham was just as anxious about meeting *them* as they were about meeting him. "Joining a new team is always quite daunting, quite scary," Beckham admitted. "I wish I had a chance to meet the players before going over, but it's not been possible." As for the thousands of Galaxy fans and hundreds of international media who had assembled to hear Beckham address the masses, they'd be surprised to know that the most famous athlete in the world was a self-described introvert. "I'm shy," Beckham said. "Even when I'm in England, people say, 'Why aren't you talking?' I'm not a man who'll sit there and chat and chat and chat. I'm a quiet person."

Beckham's sensitive nature—he called it his "feminine side"—was ingrained early on in his life. "I get it from my mum," he said. "My dad's sort of a man's man, but I've got more of my mum's personality. She's a lot softer, a lot more affectionate. We both get really emotional." Beckham cried when Victoria gave birth to their sons, Brooklyn, Romeo, and Cruz. He cried that awful night in 1998 when he was red-carded at the World Cup and became the Most Hated Man in England. He cried a year later when he won back his nation's affection, and he cried again when he gave up the England captaincy in 2006. "I'll even watch films and cry," he said. There would be no tears on the first day of the Beckham Experiment, the first chapter of a new era for Beckham and for American soccer itself. But make no mistake: Beckham's insides would be churning.

In the annals of American sports, it would be hard to imagine a monument to celebrity excess more extreme than the scene that took place on Friday, July 13, 2007, at the Home Depot Center. On the morning that the Galaxy introduced David Beckham as its newest member, the tableau included 5,000 fans, more than 700 media members from a dozen countries, a hovering news helicopter, 65 television cameras, and a pair of cannons belching a blizzard of blue-and-yellow confetti—with every second transmitted live via satellite around the world.

All for a soccer player. In the United States.

No country can match the U.S. when it comes to turning a mundane event into a glitz-filled Hollywood spectacle. From the moment Galaxy fans began arriving at 7 A.M. (for Beckham's 10 A.M. presentation), they started belting out songs in honor of their newest player, like the one to the tune of "Guantanamera":

One David Beckham!
There's only one David Beckham!
One David Beeeeeck-ham!

As workers put the finishing touches on a makeshift stage in a corner of the Home Depot Center, a reporter from France's Canal+ waved his arms frantically over his head and screamed ("BECKHAM!!! BECK-HAM!!! BECKHAM!!!") in an attempt to convince a young female in

Galaxy gear to do the same for his cameraman. Holding a WE ❤ BECK-HAM sign, she dutifully complied.

As the sun climbed in a nearly cloudless sky, hundreds of photographers, videographers, and reporters were still waiting for their credentials in a line snaking away from the will-call window. Even the grizzled veterans had a common refrain: *I've never seen anything like this before.* Not at the Olympics. Not at the NBA Finals. Not anywhere.

About the only person who wasn't acting as though Beckham was some sort of deity was Beckham himself. In a city where everyone who's anyone arrives fashionably late, Beckham showed up at the stadium a half hour early, even accounting for his side trip to Starbucks. The caffeine was crucial; he'd arrived at LAX Airport from London with his family only the previous night, welcomed by a swarm of media and a strobe-fest of camera flashes. While the Beckhams' three sons, all dressed in matching outfits, had left the international arrivals terminal through a side exit, David and Victoria had entered the maw of the media gauntlet, David smiling, Victoria wearing shades and her usual pout. From the moment they had set foot on American soil, it was clear that the Beckhams would draw just as much attention as they had everywhere else—maybe even more.

It was 8:30 the next morning when Beckham, resplendent in a gray suit, a white shirt, and a matching silk pocket square, walked through the door. The Galaxy was expecting him at 9.

"What the hell are you doing here already?" joked Galaxy president Alexi Lalas when they met, clapping Beckham on the back.

"I guess I left early," came the smiling reply. In addition to being a stickler for punctuality, Beckham had been told that it could take as long as an hour and a half to make the trek from Beverly Hills to Carson, and he was pleasantly surprised that he'd covered the distance in a mere fifty minutes.

They met briefly with the coaching staff, trading wisecracks that they must have been attending a wedding with all the business suits in the room, and then all they could do was wait. "He was here so early that most of the guys weren't here yet, so we walked out into the locker room just really casual," Lalas said. "As the players trickled in he was kind of just there. Some of the guys walked right past him and did a double take. You expect it to be so much more monumental. They have this perception of him that's formed by pop culture, and there he is in the locker room, and he cracks jokes and he's got jet lag and he's tired. It's important for those guys to get over that awe, if there is any, and to treat him like a player and make fun of him and relax."

In an effort to learn more about his Galaxy teammates, Beckham had discussed each one with coach Frank Yallop when Yallop and Lalas had visited him in Madrid that spring. They told him about Landon Donovan, the prodigiously talented young U.S. forward who had yet to tap his full potential; Cobi Jones, the dreadlocked winger who was playing in his last MLS season; Peter Vagenas, the cerebral central midfielder who'd been involved in both of the Galaxy's MLS Cup-winning teams; and Joe Cannon, the heart-on-his-sleeve goalkeeper whose father had been a Las Vegas lounge singer.

Of all the petri-dish experiments occasioned by Beckham's arrival in MLS, the most fascinating would be how one of the world's most famous and highest-paid athletes interacted with teammates who made as little as $12,900 a year. It was an arrangement that would test every bit of Beckham's desire to be just one of the lads. "It doesn't make me feel strange," Beckham said about the income disparity. "I'm never going to be a player who distances himself from other players just because we earn different money. So for me that part of it is never going to be a problem."

In fact, Beckham added, he wanted to reprise the warm atmosphere that he'd enjoyed at Manchester United (where he and six teammates rose from the youth ranks to the senior team) but found lacking during his days at the comparatively chilly Real Madrid. "It's important for me to get to know the players and also for Victoria to get to know the players' wives and girlfriends," he explained. "Hopefully when we do move to the U.S. it's going to be more like it was at Manchester, where on Sundays we used to take our sons to one of the other players' houses and have a barbecue. I'm hoping it's going to be that sort of vibe, because it would be great to have that again."

He was only one man, a thirty-two-year-old transplant from England with common-guy visions of taking his sons to Disneyland and the beach, of making his first treks to Vegas and the Napa Valley wine country, of organizing late-night runs to the local fast-food joint. "In-N-Out Burger. Ohhhh . . ." said Beckham, imagining his new life. "That's another great experience. I went inside the last time I was there."

David Beckham could be disarmingly *normal*. It was part of his transcendent appeal, of course. But when literally thousands were coming to worship at the altar of Beckham's global celebrity, it was just as clear how many people had something significant at stake *in one man*, how many reputations and careers and futures were riding on the Beckham Experiment. All those dependents were here today: fans and agents and publicists, friends and family members, sponsors and businesspeople, staffers and executives for the Galaxy and MLS. And, not least, Beckham's new teammates, who were only now, just after 9 A.M., filing into the team's modest locker room.

One by one, Beckham shook their hands (*I'm Chris, I'm Kyle, I'm Joe*) until he came to forward Alan Gordon.

"Hey, I'm Alan," Gordon said. But when Beckham tried to move on to the next player, Gordon kept holding his hand. "And *you* are?"

Beckham smiled sheepishly. "I'm David."

Everyone laughed. It was a classic Gordon move, an ice-breaker that lightened the mood in the locker room. Gordo, as his teammates called him, may have been making only $30,870 a year compared to Beckham's $6.5 million, but he wasn't starstruck by anyone in Los Angeles, and his own good looks—flowing dark hair, chiseled jaw, deep SoCal tan—combined with a subversive sense of humor helped him to pull in men and women alike. Why, the day after Beckham had signed with the Galaxy six months earlier, Gordon had "played the dumb guy," as he put it, while sitting at a bar next to a woman who gushed over Beckham's image on the television screen.

"Omigosh, David Beckham's coming!" she said.

"Who?" came Gordon's reply.

"He plays for the Galaxy."

"Oh, the Ga-lax-y. That's the . . . soccer team?"

Gordon wanted to know what people really thought about the Galaxy—if they thought anything at all—so he'd play the dumb guy on a regular basis in bars and restaurants. He was always making light of his anonymity, a circumstance that was perhaps about to change in a big way. An admittedly slow 6'3", 192-pound target man with an up-and-down scoring touch and a penchant for injuries, the twenty-five-year-old Gordon was the typical mid-level MLS player, circa 2007. His microscopic salary was a result of the league's salary cap, which limited each team to $2.1 million for its entire roster (with one exception beyond the cap allowed for a player like Beckham). How do you live in L.A. on a near-minimum-wage income? Gordon had to share an apartment in Redondo Beach with forward Gavin Glinton (salary: $50,000) and defender Kyle Veris ($17,700), and for the past three years Gordon had earned extra money by coaching a girls' soccer team on the side, many days racing from Galaxy practice to the girls' practice on the crowded L.A. freeways.

By his own account Gordon had been a teenage delinquent, a seventeen-year-old no-hoper in Gilbert, Arizona, who'd moved out of his single father's house, been arrested multiple times for shoplifting and marijuana possession, and once even collapsed on the field in a club soccer game during his junior year after an all-night drug binge. "I was doing every drug you could think of," said Gordon, who was convinced that soccer had saved his life. A coach from Yavapai College in Prescott, Arizona, spotted him at a tumbleweed club tournament in 1999 and offered him a scholarship. Gordon moved in for six months with his high school coach, quit drugs cold turkey, excelled at Yavapai and then at Oregon State University, won Rookie of the Year honors after scoring seventeen goals for the second-tier Portland Timbers, and signed with the Galaxy in 2004. He had been good enough to stick with the team for three years ("He's got a soft foot for a big man," said Lalas), despite dealing with all the injuries and sometimes brutal public criticism. Fans on the Galaxy's message board at Bigsoccer.com had dubbed Gordon "Snowshoes" and "Flash" due to his lack of speed, while a columnist at ESPN.com had suggested the Galaxy would do better to replace Gordon with the U.S. women's striker Abby Wambach.

Now the onetime no-hoper would be receiving crosses from none other than David Beckham, and it would be up to him—Alan Freaking Gordon, of all people—to summon the skills to finish them. Indeed,

Gordon knew there would be plenty on the line for him now that Beckham had arrived. Play poorly, and the Galaxy wouldn't renew his contract at season's end. Play well, and he could stay in L.A. for another season—and maybe even draw some interest from overseas clubs. "People are watching everywhere," Gordon said. A former college teammate living in England had called to say he'd seen Gordon on TV there in the Beckham news coverage. "This is either going to be the best thing ever or the worst thing ever for me," Gordon reasoned. "If you do really well, everybody's going to see you do it. But if you don't do well, everybody's going to see it, and they're going to think you suck."

After most of the Galaxy players had met Beckham, Landon Donovan strode into the locker room through the training-room door. As soon as he walked in, Donovan could feel a buzz in the room, a thrum of excitement that was different, palpable. He looked around and noticed that his teammates all had smiles on their faces, a rare occurrence in a season that had started poorly. Donovan saw Beckham, walked over, and offered the Englishman a smile and a handshake: "Welcome to Los Angeles. It's good to have you here." They exchanged some small talk. Even Donovan sensed that it was a little awkward at first.

That would have to change. If the Beckham Experiment was going to work—if the Galaxy was going to not just sell jerseys but win games—Beckham would need a cold-blooded, world-class finisher on the ends of his passes. Nobody could deny Donovan's game-changing potential, especially in MLS. At twenty-five he was on the verge of becoming the U.S. national team's all-time leading goal scorer, and he had already guided his teams to three MLS Cup championships. Blessed with explosive speed, refined technical skills, and a laserlike finishing ability, Donovan burst onto the global scene as a twenty-year-old at the 2002 World Cup, where he scored two goals during the U.S.'s surprise run to the quarterfinals. By the summer of 2007, most American soccer aficionados considered Donovan, a native of Ontario, California, the most talented field player the U.S. had ever produced.

But critics argued that Donovan had squandered his chance to become the first U.S. superstar in European club soccer. On two occasions

(1999–2001 and 2005), Donovan had played for Bayer Leverkusen of the German Bundesliga, and on two occasions he had fought homesickness, failed to earn a regular lineup spot, and returned home to MLS teams in California. Donovan's tentative performance during the 2006 World Cup, in which the U.S. had made a first-round exit, only reinforced the notion that his age-group contemporaries (such as Michael Essien of Ghana and Chelsea FC) had left Donovan behind. His detractors now derided him as soft, nicknaming him "Landycakes."

Would Donovan and Beckham hit it off? "I've heard he's a great guy," Donovan said of Beckham. "And I think it'll be interesting to see how he integrates socially into the team. Will he want to come out? Will he bring the kids? Will he bring Victoria? Some of the guys like to hang out off the field, too, so I think he'll get pulled into that if he wants to."

Donovan was just as curious about how he and Beckham would interact on the soccer field, not least because he knew his own reputation could rise if the Beckham Experiment proved successful. Tim Leiweke, the CEO of AEG, which owned the Galaxy, argued that Beckham would make Donovan a world-class player. "That's the theory, right?" Donovan said. "He'll come in and I'll get better service and more of the ball. But who knows? It's going to be weird the first time we play a game. There's going to be so much excitement and promotion going on. Are guys going to get rattled on our team? On the other team? How's it going to pan out? It's not as easy as you plug him in and he hits a long-ball and I go score."

Donovan talked a good game, insisting that he and Beckham could be beneficial for each other. Yet Galaxy officials (including coach Frank Yallop) were acutely aware of the potential for tension between the team's alpha dogs. How would Donovan handle being replaced as the Galaxy's main attraction? A year after becoming the Galaxy's captain, would Donovan give up the captain's armband to Beckham—who, after all, had captained England for nearly six years? And while Donovan earned a salary of $900,000 a year, far greater than what the rest of their teammates were paid, would he begrudge Beckham's eight-figure annual income, especially if Donovan, not Beckham, ended up being the Galaxy's best player?

"As long as he comes to play and works hard, I don't think anyone cares," Donovan said. "Guys are astute enough to understand why he's making what he's making. It would be kind of a nice gesture if he came in and just splashed the locker room with cash for some of the younger guys, but I don't think it's going to be a big issue."

Pause. Smile.

"And he'd better be picking up meals and shit, too, or else I'll call him out on it."

Outside, as the clock approached 10 A.M., the more than 5,000 fans and 700 media members were transforming the scene into a frenzy. Victoria Beckham sashayed onto the field, and a battery of photographers began jostling like a school of starved fish at feeding time. Her look was pure Posh: a knee-length fuchsia sheath dress, an oversized Birkin bag in the same electric shade, huge black Jackie O sunglasses, a new blond bob hairdo that would soon take over America, and six-inch stiletto heels that would have dug into the grass had she not been so perilously thin.

Victoria knew what to do. Facing the wall of photographers, she stuck one knee in front of the other and placed her left hand on the hip of her dress. In an odd way, the pose looked a lot like the one her husband assumed before one of his signature free kicks. Her face was fixed, unsmiling, a Blue Steel gaze that David favored as well, the better to avoid showing their not-quite-perfect teeth in photographs. And then she held it. All of it. For sixty seconds. It was affected. It was preposterous. It was perfect.

The Galaxy fans roared. "One of us! One of us! One of us!" they screamed, and Victoria waved in appreciation, both sides apparently unaware of the chant's over-the-top absurdity.

From the moment David Beckham began dating Victoria Adams at the height of the Spice Girls craze in 1997, they had been daily fodder in the British tabloids. After the period of national grieving over Princess Diana's death in August 1997, the royal family appeared drab next to the new pop couple. (The tabs dubbed their twenty-four-acre spread Beckingham Palace.) Introduced by Victoria to the fashion world, David embraced its trappings; he was photographed wearing a sarong while staying at Sir Elton John's vacation house in France. "Kids love each change of hairstyle, and I think he has taste," the British author Nick Hornby told me once. "Maybe not your taste or my taste, but a real instinct for keeping himself looking cool in the eyes of five- to twenty-year-olds." Victoria's influence—over those instincts and most everything else in David's life—was, to use one of her favorite words, major.

The move to their new $18.2 million home in Beverly Hills was certainly good for Victoria, who had never embraced Madrid during David's four years in Spain—and whose refusal to move there at first may have contributed to David's highly publicized alleged affair with a nanny named Rebecca Loos, which he denied. Though her solo singing career had been a washout, Victoria and her handlers had a masterly touch for keeping her in the public eye, and she was now designing jeans, sunglasses, and perfume. The Spice Girls had announced that they were getting back together for a reunion tour starting in December 2007, and Victoria was also filming a one-hour reality special about her life in L.A. that would appear on NBC. Yet there was insurance even if Victoria's career didn't catch fire Stateside. After all, she was now living in a celebrity-obsessed culture in which you could be famous for being famous, and her new best friends included such A-listers as Katie Holmes, Eva Longoria Parker, and Jennifer Lopez.

For the Galaxy, it was vitally important to create a welcoming environment from the start, not just for David, but also for Victoria and the Beckhams' three sons: Brooklyn, eight; Romeo, four; and Cruz, two. As Lalas explained, "When Victoria's happy, the Beckham world is a whole lot happier place." And on this day, at least, as the media beamed her image around the world, Victoria was undeniably happy. On her way out of the Home Depot Center, she would stop in the Galaxy team store to buy so many soccer balls, warm-ups, T-shirts, and Beckham jerseys for family members that her assistants could barely get them out the door, past a swarm of paparazzi, and into the black Lexus SUV waiting for her outside.

Her total bill: $583.

Now that Victoria had warmed up the crowd and taken her seat in the VIP section in front of the stage, it was time for the main event. First came the music, a thumping beat over the stadium's sound system, with the same phrase repeated over and over: "HELLO, AMERICA." Then David Beckham emerged from the tunnel, flanked by various soccer officials, and made his way through a wall of sound—cheers, music, and high-pitched screams—to the stage.

The men in suits kept their remarks mercifully brief, given the direct sun beating down on the proceedings. Leiweke, the CEO of the Galaxy's ownership group, announced that 250,000 new Beckham jerseys had been ordered from Adidas. Then came MLS commissioner Don Garber ("This is truly a historic day. It's a moment we should all cherish"), followed by Galaxy coach Frank Yallop ("It's been a long wait, believe me. The team cannot wait to get him on the field"). Then Lalas took the podium, welcomed past and present Galaxy players in the audience, and cut to the chase. "If you have a camera," he announced, "this might be a good time to take the lens cap off." And with that, Lalas introduced Beckham, pulled out the new white Galaxy number 23 jersey, and presented it to the man of the moment. Beckham raised the jersey to the sky, the music blasted once again, and the giant confetti cannons on both sides of the stage erupted, spewing tens of thousands of pieces of blue-and-yellow paper into the air.

Sitting next to Victoria in the VIP section, his white shirt untucked in the classic SoCal style, Simon Fuller stood along with everyone else and applauded. Like the scene unfolding around him, Fuller didn't do subtle. Long before he became Beckham's manager, the *American Idol* creator had turned the Spice Girls into a global juggernaut through clever promotion, lucrative-if-disposable spin-offs (like the movie *Spiceworld*), and a drill sergeant's demand for long work hours from Victoria and her bandmates. Not for nothing was Fuller often identified by the British tabloids as a Svengali. Yet for all his success, Fuller studiously avoided the spotlight himself, rarely gave interviews, and seemed content to be mistaken by nearly everyone for Simon Cowell, the hypercritical judge on *American Idol*.

It was Fuller who insisted that the press release announcing Beckham's signing include a line that his five-year deal could bring him

$250 million, even though media around the world misinterpreted that claim to mean *his Galaxy contract* was worth $250 million. In fact, whereas Beckham's endorsements, jersey royalties, and other revenue streams *might* bring him $250 million in a best-case scenario, Beckham's Galaxy salary would pay him far less ($32.5 million) over that span.

Nor did Fuller shy away from rhetorical grandstanding, proclaiming that the "grand vision" for Beckham's move across the Atlantic was his idea. Fuller's frequent use of the term "we" to describe David Beckham was revealing—and more than a little bit eerie. "I thought, well, if we're going to America for a grand vision, there are ways of structuring a deal that make it not a ridiculous move," Fuller said. "I think it led me to coming up with a very creative deal that I worked out together with [AEG bosses Tim Leiweke and Phil Anschutz] that really worked for everyone and evolved into probably the biggest sports deal of all time. That's because as we started to go down that road there's a lot of interest in soccer doing well in America, whether that's from big sports companies like Adidas or whether it's through sponsors that want to be in sport and feel that soccer is a great sport to be in, or whether it was David's existing sponsors that have years of a relationship with him that want to take that relationship to another level by going to America."

The business relationship between Fuller's 19 Entertainment and the Galaxy's owner, AEG, was based on far more than just David Beckham. AEG was one of the top two music concert promoters in the United States and owned some 130 concert venues around the world, while 19 represented some of the world's most popular recording artists, including Amy Winehouse, Carrie Underwood, and all the other stars of the *American Idol* franchise, to say nothing of the Spice Girls. It was no coincidence that AEG had signed on to promote the Spice Girls' reunion tour, which would kick off its U.S. swing that December at the AEG-owned Nokia Theater in Los Angeles and continue with seventeen dates the following month at the AEG-owned O2 Arena in London. In other words, Victoria's career interests were inextricably linked to David's move to America. "The more we talked and thought about it, the more it resonated with everything that we were doing and wanted to do," Fuller explained. "It works for Victoria because America is a place she loves and she spends a lot of time there. It was an idea that grew and grew, and it became a reality."

Beckham didn't speak long: two minutes and twenty-three seconds, to be exact. But he didn't put a foot wrong, thanking the fans, pledging himself to the Galaxy for the five years of his contract ("and maybe a few years later"), and even apologizing for his native Briticisms. "I've always looked for challenges in my career," Beckham said, standing confidently at the microphone. "My family have now moved to Los Angeles, something we're looking forward to, something we're very proud of, and in our life everything's perfect. For me the most important thing in life is my family. The second thing is the football." He grinned. "Sorry, the soccer. I'll get used to that."

The man could work a room—and a stadium. So much for nerves. "Thank you to everyone," he concluded, "who's made my dream come true."

Now that the photographers had their money shot—a beaming Beckham raising his Galaxy jersey as the confetti flew—things quickly devolved into delicious farce. Los Angeles mayor Antonio Villaraigosa was introduced and roundly booed by the Galaxy fans, the result of his previous public support for intracity rival Chivas USA. Burnishing his huckster credentials, Lalas announced that new Galaxy jerseys were available at all Sports Authority retail stores. Then he ended the formal stage show by making like International Olympic Committee president Jacques Rogge: "Thank you, and let the games begin!"

Let the games begin? Classic.

Ever the showman, Lalas had been part of the American star-making factory before. "I lived the power of a World Cup," he said, "and unlike any event in the world it can change your life." Thirteen years earlier, the red-maned, Uncle Sam–bearded Lalas had become the U.S. poster boy of the 1994 World Cup, a guitar-strumming defender who helped lead the underdog hosts to an upset victory over Colombia and a berth in the second round. Overnight, it seemed, Lalas was in demand. "Letterman, Leno, free drinks around the world. All the usual clichés," he said. "Wine, women, and song. Never has so much been done with a modicum of talent, a little facial hair, and a guitar."

Lalas became the first American in the modern era to play in Italy's Serie A, for Padova, and even after his retirement from the game he was viewed abroad as a symbol of U.S. soccer. In 2005, while reporting a story on Arab-Israeli soccer star Abbas Suan in a dusty town not far from the Lebanese border, I asked Suan if he knew anything about American soccer. Without missing a beat, he pulled a long imaginary beard down from his chin. *Lalas.*

The beard was gone now. Lalas had cleaned up, gone corporate, and yet in other ways the Galaxy's highly quotable front man hadn't changed a bit. A guitar bearing the new Galaxy logo—the one Lalas helped design—was one of the first things you saw in his office. "I'm still a mess on the inside," Lalas joked, and at thirty-seven his shtick was more or less the same now that he was a suit: to shoot off his mouth and promote the sport by any means necessary. For this was Lalas's article of faith: If soccer was going to succeed in the United States, it needed more than just skilled players. It needed personalities, celebrities, *entertainers.* Wasn't entertainment what the *E* in AEG stood for? "That's what I love about sports," Lalas said. "I love the criticism and the analysis and the rumor and speculation and innuendo, not just about what the guy did on the field but what the guy did off the field. That's personality. That's excitement. That's fuckin' entertainment. I don't think enough players are encouraged to express themselves."

Yet Lalas had won his share of enemies and detractors as a soccer executive, and his outlandish statements struck some observers as the remarks of a buffoon. Lalas had already earned mocking headlines in the U.K. for claiming that MLS's parity made it far more competitive (and, in his view, entertaining) than the English Premier League. And despite Lalas's bold proclamations that he wanted the Galaxy to become MLS's first global SuperClub ("get it right: big *S*, big *C*, all one word"), his teams had yet to win many games. In Lalas's three full seasons as a GM with AEG-owned clubs in San Jose, New York, and Los Angeles, his teams had never advanced beyond the first round of the playoffs. Nor did it help that this season's Galaxy, which had failed to reach the postseason in 2006, had gotten off to a dreadful 3–5–4 start. Lalas wasn't stupid. He knew that his job could be in serious danger if the Galaxy didn't start winning with Beckham. Even his own players had their doubts about Lalas. As Donovan said, "I think Alexi's in over his head."

"Welcome to David Beckham's America," announced Pat O'Brien, the former CBS sportscaster turned Hollywood celebrity news host, kicking off a breathless report into one of dozens of television cameras on the stadium turf. It was almost 2 P.M. now, and over O'Brien's shoulder Beckham was about to complete a task that was remarkable by any measure: providing exclusive sound bites over a nearly two-hour period to more than sixty global broadcast outlets, from *Access Hollywood* to CNN to Al-Jazeera—in the searing ninety-degree sun, no less, with his suit coat still on and his shirt collar still fastened tight. It was a wonder that Beckham hadn't fainted.

Beckham's capacity for working the never-ending rope line was breathtaking. From a publicity standpoint, Beckham's first full day in America had come off as a Hollywood blockbuster. There had been no gaffes, the media turnout was even greater than expected, and Beckham had been charming to a fault. He was on the cover of the newest edition of *Sports Illustrated*, his wife was soon to appear in her own NBC prime-time special, and in a week he'd be making his Galaxy exhibition debut against Chelsea on national television in front of nineteen ESPN cameras, including a Celebrity Cam and a special Beckham Cam. The man himself appeared genuinely thankful for the outpouring of interest, and even a bit overwhelmed. But Beckham also knew the work that lay ahead. "The hype is there at the moment, and the hype will be there for maybe six months," he said. "But to keep the interest in soccer—that's going to be the challenge."

And yet, as I thought back to Beckham's fifteen-minute exchange with me and thirty other national print reporters in "Event Suite No. 2" that afternoon, I couldn't help but recall that you can only stage-manage celebrity perfection so much. In fact, if you sat next to Beckham and looked closely, you'd see that his otherwise immaculate $3,000 gray suit was missing a button on its right cuff. For most people this would be no big deal, but for an international fashion icon as detail-obsessed as Beckham it was shocking, the sartorial equivalent of forgetting to wear pants, a reminder that despite appearances to the contrary not everything was perfect in David Beckham's world.

Not that you would know judging from the questions tossed his way in the room that day. A reporter from *People* magazine asked Beckham about his much-publicized friendship with actors Tom Cruise and Katie Holmes. ("They're good friends of ours, and they've welcomed us so far really, really amazingly.") Another questioner asked if Beckham wanted to become an actor. ("I'm just here to play football, to play soccer, sorry.") And another asked about the brand of Beckham's suit. ("Burberry.")

On July 13, 2007—Friday the thirteenth—not one of us in the room asked about his injured left ankle.

CHAPTER 2

THE BECKHAM SWEET SPOT

O n the morning of July 16, three days after David Beckham's intro-duction to the U.S. sports scene, Galaxy midfielder Chris Klein ar-rived at his locker at the Home Depot Center and discovered a red envelope on his chair. The Galaxy players were used to finding messages on their chairs, which served as a sort of mailbox for memos from man-agement or fan requests or solicitations to make a public appearance. Sometimes the locker-room "mail" was worth reading. More often it ended up in the trash can.

But Klein quickly realized that this red envelope was something dif-ferent. For one thing, he noticed that nearly thirty other identical red envelopes had been placed with care on the rest of the chairs in the Galaxy locker room, like seating assignments at a wedding reception. His curiosity piqued, Klein opened the envelope. Inside was an invita-tion in gold script on red velvet. The first line caused Klein to do a dou-ble take: *Tom Cruise and Katie Holmes and Will and Jada Pinkett Smith request your presence . . .*

Four of Hollywood's biggest stars were inviting the Galaxy players and their plus-ones to the entertainment world's A-list party of the summer: a bash at the Museum of Contemporary Art's Geffen Contem-porary gallery welcoming David and Victoria Beckham to Los Angeles. For one night, at least, the Galaxy players—some of whom earned as lit-tle as $12,900 a year and still lived with their parents—were the only non-boldfaced names on an exclusive guest list that included not just Cruise and Smith and their famous wives but also Eva Longoria Parker, Jamie Foxx, Jim Carrey, Bruce Willis, Stevie Wonder, Rihanna, Demi Moore, Ashton Kutcher, Queen Latifah, Adrian Grenier, Eve, and

Brooke Shields. Sitting at his locker, Klein studied the invitation and came to the only logical conclusion: *This is fake. This has to be fake.*

Klein was one of the league's steadiest veterans, a thirty-one-year-old right-winger who'd been good enough to play twenty-two times for the U.S. national team, and he was earning a Galaxy salary ($187,250) that was high by MLS standards. Yet he had also been in the league long enough to know that attending Hollywood parties with Will Smith and Jim Carrey was a scenario about as likely as his scoring a goal to win the World Cup. That night, Klein couldn't help but marvel to his wife, Angela, about the worlds that were now colliding with Beckham's arrival. "We're invited to a party hosted by Tom Cruise," he told her. "That's surreal. That just doesn't happen."

This was the Beckham sweet spot, the powerful concoction of sports and celebrity that had vaulted him into the pantheon of global superstardom ever since the golden-haired young Manchester United midfielder had begun dating Spice Girl Victoria Adams in 1997. The Beckham sweet spot was a cultural phenomenon, evidence that celebrity didn't just add to an athlete's appeal, it had a multiplier effect in today's glitz-obsessed times. In a nation that worshipped celebrities but had never paid much attention to soccer, the Beckham sweet spot provided even more reason for the Galaxy to pursue its newest acquisition, as Alexi Lalas was quick to acknowledge in the days following Beckham's arrival. "We are seeing in full force the power of celebrity in sports, the combination of the purist loving what the person does on the field and some random person who is interested because of the celebrity," Lalas said. "You want to appeal to as many people as possible, and that's how you do it."

As much as Simon Fuller wanted to package Beckham as an athlete, he had a deep and abiding belief that Beckham's appeal could translate in America on a number of levels. "For me it's about the fundamentals," Fuller said. "It's about being the best, about being passionate, about being honest and representing the values we all strive to achieve. David has all those. He has a great family, he's got three amazing sons. No one's devoted to a sport more than David. He's also glamorous and he's iconic, and America historically reveres stars, whereas some countries sort of actually don't like their stars very much. I'm not saying it's going to happen overnight, and it may take . . . who knows? But he passes the test. If you analyze him in a fair and open-minded way, he comes out with flying colors."

In fact, when it came to soccer in America, most mainstream observers thought the Beckham sweet spot was more potent than anything Pelé brought to the table in the 1970s—and, for that matter, far more alluring than what the world's other top soccer stars could have managed in 2007. "Pelé is an athlete. Beckham and his wife and their whole aura is entertainment, of which sports is but one piece," said David Carter, the executive director of the USC Sports Business Institute. "In a celebrity-crazed era that we're in, they roll into Southern California in a rather unique situation. I don't think you see that combination in sports very much. That's what makes the Beckhams different. They're coming to town ready, literally and figuratively, for prime time."

On the third weekend of July in 2007, David and Victoria Beckham planned to unleash the full fury of their carefully coordinated powers. On Saturday night, after one of the most expensive promotional campaigns in ESPN history, David would take the field for the Galaxy for the first time, in an exhibition game against Chelsea, the English Premier League powerhouse. On Sunday night, the celebrity crowd (along with the Galaxy players) would relocate from the Home Depot Center to the party hosted by Cruise, Holmes, and the Smiths—Creative Artists Agency stablemates whose unquestioned star power would help the Hollywood media classify the Beckhams, by association, at the top of the celebrity food chain. And on Monday night, after *Access Hollywood* and *Entertainment Tonight* had beamed images from the Sunday party into living rooms across the U.S., NBC would broadcast the hour-long reality special *Victoria Beckham: Coming to America.*

Three nights, three major events, two chances to culminate a buzz-building media rollout with, it was hoped, high television ratings for David and Victoria. There was a science to creating American celebrities, and the Beckhams had complete faith that Simon Fuller was the master of that science. But for David, in particular, finding the right mix of all those ingredients was a tricky balance. Unlike Victoria, whose main concern was avoiding under- and overexposure, David also had to keep his sports and celebrity components as finely calibrated as the gears of a brand-new Ferrari. Dial the celebrity volume too low, and Beckham risked losing the ineffable qualities that separated him from other athletes. Dial it too high, and he risked losing his credibility as a sportsman. As Beckham had learned over the previous decade, he had to earn that credibility constantly on the field of play. Otherwise the machine could turn against him, and then a slew of pundits—coaches, commentators, fans—would criticize him for allowing his fame to detract from his game.

Beckham and his handlers understood that delicate balance, and as such the priorities that he had to project. In other words, soccer always came first. "Of course, everyone knows it's not just about the soccer with me," Beckham said. "First and foremost, it is about the soccer. But everything that comes with me is a bonus for the MLS. The attention that we have got is not just from the sports world, it's from all parts of the media, and that's great. It's not a bad thing to have the celebrity side come out in a sport. It gives a bit of glamour and glitz, and some people like that."

This was the formula that had made him *David Beckham*. This was the package that would conquer America, by the grace of God—or Simon Fuller, who might have been one and the same. When you looked closely at what Fuller was trying to achieve with Beckham, the audacity of his "grand vision" was remarkable. The guy who managed the Spice Girls was going to make soccer matter in America? Seriously? It would have been far easier for Fuller to position Beckham as a celebrity in the United States than as a soccer player. America cared about pop stars, and packaging pop stars was Fuller's area of expertise. Sports? Not so much. By casting the goals of the Beckham Experiment in soccer terms from the start—and seeking to convince Americans to care not just about Beckham but about an entire sport—Fuller and Beckham were setting an awfully high bar for themselves. *I'm moving to America because of the soccer. . . . Shoot for the stars, and if you don't hit them, then it was fun trying. If you do hit them, then you've made history.* For the Beckham Experiment to be successful, it wouldn't be enough for Beckham to become an American celebrity or to earn boatloads of dollars. He had to change American soccer. He had to leave a legacy that would exist long after he was finished playing for the Los Angeles Galaxy. In the end, those were Beckham's and Fuller's own terms for the way his impact would have to be measured.

It was a stretch to say that Fuller was "arguably the world's most intelligent businessman," as Victoria claimed, but he was a smart man, and he knew that positioning David as a sportsman, not a pop star, would require a shrewd media strategy. And so, months before Beckham's arrival, 19 Entertainment took the initiative, approaching *Sports Illustrated* with the desire to make Beckham available for a significant feature story and photo shoot whose release would coincide with his Galaxy debut. The *SI* spread would be Beckham's big bang media-wise, providing 20 million readers with his first public images in the new Galaxy uniform, and Beckham would do no other U.S. sports interviews published in advance of the *SI* story. Fuller's hope, of course, was for Beckham to make *SI*'s cover—one of the ultimate stamps of American sports relevance—and for the story to present Beckham as an athlete above all else.

Just in case that desire was not made clear enough, Beckham's publicists reiterated the Beckham-as-athlete mantra on numerous occasions. And so, too, did Fuller. "For David and for me, we have to fit into the American way, and we have to be convincing and compelling," Fuller said. "We know we've got to prove [ourselves] to a hard taskmaster nation in sport, because sport is like a religion in America. We've got to earn our stripes, and we really want to earn them. And whatever razzmatazz and hoopla there is about David arriving—and David's always attracted a lot of media attention—it has never interfered with his football and his passion for the sport and the fans and the recognition of sport having all the integrity. So I hope people don't confuse the flashing lights with his dedication to the sport. He has a huge love of sport, and I just hope that gets recognized. That's why we're very respectful of you and your magazine, because you're all about the love of sport, and that's what he's all about, and that's why I understand myself. It's important."

If you're counting, those were six mentions of the word *sport* in one paragraph. But the effort paid off. The cover of the July 16, 2007, issue of *Sports Illustrated* featured Beckham posing in his white Galaxy uniform with a red carpet and velvet-rope line in the background. The cover line read: "DAVID BECKHAM: Will He Change the Fate of American Soccer?" It was the first time a player in an MLS uniform had appeared on the cover of *SI*. Beckham had been chosen for the honor that week ahead of Roger Federer, who had just won his fifth consecutive Wimbledon title.

In the summer of 2007, David Beckham was not the planet's highest-paid athlete. (That was Tiger Woods.) Nor was he its finest soccer player. (That was either Brazil's Kaká, Portugal's Cristiano Ronaldo, or Argentina's Lionel Messi.) Yet Beckham was undoubtedly earth's most-talked-about sportsman, more Madonna than Maradona, a (mostly) silent oracle whose all-purpose celebrity transcended race, gender, nationality, sexual orientation, and sports itself. "Whereas Tiger Woods and Michael Jordan are respected, Beckham is loved, adored, worshipped in some parts of the world," said Ellis Cashmore, a Staffordshire University professor who taught a course on Beckham's cultural influence. "He has an almost godlike status."

Almost? In the first years of the twenty-first century, there was little need to attach a qualifier. At a Thai monastery, Buddhist monks kneeled before a gold-plated Beckham. In Japan, nightclubbers donned plaster casts in homage to their idol's injured right wrist. When Nelson Mandela met Becks in Johannesburg, you'd have judged by the coverage that the privilege was entirely Mandela's. Like Kim Jong Il's mug in North Korea, Beckham's face was everywhere in the U.K. Depending on your reading preferences, he "[set] the nation's emotional agenda" (*The Observer* of London) or inhabited "the sentimental terrain once occupied by Diana, Princess of Wales" (royal biographer Andrew Morton). It was a lot to ask of a soccer player.

To understand England's hysteria over Beckham was to realize how closely it was tied to the fanatical hatred of him in 1998. At the World Cup in France, Beckham's first major tournament, England faced its bitter soccer and military rival, Argentina, in a winner-take-all second-round game. When Beckham was ejected early in the second half for kicking Argentina's Diego Simeone, contributing to England's elimination from the tournament, the public onslaught that followed went beyond your ordinary media lynching. Rallied by the tabloids, fans hanged Beckham in effigy outside a London pub. An Islington butcher put two pig heads in his front window, one labeled DAVID and the other VICTORIA. For months Beckham was subjected to death threats, chants wishing cancer upon his son, even a piece of "fan mail" bearing a bullet with his name inscribed on it.

Though Beckham returned to Manchester United later that summer, ending speculation that he might have to join a team on the Continent, he kept his head down, his mouth shut. "It was hard concentrating on football," he recalled. "It was like, *I'm a soccer star. Nobody was killed. This isn't right.*"

Beckham's detractors tried hard to spin the hype machine into reverse after the World Cup debacle, seizing on anything at hand: his wife, his fashion forays, his high-pitched Essex accent. "But they were flailing about a bit, to be honest," said Nick Hornby. "That's why the hatred of him was so inflated. People wanted to loathe him, but they couldn't get a handle on anything. A brief moment of indiscipline against Argentina, and people are hanging effigies? If it had been any other English player, all the focus would have been on Simeone. Kicking Argentines is generally approved of, but not in this specific case."

Then something odd happened. Through a combination of PR savvy, quiet dignity, and, above all, unimpeachable play, Beckham turned the media coverage on its head. Running tirelessly, serving exquisite crosses into the penalty box, scoring timely goals, he helped lead Manchester United to an unprecedented Treble in 1999, winning the English Premier League, FA Cup, and European Champions League trophies. Within two years he'd be named captain of England—forcing fans to suspend all hostilities in the name of national pride—and his last-second free-kick goal against Greece clinched England's berth in the 2002 World Cup in the most dramatic fashion possible. When Beckham buried a penalty kick to beat Argentina at the World Cup in Japan, his transformation from pariah to paragon was complete.

Redemption had proved lucrative. In the five years before his move to America, Beckham had earned an estimated $150 million (nearly three-fourths of it from such endorsers as Adidas, Pepsi, Gillette, and

Motorola), making him the world's highest-paid soccer player. The key to Beckham's popularity was his ability to function as a one-size-fits-all vessel for his fans' hopes and dreams. It was revealing that he didn't say a word in the 2002 film *Bend It Like Beckham*, serving instead as a listening post—in the form of bedroom wall posters—for the deepest secrets of a teenage Anglo-Indian girl.

"He's this phantom of the imagination," Cashmore explained. "Because he doesn't actually come out and say anything, he gives the people carte blanche to construct their own David Beckham." To claim that Beckham didn't say anything was a bit uncharitable. Granted, like Woods and Jordan, he wasn't Muhammad Ali refusing induction into the Army. "I try to stay away from as much politics as possible," said Beckham, who admitted that he didn't vote in elections. Yet his open-mindedness often featured a candor you'd never expect to hear from Tiger or Michael.

Consider his stance on homosexuality. Beckham happily spoke out against the raging taboo of male locker rooms worldwide. "Being a gay icon is a great honor for me," said Beckham, who once posed suggestively for the cover of the British gay magazine *Attitude*. "I'm quite sure of my feminine side, and I've not got a problem with that at all. These days it's the norm, and it should be. Everyone's different, everyone's got their thing."

And Beckham's thing was, well, everyone. Race? One British TV show, citing his cornrows and chunky jewelry, dubbed him "an honorary black man." Religion? He was one-fourth Jewish. Women's soccer? His David Beckham Academy set up soccer schools in London and Los Angeles for girls and boys alike. "People always say to me, 'Why girls?'" Beckham explained. "And I say it's important that girls get involved in sports."

The person who had the biggest influence on Beckham was his wife, whose own fallen star after the Spice Girls breakup in 2000 had caused U.K. pundits to suggest she was using her husband as a prop to boost her career. (Or, as *The Guardian*'s Julie Burchill none-too-delicately put it, "Beckham has been grotesquely, massively pussywhipped by his talentless ambition-hound of a wife.") If you asked Victoria how she had changed David's life, she steered clear of such trivial matters as love, family, and maturity. "I've changed his dress sense," she said, munching on a strand of grapes at a New York City photo shoot. *"Drastically."* Her face was blank. Was she in on the joke? Or was that really all there was to it? It was impossible to tell.

By all accounts, though, theirs was a strong, stable marriage during David's Manchester United days, which made him a welcome contrast to such previous English soccer stars as Paul Gascoigne (who beat his wife and spent his free time getting hopelessly drunk with a sidekick named Five Bellies) and George Best (the Manchester United playboy star of the late 1960s who once famously quipped, "I spent a lot of money on booze, [women], and fast cars. The rest I just squandered"). David's alleged affair with Rebecca Loos in 2004 called the notion of his idyllic marriage into question, but frantic PR work minimized the fall-out, and Beckham held on to his female fans, not least because he was clearly infatuated with his sons. "David is a model dad," Victoria said. "If I leave him with the children, he'll look after them just as well as I can."

Naturally, Beckham's New Age family-man side appealed to house-wives and grandmothers. Yet by pursuing so many nontraditional sports demographics, he had long run the risk of alienating hard-core soccer fans. For no matter how gorgeous he may be, the sportsman must constantly prove his superiority in the arena. Beckham certainly had his flaws: ordinary speed, weak heading skills, not much of a left foot. But for someone regarded as a pretty boy, his capacity for work was breathtaking. Simply put, he ran his butt off. Beckham, for all his beauty and all his endorsements, was not the male Anna Kournikova, a winless wonder. Not when he had won six English Premier League tro-phies, two FA Cups, and one European Cup with Manchester United and one Spanish La Liga championship at Real Madrid. Not when the world's national team coaches had twice voted him the second-best soc-cer player on the planet (behind Rivaldo in 1999 and Luis Figo in 2001). Not when he could serve a bending, thirty-yard cross on the run as well as any player in the world. And certainly not when he possessed a phys-ical genius for spinning an inert ball into a remote corner of the goal, a skill that inspired a movie to be made in his name.

Still, striking the right balance between what Beckham called "the sporting side" and "the celebrity side" had been a perpetual challenge, one that led to his departure from Manchester United in what became the world's most publicized sports story of 2003. It was a deeply personal divorce. If you asked Beckham to pick the most significant moment of his childhood, he didn't hesitate. He was eleven, a working-class kid from East London who'd just finished playing a game for Ridgeway Rovers, his Sunday League team: "My mum came up and said, 'It's good that you've played well today, because Manchester United were watching you, and they want you to come down and have a trial.' I just stood there and cried."

In European soccer, if you survive the Darwinian winnowing process, if you come up through the youth ranks and stay with your team, the attachments run deep. Beckham began training with Manchester United at fourteen, signed a contract at sixteen, and joined the starting lineup for good at twenty, in 1995. For fourteen years Man United—the world's most popular sports franchise, the team he grew up supporting—was the only professional home Beckham had ever known. With more than 200 official fan clubs and an estimated fan base of 50 million, Manchester United had been the launchpad for Beckham's rise as a global phenomenon. What's more, Beckham had developed what he called "a father-son relationship" with United coach Sir Alex Ferguson, a bond that helped make up for Beckham's sometimes icy relations with his own father, an East London heating engineer. Beckham's parents, Ted and Sandra, would divorce in 2002, and David, Victoria, and the kids spent far more time with David's mother.

For Ferguson, a no-nonsense taskmaster raised in the shipyards of Glasgow, Scotland, *old school* wasn't a marketing catchphrase. It was standard operating procedure. During an interview in 2003 just two months before Beckham left Manchester United, Ferguson told me he had read *When Pride Still Mattered*, David Maraniss's biography of the legendary NFL coach Vince Lombardi. "I saw myself," Ferguson explained. "Obsession. Commitment. Fanaticism. It was all there." Like Lombardi, Ferguson was ruthless, maintaining ironfisted control of his team despite his players' rising salaries. "I never have a problem with egos," said Ferguson, who had been the Man United coach since 1986.

"You know why? Because you have to win. You can't escape the field. And if the money has affected them, they have to go. Easiest decision ever made."

In the spring of 2003, it was clear that the relationship between Beckham and Ferguson had begun to unravel. The coach had benched Beckham for the season's two most important games, against Real Madrid and Premier League archrival Arsenal, and the tabloids had feasted on a locker-room incident in which Ferguson, livid after a loss, had kicked a soccer shoe in anger, dinging Beckham in the forehead and opening a gash above Beckham's eye. But the wounds were deeper than that. To hear Ferguson discuss the teenage Beckham was to hear a tale of youthful innocence and talent corrupted—or at the very least distracted—by fame. "He was blessed with great stamina, the best of all the players we've had here," Ferguson said. "After training he'd always be practicing, practicing, practicing. So there's a foundation there that never deserted him. And then . . ."

It was a long pause, one of those times when silence communicated more than words ever could. Suddenly you realized, in that fleeting moment, how deeply Ferguson longed for the schoolboy Beckham, for a simpler era, for a time when his star wasn't spending his free hours with Elton John, Jean-Paul Gaultier, and the Naked Chef.

". . . his life changed when he met his wife, really," Ferguson finally continued. "She's in pop, and David got another image. And he's developed this *fashion thing*." (He said "fashion thing" in the bewildered way you'd expect to hear from, say, Vince Lombardi.) "I saw his transition to a different person. So long as it doesn't affect his football side, it doesn't bother me at all." Clearly, though, Ferguson had decided: The glitz had indeed affected Beckham's football side. *You can't escape the field*.

Real Madrid bought Beckham from Manchester United in June 2003 for $41 million—a bargain when you consider that Beckham was the main reason for Real's huge increase in merchandise sales during his four years with the club, a total reported by *Forbes* magazine to have exceeded $1.2 billion. From a star-power perspective there had never been a soccer team assembled like Real Madrid's *Galácticos*, which featured not just Beckham but three FIFA World Players of the Year: France's Zinédine Zidane, Brazil's Ronaldo, and Portugal's Figo. Defying skeptics who predicted he'd struggle on a team full of soccer magicians, Beckham won over the hard-to-please Real Madrid fans from the start with his relentless work rate and free-kick mastery, as if he was trying to prove a point to Ferguson in every game.

But while the *Galácticos* captured the world's imagination, at times displaying some of the most inventive soccer ever witnessed, they failed to win any significant trophies during Beckham's first three seasons. Once again, it appeared that the scales of Beckham's career were tipped too much toward commerce and fame at the expense of athletic achievement. When Beckham stunned the soccer world by signing with the Galaxy in January 2007, European cynics wrote him off as irrelevant to the sport's highest levels, a de facto retiree settling for easy money in a backwater league. Beckham's career with England's national team appeared over—new manager Steve McClaren had dropped him after the 2006 World Cup—and his club coach at Real Madrid, Fabio Capello, announced he would never play for the team again. "David Beckham will be a B-list actor living in Hollywood," sniffed Madrid president Ramón Calderón, concluding that the Beckham sweet spot would disintegrate without the fuel of top-level soccer.

But Beckham had always shown an uncanny knack for reinvention, and in no time he was plotting his latest comeback. "At that point in the season, I was surprised at many things that were said about me behind my back that hurt me at the time," Beckham told me. "But I've always come back from adversity, and I've always had the mentality of proving people wrong. I had to think, 'Okay, even if I don't play for Real Madrid again I'll still carry on training and working like I always have, just in case I do get a chance again.'"

Refusing to lash out at his critics, Beckham earned back his starting position, to say nothing of his teammates' respect, and helped lead Real Madrid on a fairy-tale run from fourth place to the La Liga title. "At his darkest moment he rediscovered himself and found arguably the richest vein of form since his greatest days at Manchester United," said Ray Hudson, who broadcast the Spanish league in the U.S. for GolTV. "That in itself is a feat of unbelievable character. I call it testicular fortitude. Whether you love him or you hate him—and I've never been his most ardent fan—it's inarguable that he was as deadly as he's ever been."

The prodigal son rejoined the England national team in May 2007, producing three gorgeous assists in two games, and his rehabilitation was secure. Suddenly, the same people who'd buried Beckham's career five months earlier were begging him to stay in Europe. Too late. When Real Madrid contacted the Galaxy a few weeks before his arrival in America about reacquiring Beckham, the conversation was a quick one. "We made it very clear," said Tim Leiweke, the chief executive of the Galaxy's ownership group. "My Spanish was not tested." As he spoke, Leiweke was straining nearly every facial muscle *not* to look smug over pulling off what now appeared to be a steal of a deal—and not entirely succeeding.

But could you blame him?

CHAPTER 3

THE $250 MILLION
FAIRY TALE

By just about any measure, whether it was monetary value, global news coverage, or the sheer forehead-smacking surprise of it all, Tim Leiweke's move to acquire David Beckham for the Los Angeles Galaxy was one of the most audacious sports signings of the early twenty-first century—and the main reason the *Sports Business Journal* named Leiweke the Sports Executive of the Year in the United States. Perhaps the most powerful figure in American soccer, Leiweke had cut his teeth promoting indoor soccer during its heyday in the 1980s before moving on to executive positions in the NBA and, eventually, the CEO position at AEG. Leiweke was in charge of AEG's manifold global projects, from the traveling King Tut exhibition to Celine Dion's Las Vegas show to the ownership of two MLS soccer teams (the Galaxy and the Houston Dynamo), the National Hockey League's Los Angeles Kings, and downtown L.A.'s Staples Center, among dozens of other arenas around the world. Equally at ease when speaking to Chinese politicians or superstar entertainers, Leiweke was the kind of mogul who ended conversations by saying, "I get to go see Prince now."

As Leiweke recounted his five-year Beckham pursuit the day after news of the deal had stunned the sports world, it was clear that it had been a rollicking adventure. Leiweke had begun laying the groundwork for signing Beckham in 2002, when he first met Beckham's best friend, Terry Byrne, in London (where AEG had several major projects). They began discussing Beckham's interest in starting a soccer academy for boys and girls with branches in London and Los Angeles. Leiweke and Beckham met in person at an Adidas shoot at the Home Depot Center in 2003, and they soon went into business together on the David Beckham Academy. Meanwhile, Leiweke spoke regularly with Simon Fuller. "We have a long relationship with Simon because of our music business and *American Idol*," Leiweke said. "So Simon and I were sitting around talking about vision. Wouldn't it be great one day with David? How would he do in America? It all started with that."

In 2004, Victoria and David Beckham invited Leiweke to a casual dinner at their mansion outside London (aka Beckingham Palace) with Fuller, Byrne, and several others. Knowing that the Beckhams enjoyed fine red wine, Leiweke brought a high-end California cabernet, and the evening went so well that he and his AEG lieutenants stayed until nearly midnight. "That to me was the turning point," Leiweke said. "Because it was very clear that night: David looked at us and you could tell he felt we had a chemistry between our company and him and his family." From the start, the relationship involved not just AEG and David, but rather Beckham *and his family*. Indeed, from Leiweke's perspective the best part of the evening was the connection he had with Victoria. It was the first time they had really spoken to each other, and they spent much of the dinner talking about the music industry and AEG's music division. Ultimately, AEG went into business with Beckham on the David Beckham Academy, investing more than $20 million in the London branch alone.

There were other dinners as well. An MLS All-Star team's 5–0 loss to Real Madrid in August 2005 was forgettable for Leiweke and embarrassed MLS executives in just about every respect but one: That night the Beckhams had a fashionably Spanish 1 A.M. dinner at a Madrid restaurant with Leiweke, MLS commissioner Don Garber, and deputy commissioner Ivan Gazidis. "Tim had already done the academy deal, and we filled David in on our league," said Garber, who described the conversation as a pleasant one about the U.S. and the growth potential for soccer. Beckham's interest continued to grow.

With the relationship established, the events building to Beckham's signing began in earnest in November 2006, when MLS owners passed the Designated Player Rule. The rule, long called "the Beckham Rule," gave each team one slot for a player who could earn unlimited wages beyond the salary cap. The Beckham Rule had been Leiweke's baby, even though it took him two years to persuade MLS owners to go along with it. In 2005, the owners shot down Leiweke's plan, arguing that the league wasn't ready for such a jolt to its original slow-growth strategy. A year later, though, buoyed by Red Bull and Adidas's eight-figure investments in MLS and the league's new TV rights deals with ESPN, Univision, Fox Soccer Channel, and HDNet, Leiweke got his wish and MLS owners signed off on the Beckham Rule.

At the same time, Beckham's talks with Real Madrid to negotiate a new contract had stalled. FIFA rules stipulated that players could not begin negotiating with other teams until the final six months of their contract, and Leiweke swore that no pre–January 1 tampering by the Galaxy took place. He and Beckham "did a complete shutdown" between July and the end of December, Leiweke said, eliminating all contact with each other. Still, he added, Beckham's people "were very aware that if the time came and they didn't get a deal done at Real Madrid, we were ready to jump in."

In December 2006, Leiweke had a conversation with Philip Anschutz, the Galaxy owner who had named Leiweke to run AEG. "We're going to have a moment of truth here on January 1 when we begin negotiations," Leiweke told his boss. "I believe it's going to happen very quickly, because I think David will have made up his mind by then. He could re-sign with Real Madrid before January 1, but if we get to January 1 he's ours."

Leiweke showed Anschutz the offer he wanted to make to Beckham. Anschutz initially hadn't liked the idea for the Designated Player Rule, believing that slow growth over the long term was a better blueprint for MLS than simply buying superstars, the lightning-in-a-bottle strategy that had contributed to the NASL's demise in the early 1980s. But Leiweke's salesmanship was convincing, both for fellow MLS owners and for Anschutz himself. When the Beckham Rule was finally passed at the MLS Board of Governors meeting the day before the league's 2006 championship game, Anschutz turned to his top lieutenant and shook Leiweke's hand. "You're right, this *is* a good idea," he said. "We need to do this for the league, because if we're ever going to expand our ratings and our audience and get credibility in our country, we're going to need a star to break through."

Now, at their meeting in December, Anschutz looked at the Beckham contract proposal. "Can you hit these numbers?" he asked.

"We can hit these numbers," came the reply.

What followed was a ten-day "mad dash" (Leiweke's term). On New Year's Day, Leiweke initiated the process with Fuller and superagent Jeff Frasco of CAA Sports, the new sports arm of the powerhouse agency that represented not just the Beckhams but some of Hollywood's biggest stars, including Beckham friends Tom Cruise and Will Smith. The next day, Leiweke and his team spent four hours at the CAA Sports office in Los Angeles, and negotiations continued steadily over the next several days. "Finally, over the weekend it became pretty evident to me, *I think we're going to pull this deal off,*" Leiweke said. "We were getting into a lot of details that you wouldn't normally get into unless you were about to make a deal." All along, the only question was whether Beckham would decide to take the safer route and extend his contract with Real Madrid.

Both sides' lawyers pulled all-nighters on the last two nights before Beckham signed. Leiweke had to fly to New York City for an unrelated meeting, and on January 10 he returned to LAX Airport, where he signed the Galaxy's end of the contract offer at a hotel courtesy-phone counter next to the baggage claim at 9:30 P.M. Pacific time (6:30 A.M. Madrid time). "This thing had to *go,*" Leiweke said. Beckham and his representatives were going to meet with Real Madrid on Thursday, and Leiweke had to make sure they knew AEG was committed to the deal. "David was going to make a decision on Thursday morning, and we were on pins and needles," Leiweke said. "We needed them to walk out of the meeting and tell us we had a deal, because we were worried they'd go into the Real Madrid meeting and call us up and say, 'We just signed for another two years at Real Madrid.'"

Leiweke was up at 4 A.M. Pacific time the next morning, expecting to hear good news from Beckham's reps in Madrid. None came. One of Beckham's attorneys had been delayed by two hours on his flight from London to Madrid, which set back the Real Madrid meeting two hours, which caused all sorts of problems for AEG. Leiweke had arranged for full-page color advertisements in several U.S. newspapers, and the deadline for Friday's *New York Times* was at 6 A.M. Pacific on Thursday. If AEG didn't lock in the ad by then, it would face a $100,000 fee to cancel it afterward. By 6 A.M., Leiweke's top marketing exec had run out of patience. "What do you want me to do?" he asked. "Are we going to run the ad or not?'"

"Pull the ad," Leiweke replied.

But then the *Times* did something serendipitous. It gave him a twenty-minute extension. And ten minutes later, at 6:10 A.M., Leiweke received a call from Fuller and Frasco.

"Run the ads," they said.

"We've got a deal?"

"We've got a deal. We had the meeting. David's made his decision. We've informed Real Madrid that he's leaving."

Within minutes the news was already going global. At age thirty-one, David Beckham was jumping from Real Madrid to the Los Angeles Galaxy of Major League Soccer.

By 5 P.M. the next day, sitting in his office across the street from the Staples Center, Leiweke looked less tired than most men who had barely slept in a week. "It wasn't until finally today when David was talking to the media at the press conference that I finally realized, *My God, we just did this,*" he said. "We went through two years of arguments within Major League Soccer: Is the Designated Player a good idea or a bad idea? *Two years*. We went through everything with David on his vision and the academy, telling him: If you ever make a decision that you want to come, it's going to work. Here's why, and let us know. We went through all the rumors of other clubs' interest, went through the hell of the ten days negotiating the contract, and when you sat there today and opened up the paper and saw five pages of articles in the *Los Angeles Times* . . ."

He stopped. Looked up. Smiled. Outside, the Staples Center marquee featured Beckham kneeling in full goal-celebration glory below the news: BECKHAM COMES TO AMERICA. The world's ultimate sports celebrity was moving to the world's ultimate celebrity city, and in less than two days the Galaxy had already sold 5,000 new season tickets. Half a decade after beginning his pursuit, Leiweke had finally landed his man.

As the world learned of Beckham's signing on January 11, 2007, the only news more surprising than the move itself was the almost inconceivable price tag. Was the Galaxy press release right? Could the first Associated Press wire story and a blizzard of other media reports possibly be correct? Was Beckham's five-year deal really worth a potential $250 million? Would a soccer team in a money-losing league really have to cough up *a quarter of a billion dollars*?

The answer to the last question was no, not even close. According to figures released several months later by the MLS Players Union, Beckham's salary with the Galaxy was actually $32.5 million over the entire length of the contract—hardly chump change, but not $250 million and still less than the salaries of a lot of U.S. sports stars. Nor would Beckham's income bankrupt MLS. According to the Designated Player Rule, MLS's owners (who shared the costs for all player salaries) had to contribute only a total of $400,000 a year for each of the league's Designated Player exceptions whether or not their own teams used the slots. The rest of Beckham's salary came from AEG. The result: AEG was on the hook for $30.5 million of Beckham's five-year contract, while MLS owners had to pay only $2 million. With his estimated $8 billion net wealth, Phil Anschutz—one of the world's richest men—could certainly afford to pay for his new star.

There was more to Beckham's deal than his salary, however. In an arrangement that was similar to the movie deals of Hollywood action-movie stars, Beckham would also earn percentages of Galaxy jersey sales and ticket revenues, income that could more than double his Galaxy salary at the end of each season. So where was the other $170 million or more of Beckham's putative $250 million supposed to come from? Endorsement deals. For Beckham's sponsors (which included Adidas, Pepsi, Motorola, and the fragrance maker Coty), his move to the potentially lucrative U.S. market was worth a more significant investment in Beckham himself. In a clever piece of high-dollar synergy engineered by Fuller, the $250 million figure represented the best-case scenario *provided by Beckham's own handlers* for his total income over the five-year period.

Fuller insisted that the Galaxy include the $250 million figure in its press release announcing Beckham's signing, and the number was repeated again in *David Beckham: New Beginnings*, the not-so-independent hour-long "documentary" produced by Fuller's 19 Entertainment that aired on ESPN before Beckham's Galaxy debut against Chelsea. After all,

$250 million certainly reflected well upon Fuller's negotiating acumen, and it was a short but effective rejoinder to anyone in Europe who wondered why Beckham would join a lower-level league like MLS. What's more, since Beckham's contract itself was top secret, it forced the media to either repeat the $250 million figure at face value or do the sort of digging for facts that required time, effort, and access.

From a factual perspective, the media's widespread use of the phrase *$250 million Galaxy contract*—a practice that gained critical mass on the day Beckham signed and continued into 2009—was shockingly bad journalism. When reporting athletes' contracts, the standard practice is to include the length of the contract (in years) and the amount of money the team is paying the athlete. An athlete's endorsement deals are never taken into account, the better to avoid confusion over the size of a team's investment. Case in point: At the time of Beckham's signing, LeBron James had a four-year, $60 million contract with the NBA's Cleveland Cavaliers. At no point was it ever stated in the media that James had a $210 million Cavaliers contract, even though James also had $150 million in endorsement deals with such companies as Nike, Sprite, and Glacéau. Yet for some reason many media members swallowed the Beckham figure whole.

In the end, Fuller's $250 million mantra served its purpose, and the vast majority of the public came away believing that Beckham's base salary with the Galaxy was eight times its real size. Having promised Fuller that he wouldn't leak any contract details, Leiweke himself professed not to care ("This is an economic deal that makes sense for everybody" was all he would say), but for MLS the "$250 million contract" became an ongoing headache. Not only did it make the league look like it was overpaying for Beckham, but it also gave the impression to overseas soccer stars (and their agents) that MLS teams were now willing to toss around obscene sums of money when in fact they were not. That gap between perception and reality would create problems when the Galaxy brought in foreigners who thought it was the Manchester United of MLS, and it also helped explain why MLS was still lacking in star power at the start of the 2009 season: Of a possible fifteen Designated Player slots, only five were filled.

As vocal as Fuller and the Galaxy had been from the start about

Beckham's potential income, there were two other important provisions of Beckham's contract that wouldn't become public knowledge for many months. For starters, Beckham had the option to buy an MLS expansion team at a fixed price whenever he stopped playing in the league—an allowance that the league's owners had never given to a player before. "Our partners all had to sign off, and they did," Leiweke said. "We had a couple of interesting board calls, but they did." Giving Beckham the option was smart business by MLS: It would increase Beckham's incentive to raise the league's profile, and it might also curtail Beckham's participation with the Players Union during what were sure to be contentious negotiations for a new collective bargaining agreement in 2009. If MLS's most powerful player was going to be an owner himself, the thinking went, he might not push for too many concessions from the league's owners.

The other unpublicized contract provision seemed like a formality. Despite public assurances from Beckham's handlers and Leiweke to the contrary, Beckham did indeed have an opt-out clause in his contract. The final two years of his five-year Galaxy deal were option years that were under Beckham's control, meaning he could walk away from the Galaxy after the 2009 season as a free agent if for some reason things had gone horribly wrong.

In the heady days of July 2007, however, when the Beckham sweet spot was beguiling America, such a scenario was impossible to imagine. The financial impact of his arrival was staggering. "David has already paid for himself," Leiweke claimed, citing the 250,000 jerseys shipped, the Galaxy's 11,000 season-ticket holders, the stadium's sold-out luxury suites (forty-two in all), and the team's new five-year deal worth an estimated $20 million with jersey sponsor Herbalife.

But while Leiweke had earned a reputation for visionary thinking and taking big risks, he had acquired another one for slinging hype. Much like NASL commissioner Phil Woosnam, who had proclaimed in 1977 that his league "will operate on a par with the NFL" by 1987, Leiweke had a habit of making grand pronouncements about the future of MLS in relation to the other U.S. sports leagues. In 2005, Leiweke had famously predicted: "If within ten years from today Major League Soccer is not top four and hopefully top two or three . . . in this country, we will have failed." Likewise, Leiweke outdid himself in 2007, on the day the Galaxy announced Beckham's signing: "David Beckham will have a greater impact on soccer in America than any athlete has ever had on a sport globally." Really? "That's probably asking too much of David," Leiweke admitted later. "But you know what? We'll stick to it."

Nor was the impact of Beckham's signing on AEG limited to sports, or even to AEG's music-business relationship with Fuller's 19 Entertainment. It went far beyond that, in fact. Leiweke was already leveraging his Beckham association to raise AEG's profile in places such as China, where the company had been working aggressively in Shanghai and Beijing for years to receive clearance to build arenas and stadiums. "Suddenly we're known as the company that owns the team that David Beckham is going to play for, so our world changed," said Leiweke. "Maybe the change is they realized we are the kind of company that can do things others choose not to even dream about or accomplish. That's part of what David has contributed. We certainly have more credibility when we throw the crazy idea on the table."

Of course, the money for the Beckham Experiment wasn't coming from Leiweke's pocket. In the end, strangely, the only major Galaxy figure who hadn't been at the HDC for Beckham's unveiling was the man who paid for it all. Anschutz, the Galaxy's Denver-based owner, was a giant in the oil, telecommunications, railroad, newspaper, and entertainment industries. A right-wing evangelical Christian who had become a soccer fan during the 1994 World Cup, Anschutz had saved MLS from extinction by owning as many as six of its teams earlier in the decade. But Uncle Phil, as U.S. soccer fans called him, was also a famously media-shy mogul who hadn't given an interview in more than thirty years. There was no way he'd attend an event crawling with 700 media members. "That's Phil," said Alexi Lalas. "He rolls way under the radar. Mr. Anschutz has a whole other empire that has absolutely nothing to do with soccer."

Truth be told, Anschutz and Beckham had never met.

Not long before his U.S. arrival, Beckham saw *Once in a Lifetime*, the 2006 documentary film that depicted the rise and fall of the New York

Cosmos and the North American Soccer League. He marveled at scenes of the Cosmos partying with Mick Jagger at Studio 54, of soccer fans filling Giants Stadium . . . and of the league disintegrating just a few years later. "It's incredible what that time was like for the Cosmos and Pelé," Beckham said. "But I think the league is definitely more stable than it was back then, when you had a huge amount of money just being put into one team."

If you asked any MLS executive why the Beckham Experiment should be more successful than Pelé's, the word you heard was *infrastructure*. "Back then we didn't have an infrastructure that was prepared to take advantage of the opportunity," said Leiweke. "Pelé was able to hide the lack of true deep roots you needed to be successful. That's how great Pelé was, but you knew the minute he left it was over." Unlike the NASL, the twelfth-year MLS had seven teams (and counting) playing in their own soccer stadiums; four national TV contracts; a country with 42 million Hispanics (many of them soccer lovers); a base of competitive homegrown players (for a U.S. national team that had reached five straight World Cups); and a single-entity business model that prevented teams from spending themselves into bankruptcy by bidding against one another for free agents.

But there was a flip side to "soccer socialism," the collective planned economy that governed the league. MLS's owners may have included billionaires such as Robert Kraft, Philip Anschutz, Stan Kroenke, Jorge Vergara, and Dietrich Mateschitz, but the league's $2.1-million-per-team salary cap kept MLS from competing for top players on the world market. (The budget for player salaries at Chelsea, for example, was an estimated $200 million.) MLS was still losing money and television ratings were anemic (ESPN2's Thursday-night MLS game averaged a 0.2 rating), but seven new ownership groups had come on board from 2004 to 2007, and the plan was to expand from thirteen teams to eighteen by 2011. "You couldn't sign Beckham in 1996 when the league started," said MLS commissioner Don Garber, "not before you had the right facilities, the right television contracts, and the right brands with our teams so we really understand how to build this business." Even Pelé himself was encouraged. "Now things here are more organized," he said. "The league is set up, but they need more good names in the other cities to continue to promote the sport."

The eternal challenge for soccer in the United States had always been to convert the widespread interest in playing the game—the U.S. had nearly 18 million registered players in 2007—into a desire to watch soccer as a spectator sport. But the equation had started to change. The World Cup was now a major event on the U.S. sports calendar, earning magazine covers and solid television ratings, and summer exhibition games involving top European clubs filled NFL stadiums. Why, the Mexican national team played more games in the United States than it did in Mexico, the better to take advantage of higher ticket prices (and significant demand) north of the border. To hear some MLS executives, the ground rules had changed, and now the goal was to use Beckham (and other players) to convince those soccer fans that MLS was not an inferior product.

"It's already established in the grassroots now," argued MLS deputy commissioner Ivan Gazidis. "What we hope from David Beckham is something a little bit different, which is that he can help us connect with those people who are already fans of soccer that aren't yet fans of Major League Soccer. That's our single biggest challenge as a league. The soccer audience exists: Look at the World Cup ratings or the number of people who show up for the Mexican national team or FC Barcelona or Real Madrid. We need to have those people embrace Major League Soccer, and that's a process. David Beckham can help us achieve that and have a dramatic effect on soccer in this country."

Ever since Beckham's signing, pundits in the snarky British media had taken repeated potshots at MLS, arguing that Beckham wouldn't be sharp for national-team games if he was toiling in what was invariably described as "a semi-retirement home" (*The Guardian*) or "a Mickey Mouse league" (*The Independent*). The catcalls got even louder when the U.K. media, which had descended on Los Angeles for Beckham's debut against Chelsea, got a sneak preview of the Galaxy four days earlier in a horrific 3–0 exhibition loss to the Mexican club Tigres. More than one visiting British pundit called the Galaxy "a pub team." Nonsense, replied the Galaxy's Lalas. "It irritates me so much I want to put my fist through a wall—or through a television set playing *Benny Hill*," Lalas said. "It's such an ignorance that's fueled by an arrogance that exists over there." True, English insecurity about the U.S.'s rising global soccer influence was at an all-time high, not least because wealthy Yanks had bought three English Premier League teams (Manchester United, Liverpool, and Aston Villa) in the previous two years. But while the quality of MLS was clearly below that of the top teams in Spain or England, young Americans like the Galaxy's Landon Donovan and New York's Jozy Altidore and a crop of new imported stars (led by Beckham, New York's Juan Pablo Ángel, and Chicago's Cuauhtémoc Blanco) were making sure the level of play wasn't nearly as bad as most British commentators might have thought.

For his part, Beckham maintained that MLS's less-crowded schedule would keep him fresh for international duty. If he had any second thoughts, he wasn't voicing them. "The majority of my friends are like, 'As long as you're happy, that's the most important thing,'" Beckham said. "A couple of them think that I should still be playing in Europe, because they know I can play at the highest level for at least another three years. But those people also think I'm doing the right thing, because they can see that I'm happy. I've made the decision and I've got no regrets."

Now six months of anticipation was supposed to culminate in big box-office on Beckham's megahyped opening weekend on July 21–22, 2007. The Chelsea game might have struck traditional soccer fans as a meaningless friendly, but few moments could have been more important for the Beckham Experiment. There was only one chance to make a first impression, and given the money invested it had to be a good one. After all, Beckham's television audience numbers would set the bar for future interest and advertising-rate charges by ESPN. With so many celebrities and sports stars on hand, with so much national promotion, the Beckham sweet spot would never be larger.

All Beckham had to do was play. But that was the problem. Although Beckham knew just how important it would be for him to take the field that Saturday, he also knew that his left ankle was injured far more seriously than anyone had imagined.

CHAPTER 4

AMERICAN IDLE

"You have to wonder what's going on in sports. Baseball's greatest hitter has got this steroid thing going. You have an NBA ref fixing games, NFL dogfighting rings, the Tour de France leader just got kicked off his team. One more scandal and Americans could actually start watching soccer."

—JAY LENO, *The Tonight Show,* July 2007

"No question, they are the It couple right now, and we are your Posh and Becks source!"   —MARY HART, *Entertainment Tonight,* July 23, 2007

Alexi Lalas needed a drink. Or a day off. Or, at the very least, a good night's sleep. His teal necktie unknotted, his hands stuffed into his pockets, Lalas slumped against the wall outside a luxury suite at Dick's Sporting Goods Park in Commerce City, Colorado, a suburb of Denver. It was July 19, two nights before David Beckham's scheduled debut against Chelsea, and Lalas had just spent ten minutes during halftime of the MLS All-Star Game answering a barrage of reporters' questions about perhaps the worst possible scenario: What if David Beckham couldn't play in the most publicized game in MLS history, a made-for-TV event designed solely for him?

Tim Leiweke, Lalas's boss, kept calling him for updates on Beckham's injured left ankle. The coordinating producer for ESPN was lighting up his BlackBerry asking the same question. And who knows how many journalists and Galaxy sponsors might call in the next forty-eight hours? "We're getting pressure from so many places," Lalas said. "But we can't make him play."

One of the most meticulously packaged rollouts in sports history was falling apart. Beckham had sprained his left ankle six weeks earlier, on June 6, while playing for England in a Euro 2008 qualifier against

Estonia. In most cases, Beckham would have sat out for a few weeks to let the ankle heal, but Real Madrid had two games left in an epic race for the Spanish league title, and Beckham wasn't about to miss his finest hour in La Liga. He played four days later for Real, aggravating the injury, and before the must-win season finale he took three cortisone injections in his ankle, a risky step that numbs the pain but can weaken the joints and cause structural damage.

As a rule, Beckham refrained from using painkillers, believing they were unnatural and potentially dangerous. But this was no ordinary circumstance. "I would have sort of done anything to play in that game," Beckham said. "It wasn't healthy, and it wasn't maybe the right thing to do long-term, but I did it, and at the end of the day I'm glad I did it, because I played in the game for sixty-five minutes and we ended up winning the league. It's something that I did at the time, but it's not obviously done me much good the last few weeks." By Beckham's own account he had "ripped the ligaments" in that last game, leaving his ankle "a bit of a mess."

It was hard to criticize Beckham for taking the injections—we hail athletes all the time for playing with pain in big games—but neither Beckham nor the Galaxy handled the aftermath well at all. In hindsight, Lalas wished the Galaxy had sent a doctor to begin treatment on Beckham's ankle during his vacation in the south of France. As for Beckham, he admitted that his arrival in Los Angeles marked "the first time I really had treatment apart from about a week of fitness work" during his stay in France. Why Beckham wouldn't have done everything possible to treat the ankle during his vacation was a mystery; perhaps he underestimated the severity of the injury. But the inaction on both sides was the start of a troubling pattern in Beckham's relations with the Galaxy: Beckham and his advisers wouldn't communicate important information to the team, and the team was too afraid of angering the man it was paying millions of dollars (by, say, interrupting Beckham's vacation) to look out for its own interests.

Although Lalas had flown into Denver with Beckham on one of AEG's private airplanes, their messages to the media about Beckham's injury that night were, laughably, miles apart. When asked during the ESPN2 halftime show about his status for the Chelsea game, a grim-faced Beckham dampened expectations: "At the moment it doesn't look good that I'm gonna play, because the swelling is still there." Minutes later, Lalas was presenting (read: spinning) a far rosier picture to reporters in the press box: "We still anticipate that he's going to play. To what extent, we don't know."

As soon as Beckham opened his mouth, television executives in Bristol, Connecticut, no doubt wanted to throw up. No company had more riding on Beckham's opening-night extravaganza than ESPN, which had stoked the hype for the Chelsea game by investing in one of the most expensive advertising campaigns the network had ever created. Shot on location in Madrid, the television spot—set to the tune of the Beatles song "Hello, Goodbye"—featured tearful Spanish fans waving *adiós* to Beckham and joyous American fans celebrating his arrival. The promo had been running almost nonstop on the ESPN networks for nearly two weeks, a fitting prelude to a broadcast package that ESPN was touting as its "most expansive initiative ever for a single U.S. domestic soccer event." On the schedule: a special thirty-minute preview edition of *SportsCenter* devoted to Beckham; a one-hour documentary called *David Beckham: New Beginnings*; a thirty-minute pregame show; and the game broadcast itself, which featured nineteen cameras, including a Skycam, a Beckham Cam, and a Celebrity Cam. Remarkably, the network whose *SportsCenter* anchors had ridiculed soccer mercilessly over the years was treating a soccer game—and a meaningless one at that—as must-see TV.

But ESPN wanted something significant in return for its Beckham investment: ratings of the sort that would dwarf the minuscule audiences it was drawing for its weekly Thursday-night MLS broadcasts on ESPN2. In 2007, ESPN was paying MLS a rights fee for the first time as part of a new eight-year, $64 million contract. (In previous years, MLS had actually paid ESPN to broadcast its games, a time-buy that gave the network no incentive to spend a dime on promotion.) John Skipper, ESPN's new executive vice president for content, was a soccer fan, and his move to purchase the broadcast rights to the 2010 and 2014 World Cups (for $100 million) came with a commitment to FIFA that ESPN would support MLS.

Not even a regular Thursday time slot and the promotional muscle of ESPN had moved the MLS ratings needle. In ESPN2's fourteen MLS broadcasts in 2007 before Beckham joined the Galaxy, the average rating of 0.2 (202,000 homes) was flat with the previous year's rating (0.2/200,000) for MLS's time-buy broadcasts. "If, before the season, you told me that we'd be at a 0.2 before Beckham, I'd tell you that I'd be disappointed," ESPN senior coordinating producer Tim Scanlan told the *Sports Business Journal*. "We clearly weren't expecting those ratings."

Should Beckham have even considered taking the field against Chelsea? Of course not. He hadn't been healthy enough to practice yet with the Galaxy, he'd be risking further damage if he played, and he was going to be in MLS for five years, after all. But Beckham knew as well as anyone: His buzz in the U.S. would never be higher, ESPN needed that big rating, and it was vital to his own interests that ESPN got that rating. Lalas knew too, which is why he didn't crack a smile that night in Colorado when it was pointed out that ESPN execs must have been about to hang themselves. "There are no sure things in sports," Lalas said wearily. "I wish I had a better answer, because we'll do anything we possibly can to get him on the field. We all live in Hollywood, so we know what a script looks like. Sometimes you have to deviate from the script and make something out of it. On Saturday we'll try to make something out of it, with or without him."

Lalas walked off down the hallway, a man muttering to himself, a man who suddenly seemed very alone.

"*Fuck.*"

Simon Fuller's 19 Entertainment knew what a script looked like, too. David Beckham was a gold-plated international *brand*, after all, and like any other elite brand, Fuller reasoned, the Beckham Brand needed to have a long-term vision, a meticulously crafted media strategy, and military precision when it came to controlling Beckham's words, images, and reputation. The tasks were far too great for Fuller to manage alone, and so he employed a small army of advisers for Beckham. There were three publicists, one in London, two in Los Angeles. There was also an agent with CAA, a personal assistant, a representative who handled appearances and endorsements, multiple Beckham Brand assistants at 19 (including a designer for Beckham's website), and a personal manager/soccer adviser.

The last figure—and easily the most fascinating of the bunch—happened to be Beckham's best friend. While Fuller was the big-idea man for Beckham's career, Beckham's regular sidekick was Terry Byrne ("my mate for fifteen years," as Beckham put it), an open-faced Brit who bore a striking resemblance to the comedian Ricky Gervais. A former London cabdriver and later a massage therapist and equipment manager for Chelsea and England, Byrne earned Beckham's everlasting gratitude for his support on the worst night of his career. It was Byrne who accompanied Beckham to the locker room after he'd been ejected from England's second-round loss to Argentina at the 1998 World Cup. And it was Byrne who stood by Beckham as the British tabloids turned him into a scapegoat who became the target of death threats. Beckham hired Byrne (a godfather to Beckham's children) as his personal manager in 2003, and Byrne had increased his stature as Beckham's straight-talking right-hand man ever since. Now that he was a business associate of Simon Fuller's 19 Entertainment, those who underestimated Byrne's power did so at their peril. "He's David's best friend, and he keeps David on the straight and narrow," said Tim Leiweke. "Without Terry Byrne believing in us, we never would have pulled this off. *Never*."

As Leiweke and everyone else with the Galaxy acknowledged, if you wanted to communicate anything important to Beckham, you went through Byrne. Yet questions swirled around Beckham's best friend, who'd signed on as Beckham's personal manager after spending two years as the director of soccer at Watford, a second-tier English club. Could Byrne keep Beckham calm through the inevitable frustrations of playing with low-skilled teammates? How much influence would Byrne try to exert behind the scenes on soccer issues with the Galaxy? And for that matter, how much sway would Leiweke give him?

For if there was a common theme among Beckham's inner circle and 19 Entertainment in any matter connected to Beckham, it was their insistence on a breathtaking degree of control. They were the gatekeepers of the Beckham Brand, and they had discovered they could make detailed (and occasionally outrageous) demands of any groups—team executives, sponsors, media outlets—that wanted a piece of the Beckham magic. If some of those demands compromised the ethics of those organizations, that wasn't 19's problem to worry about. Besides, it was remarkable how often those groups ceded control that they wouldn't ordinarily dream of giving up, kowtowing to the star power of David Beckham—who was almost always unaware himself of the ultimatums issued in his name. Beckham's advisers knew all too well: At the highest levels of celebrity, handlers were usually fired for exhibiting too little control, not demanding too much.

For months, 19's entire publicity strategy had been pointing toward Beckham's big-bang opening week in Los Angeles, which would end up being capped off by the Tom Cruise–hosted party and the game against Chelsea. The linchpins of that strategy were the spread in *Sports Illustrated*, which would position Beckham as an athlete; the promotional campaign with ESPN, along with the filming of the one-hour "documentary" (as ESPN called it in an official press release) to be shown on the network before the Chelsea game; and an advertising campaign called "Fútbol vs. Football" with Adidas, Beckham's lifetime shoe and apparel sponsor, in which Beckham and NFL running back Reggie Bush took turns teaching each other how to play their respective sports.

Fuller's original plan for Beckham didn't include his participation in any celebrity-themed media; the fear was that it would have taken away from the Beckham-as-athlete message. But the strategy changed when *W* magazine, a glossy fashion monthly, approached 19 about a provocative photo spread featuring both David and Victoria that would be released to coincide with their U.S. arrival. Victoria wasn't the draw that she once was, and the magazine would go for it only if she could persuade David to be involved as well. After she did, the shoot took place in Spain, and the results were startling: a racy series of photographs that included the Beckhams frolicking in bed in their underwear; Victoria sprawled in front of a shirtless David, her legs spread wide, on the hood of a car; and various other shots meant to evoke pre- and postcoital bliss. Some called it tacky, some called it hot, but just about everyone who saw the spread had a reaction, and that was precisely the point.

In each instance of 19's publicity strategy, Beckham's handlers demanded an enormous amount of control. They were granted final approval over the images and text in the *W* photo spread as well as the content in the Adidas campaign with Reggie Bush. As for ESPN, Fuller strong-armed the U.S. television giant into giving up control over the "Hello, Goodbye" promotional campaign and the *David Beckham: New Beginnings* "documentary." In fact, ESPN actually paid a six-figure sum to 19 for producing the show, which provided exclusive access to both David and Victoria. The practice of paying the subjects you cover may be commonplace in the rough-and-tumble British tabloids, but it was still an ethical no-no in almost every sector of U.S. journalism. ESPN had crashed over that line in 2006 by paying a production company a reported $4.5 million (an estimated $1 million of which went to Barry Bonds) to produce a show chronicling Bonds's chase for baseball's all-time home-run record. Paying 19 for *New Beginnings* was just one more example of checkbook journalism. What's more, ESPN never explicitly stated to its viewers that the show wasn't a documentary, as the ESPN press release had claimed, but rather an hour-long Beckham Brand infomercial produced by Beckham's own handlers.

As ESPN was learning, Simon Fuller may have been British, but he played classic American hardball. Frustrated ESPN staffers complained that 19 controlled every aspect of the *New Beginnings* infomercial, including hand-picking a favored British interviewer who didn't work for ESPN. What's more, they lamented, ESPN was unable to land any interview access to Beckham for *ESPN The Magazine,* despite the six-figure payment to 19 for access on ESPN television.

That was because Fuller and 19 had decided to make Beckham available instead for *Sports Illustrated*, which had a longer tradition and a bigger circulation (3.1 million) than ESPN's magazine (2 million). But then 19 made a significant misstep. It gave *SI* a list of demands—including granting 19 approval over the final product's words and photographs—that it wanted the magazine to agree to in writing before 19 would arrange the Beckham interview and photo shoot. That strategy may have worked with sports magazines in Europe and even celebrity magazines in the U.S. (Angelina Jolie had turned it into an art form), but Fuller had overplayed his hand. The magazine responded that as a news publication it did not enter into written agreements with the subjects of its stories, adding that it would use the images from the photo shoot as it pleased on its multiple platforms. (*SI*'s only concession was to let 19 have approval over the syndication of the photographs to third parties, a standard practice with top celebrities that would allow 19 to prevent, say, *Playgirl* or *Holocaust Deniers Monthly* from purchasing and using the Beckham shots.)

The exchange with *SI* was illuminating, a sign that Fuller and 19 didn't fully understand the American media elite (the list of demands was taken in some quarters of *SI* as an insult) and overvalued Beckham's status in the United States. The message from *SI* to 19 was simple—take it or leave it—and 19 decided to take it. A rep on Beckham's side admitted that 19 had never given up as much control for a major magazine article as it had to *Sports Illustrated*. Not only did *SI* refuse to guarantee Beckham (or any story subject) a place on its cover, but the magazine's hard-line stance provoked such a response of respect from 19 that Beckham's chief publicist, Simon Oliveira, didn't even try to sit in on my interview with Beckham in Madrid. (Whenever that happens on other stories, I politely say that *SI* agreed to a one-on-one interview, not a one-on-two interview.)

Ultimately, 19 was thrilled with the *Sports Illustrated* package, including the photographs, the open-minded story, and Beckham's place on the cover itself. (It certainly helped that Barry Bonds remained a few home runs shy of breaking the home-run record that week, or he likely would have taken the cover instead.) Oliveira even suggested that Beckham would love to attend a party thrown in his honor by *SI* after the Galaxy's road game against the New York Red Bulls on August 18. Although such magazine-sponsored parties were apparently common among the celebrity set—the Beckhams would attend a party thrown by *Allure* celebrating Victoria's August 2008 cover—it was hard to know how to interpret such a request: as the ultimate sign of 19's respect (*David Beckham wants to be associated with your brand!*) or as a blindingly nervy lack of manners (*David Beckham wants you to drop thousands of dollars on a party to celebrate David Beckham!*). Beckham got the cover; he didn't get the party.

Aside from the snafu over 19's rejected demands list, Beckham himself was thoroughly professional—downright charming, even—in his dealings with *SI* on the story. He arrived at the Madrid studio on May 24, 2007, a half hour early for the interview and photo shoot. Despite a persistent cough, the result of a nagging cold, he was talkative and candid during the nearly sixty-minute interview, and at the end of the hour-long photo session he thanked the half-dozen assistants individually, not once but twice. ("I've never had that happen before," one said.) It was the antithesis of a diva act.

But if there were any doubts over how closely 19 protected Beckham's image, they were answered on a call from Oliveira a few hours before *SI*'s Beckham cover was to be released publicly. Oliveira was deeply concerned that a picture of Beckham from *SI*'s Madrid photo shoot had somehow appeared on an unauthorized Beckham fansite. Had there been a leak at the magazine? Worst of all, Oliveira added, the picture— of a smiling Becks juggling a soccer ball in the new Galaxy uniform— was a disaster. Beckham hated smiley shots that showed his imperfect teeth. "It's *awful*," Oliveira said. "David won't like that at all."

"It's not awful," I said. "I don't like it as much as the actual *SI* cover shot"—in which Beckham was rocking his favored Blue Steel gaze— "but it's not awful."

After some poking around, it turned out that a producer at SI.com, not realizing the photo was supposed to be off-limits until the magazine was published, had added the Madrid shot at the end of an online photo gallery featuring a dozen Beckham pictures from over the years. The photo was buried on *SI*'s website—and not even on the front page— but the Beckham fansite had discovered and posted the image, and now Oliveira was worried that this "awful" picture would become the defining shot that got sent around the world. In the end, it wasn't: I apologized for the mistake, and *SI*'s PR department released the *SI* cover image a few hours early, allowing Blue Steel Beckham under the *Sports Illustrated* banner to be the defining global image. The crisis was averted, but Oliveira's eagle-eyed oversight was nevertheless highly revealing.

Sometimes you could understand why 19 was so vigilant about trying to influence Beckham's coverage in the media. The British tabloids, in particular, produced a blizzard of half-truths, unsourced gossip, and bald-faced lies about David and Victoria Beckham—in the sports pages and in the celebrity pages. Fuller and the rest of Beckham's advisers at 19 had been shaped (and scarred) by the razor-sharp knives of Fleet Street. "I'm in the entertainment industry," said Fuller. "I witness the greatness of the media and the destructive, negative side of the media." Although journalists and commentators were generally friendlier in the U.S., there were some exceptions, particularly at the *Los Angeles Times*. Lead sports columnist Bill Plaschke had this to say on the day of Beckham's introduction: "The Galaxy has won three of twelve games; I predict he won't take them anywhere but to the bank." Meanwhile, *Times* writer T. J. Simers began a story with this line: "The bloke is already a joke, and a case could be made, if anyone really cared, that Beckham's a thief—stealing millions from the Anschutz Empire." Then there were the sometimes bizarre questions that would surprise Beckham in interviews ostensibly about sports. Many of them, oddly enough, came from the Spanish-language media: *Do you believe in a supreme being? . . . What's your favorite kind of taco? . . . I've been told you want to adopt a Mexican-American girl.*

Whenever Beckham spoke to the assembled media, a verbal slipup could harm the Brand. As a result, the banality of a Beckham press conference could be soul-crushing, even by jock standards. Most top athletes have gone through some sort of media training, but if you attended enough of Beckham's speaking engagements it sure seemed like 19 was controlling the message with a distinct set of brutally anodyne talking points. Beckham delivered his go-to sound bites with an almost oracular gravitas, usually followed by a thin smile that called to mind the jarring grin that John McCain sometimes flashed in his speeches. Beckham's favorites included:

American patriotism. Beckham knew you couldn't go wrong by appealing to the flag-waving impulses of the Yanks. In fact, he could take a question that had nothing to do with the topic and turn it into an ode to "The Star-Spangled Banner." When Beckham was asked on ESPN2 at the All-Star Game on July 19 what he and his family wanted to do in the U.S. together, this was Beckham's actual response: "There's many things. America is such a huge country and so patriotic, and that's why I'm so honored to actually be here and be a part of this country. 'Cause I'm from England and they're very patriotic about their sports, and to be honest, the American public, the country as a whole is so patriotic, not just about sport but about the country. That's what I love about living here." *Smile.*

The "I'm not silly"/higher-level speech. Fully aware that NASL officials had predicted in the 1970s that soccer would challenge the supremacy of the NFL, Beckham always tempered his goals for MLS while making sure to profess his deep respect for the more established American sports: "I'm not silly enough to sit here and say [soccer] is going to be bigger than baseball, basketball, or American football, and ice hockey . . . because there's so much great tradition, so many great sportsmen who play these sports. But we can raise [soccer] to a certain level that's higher than it has been." *Smile.* Lalas heard so many versions of the "I'm not silly" stump speech that he couldn't take it anymore. "He needs to be silly," Lalas said. "I could argue that in many ways we've already passed hockey."

MLS is better than most Europeans think. The question about the quality of play in MLS compared to Europe inevitably came up in every Beckham press conference. And the response was the same every time: "The standard is a lot better than people have actually talked about. But, of course, there's always room for improvement in any walk of life." *Smile.* (He got bonus points for the Zen-like "any walk of life" finish.)

It's about the kids. Much like his riff on American patriotism, Beckham didn't miss a chance to talk about his charity work with children or his David Beckham Academy for boys and girls (which he neglected to add was very much a for-profit enterprise): "It's always important to be a role model for children. When I visited Harlem last year it was an incredible experience, and I tried to do everything possible that I can do to help kids and to help obviously the game. So that's my role." *Smile.*

I'm here for five years. As it became clear that Beckham's ankle injury was worse than anyone suspected—and that he would miss playing time during his all-important first month with the Galaxy—he adopted a standard line for the media and disappointed ticket-buyers, which he first pulled out during the All-Star Game interview on ESPN2: "I'm here for five years. I'm not here just obviously for the game on Saturday. It's great that Chelsea are here, it's great to have great players and a great team and a great manager here, but I think it's more important for me personally that my ankle is right, and I don't think it'll be right for the game. So maybe I'll play in some part toward the end of the game if it's all right, but we'll see." (More bonus points for using the word "great" five times in one sentence.)

Only now, two nights before his Galaxy debut, Beckham wasn't wearing his customary end-of-quote smile. He appeared devastated, in fact. Simon Fuller and 19 Entertainment had masterminded a nearly perfect media rollout, controlling almost all of it, and everything important had fallen into place—the Real Madrid title, the *Sports Illustrated* cover, the introductory press day, the Hollywood buzz—with one glaring exception. Beckham's ankle injury was a powerful reminder that no matter how much influence you may wield or how wealthy you may be, you can't control sports.

How much did the tables turn? In the hours before the Chelsea game, as the celebrity-studded crowd began arriving at the Home Depot Center, Beckham and his advisers started wondering if outside forces were trying to strong-arm *them*. ESPN.com posted a news story on the front of its website written by "ESPN News Services" and citing "sources" saying that Beckham understood the importance of his participation in the game. Whether the story was trying to communicate a message to Beckham on behalf of ESPN or the Galaxy wasn't certain, but more than a few observers began to wonder, including ESPN's own commentator, Eric Wynalda. "If I really put that through my computer as a [former] player trying to figure out where pressure should come from to get you back on the field," he said, "it certainly should *not* come from a network's desire to get ratings."

Beckham was going to play. Not for ninety minutes, and not because he wanted to, but because he knew *he had to play*. Besides, Lalas said, the Galaxy would just ask Chelsea not to have anyone go in hard to tackle Beckham. Everyone would understand. It was a friendly, after all.

"Back up! Back up! Back up!"

It was, for a few anxious seconds, a borderline terrifying sight. What began as a fun pregame moment—Beckham trotting out of the stadium tunnel, waving to a packed Home Depot Center, and taking his seat on the bench next to his Galaxy teammates—was turning into a full-blown, out-of-control human crush. Forty . . . sixty . . . then eighty photographers and Minicam operators crowded around Beckham, four and five rows deep, jostling for position, holding their cameras high over their heads like periscopes, inching closer . . . closer . . . closer, until they were clearly invading Beckham's personal space. Finally, a phalanx of security guards squeezed in with a rope line and pushed the horde backward, giving Beckham and his teammates some breathing room.

For anyone who had spent years at MLS games, who had grown accustomed to seeing small groups of dedicated fans outnumbered by thousands of empty seats, the scene surrounding Beckham's Galaxy debut might as well have been part of a separate universe. On a glorious Southern California evening, every seat in the HDC was taken, from the luxury suites to the upper-deck benches to the $500 field-side director's chairs. A VIP parade of Hollywood and sports stars, including many who'd never attended a soccer game or set foot in low-rent Carson, had turned out for the event: the Beckham family, of course, but also Katie Holmes (holding her daughter, Suri Cruise), Eva Longoria Parker, Mary-Kate Olsen, Governor Arnold Schwarzenegger, Kevin Garnett, Jennifer Love-Hewitt, Alicia Silverstone, and Drew Carey (who was actually a longtime Galaxy season-ticket holder). So many media members had applied for credentials that the Galaxy had taken the unprecedented action of setting up an auxiliary press section in a corner of the stadium. Beckham himself was decked out for the special occasion, wearing custom-made shoes by Adidas with American flags and the names of Victoria and their kids stitched into them.

But there was also a profound strangeness to it all. A game was going on, of course—and a surprisingly good one—but the excitement wasn't really about the soccer. Two-time defending Premier League champion Chelsea was in the house, but stars like John Terry, Michael Ballack, Michael Essien, Andriy Shevchenko, and Didier Drogba were relegated to supporting-cast status on this night, especially on the television broadcast. Mainstream American sports fans just didn't know them. "If I signed Zinédine Zidane tomorrow, Middle America would have no idea who he is," said Lalas. "Or he'd be that crazy guy who head-butted somebody. Well, that crazy guy who head-butted somebody happens to be one of the greatest players ever to play the game. It's sad, but it's the American culture."

Beckham was different. Beckham had crossover appeal. But Beckham's injury—and his inability to play for the first seventy-eight minutes of the game—only reinforced the surreal disconnect between the celebrity star power in attendance and the game itself. Fans who sat near the Beckham family's luxury box said the spectators in their section spent as much time looking backward at the celebrities as they did watching the action on the field. Sitting on the bench, David Beckham was unable to bridge the gap. MLS couldn't catch a break. Its most heavily publicized television broadcast before the Beckham game, the 2004 debut of fourteen-year-old prodigy Freddy Adu, had turned into a dud when his D.C. United coach surprisingly benched him.

ESPN tried to make the best of the situation, keeping up with the game action but cutting away whenever possible to its "Star Patrol" interviews, more than a dozen views of Victoria in the Beckham box, and (no lie) forty-seven different shots of David on the sidelines during the game. It was hard to tell which moment was more absurd. Was it when ESPN's Beckham Cam showed a close-up, slow-motion replay of Beckham taking his left shoe off on the bench? Was it when Beckham drew the stadium's biggest cheer thus far of the night for kicking the ball back onto the field during his second-half sideline warm-up? Or was it when ESPN announcer Dave O'Brien compared Beckham's imminent game entrance to Willis Reed's return from injury to spark the New York Knicks in the 1970 NBA Finals—one of the most famous moments in NBA history?

Yet for all the schlock, no one could dispute that Beckham's seventy-eighth-minute entry was a special moment—for him, for the fans, for the Galaxy players and organization—or that it was first-rate melodrama. In the seventieth minute, Beckham left the field to have his ankle retaped in the Galaxy locker room, and five minutes later he galloped out of the tunnel. By the time he pulled off his warm-up, the camera flashes in the stadium formed a thousand points of light. "The theater of it was beautiful," said Lalas, whose week-long existential angst melted. "And it was fun. And I don't mind telling you that it was a proud kind of moment." Beckham came on for Alan Gordon, who was now the answer to a trivia question. ("If I'd known how big a moment it was, I would have taken my time, fixed my hair, given him a hug or something," Gordon would joke.) Beckham trotted onto the field, got a low-five from Landon Donovan, and spent the next few minutes testing the ankle, favoring it slightly, employing a skipping motion when he ran that suggested he was far from match-fit.

But the cheers came stronger than ever. The fans could appreciate that Beckham was trying to play through the pain, and the teenage girls (and probably a few boys) in the crowd squealed over anything he did: clearing a ball from the Galaxy box, taking a corner kick, waving to them after the game. When Beckham launched a looping forty-yard pass to Quavas Kirk in the eighty-first minute, you got a sense of the vision Beckham could bring to the Galaxy attack. The crowd gave Beckham a rousing ovation.

Then, in the first minute of injury time, disaster nearly struck. Beckham briefly lost control of the ball near midfield, and a Chelsea reserve named Steve Sidwell, who was trying to earn a spot on the team, violated the lay-off-Beckham message and came in *hard*. Beckham, whose instinct was always to play at full speed, lunged at the ball, and Sidwell's cleats struck Beckham's right foot, sending him airborne, and then he crumpled to the ground. For a moment the exchange sucked the air out of the stadium. Horror-stricken Galaxy coach Frank Yallop thought Beckham had severely injured his knee. Slowly, Beckham stood up, grabbed his injured left ankle, and resumed playing. When the final whistle blew on Chelsea's 1–0 victory, everyone breathed a sigh of relief.

Beckham was glad to have survived a game he never should have played in, but he didn't come out unscathed from Sidwell's hard-but-legal challenge. As Beckham would say, "it definitely aggravated [the ankle injury] and put me back at least a week." He would end up miss-ing the next four Galaxy games: three in the Superliga, a tournament in-volving teams from MLS and the Mexican league, and an MLS game in Toronto.

Of course, the most important number from the Chelsea game was not the 1–0 score line. After averaging a 0.2 rating for its MLS broad-casts, ESPN's presentation of Beckham's debut earned a 1.0 rating, meaning it was seen in an average of 947,000 television homes. On the one hand, the audience was five times greater than the typical size for ESPN's MLS broadcasts, and it was the most-viewed MLS telecast ever on ESPN or ESPN2. But on the whole, the rating was massively disap-pointing, given the national media buzz and two weeks of constant pro-motion by ESPN. Freddy Adu's MLS debut had drawn a higher rating (1.3) on ABC in 2004, and the Beckham debut was beaten among that weekend's sports broadcasts by the British Open golf tournament (not surprising), a regular-season national baseball game (somewhat sur-prising), and even the IRL Honda 200 motor race (extremely surpris-ing). Why, the final game of the Women's College World Series on ESPN2 the previous month had earned a 1.8 rating. That's right: A women's softball game outdrew Beckham's debut by nearly 2 to 1.

How much had Beckham's injury and seventy-eight minutes of bench time hurt ratings? You couldn't know for certain, but it was as-suredly a significant factor. This much was now clear: Drawing U.S. tel-evision audiences for soccer would be a harder challenge for Beckham than anything Steve Sidwell could ever throw at him. At least there was one saving grace. The Beckhams' big Hollywood welcome party was the next night, and David had no doubts whatsoever that he would be able to participate.

It was, as *Entertainment Tonight* not-so-understatedly called it, "the party to end all parties, welcoming the Beckhams to the upper strato-sphere of Hollywood." On the night of July 22, 2007, blocks of downtown Los Angeles were closed down around the Museum of Contemporary Art. British and American flags flew over the valet stand. Helicopters hovered overhead, police and security officers kept curious onlookers at bay, and a multitude of paparazzi swarmed near the rope line, clamoring for the money shot, the image that Simon Fuller and the all-powerful Creative Artists Agency hoped would define David and Victoria Beckham as members of Hollywood royalty.

Posing with the Beckhams were two of America's most famous celebrity couples: Tom Cruise and Katie Holmes, the pairing so ubiquitous that the tabloids called them TomKat, and their cohosts for the event, Will and Jada Pinkett Smith. The three men were all dashing in designer suits, while Victoria and Pinkett Smith wore short black dresses and Holmes opted for a stunning red vintage gown. Mainstream Americans might have had a hard time grasping the finer points of professional soccer, but they understood (and consumed) megawatt star power with a zeal that bordered on fanaticism. And compared to sports, with its unplanned injuries, unscripted action, and pesky upset defeats, controlling this celebrity party stuff was easy. All you had to do was get the right people to show up.

No figure was more instrumental in that process than Cruise, who had flown in for the event from Germany, where he was filming the World War II movie *Valkyrie*. Cruise and the Beckhams had met four years earlier, and it wasn't long before Cruise flew to Spain to attend a Real Madrid game as David's guest. "We sort of just got to be friends from then on, really," Beckham told me. "And obviously Victoria got to be friends with Katie. It's nice to have someone that you've actually got a lot in common with and get along with and have the same ideas and feelings about your job and your family. He's a good-hearted person, and he's been good to me for the time that we've known each other."

Indeed, Cruise had become one of the most influential people in Beckham's life. Both David and Victoria shared Cruise's rep, the Creative Artists Agency, the most powerful collection of agents in Hollywood. David took Cruise's recommendation and hired the actor's Los Angeles–based public-relations firm, Rogers & Cowan, to help handle the U.S. media. And Beckham revealed that he had gone to Cruise for advice on the two nights before he signed the contract to join the Galaxy. "I speak to Tom most days of the week, just chatting about work and the kids and Victoria and Katie," Beckham said. "I asked him certain things about living in L.A. and what the experience could be like, and he gave me his advice as a friend and told me the good things and a couple of things to be aware of. He was just being a mate."

If Terry Byrne was Beckham's best friend, Cruise and Holmes had turned into the Beckhams' favorite couple. Victoria had attended the Cruise/Holmes wedding in Italy (David missed out due to soccer commitments), and Cruise and Holmes had sat with Victoria in the stands at Beckham's title-clinching last game at Real Madrid before staying out to celebrate until 6 A.M. the next day. When Victoria picked the Beckhams' house on San Ysidro Drive in Beverly Hills, it was less than five minutes from their new neighbors, Cruise and Holmes. David even acknowledged that Cruise had influenced the decision to name the Beckhams' third son Cruz. "I must admit, when we met Tom, I remember turning around to Victoria and saying, 'Cruise is a great name, but we could spell it *different*,'" Beckham told me. "And also living in Spain, Cruz spelled the way it is is Spanish. So that's why we got it."

Of course, the more time the Beckhams spent with Cruise and Holmes, the more skeptics questioned whether Cruise saw David's vast global appeal as a potential vehicle to spread the message of the Church of Scientology. Cruise was a vocal believer in Scientology, the controversial faith founded by the science-fiction writer L. Ron Hubbard, and Holmes had become a Scientologist before marrying Cruise. The faith had gained a measure of popularity in Hollywood—members included John Travolta, Kirstie Alley, and Lisa Marie Presley—but in some countries (Germany, for one) government officials viewed the church as a dangerous cult. Did David Beckham have any interest in joining Cruise as a Scientologist? "No," Beckham told me. "It's something obviously I respect, because Tom's explained to me and Victoria what it's all about, but he's never turned around to us and said, 'That is what you should be doing,' because he would never do that. He and Katie have their beliefs, and I totally respect that, but me and Victoria have also got our own."

In Beckham's interactions with Cruise, at least one conversion *had* taken place, however. "I think Tom's getting into soccer," Beckham said, flashing a wide smile. "He'll send me a message after every game that I've played now, and he'll say: *What an amazing game!*" If Beckham could have the same effect on a few million other Americans, then the Beckham Experiment might just have a chance.

That Cruise had flown all the way from Berlin to attend the party suggested how important the occasion was for him. Yet the presence of Will and Jada Pinkett Smith as headlining cohosts was more puzzling. Will Smith was one of the most bankable movie stars in Hollywood, an entertainer blessed with reservoirs of charisma, but neither he nor his wife had more than a cursory relationship with the Beckhams, and nothing close to the ties that Cruise and Holmes had. Although Cruise and Holmes would regularly be seen with the Beckhams in the months ahead—hosting them at their home in Telluride, Colorado; spending Thanksgiving together in New York City; joining them in Napa Valley wine country to celebrate Victoria's birthday—the Smiths were rarely, if ever, spotted with the Beckhams by the paparazzi that constantly followed them.

The main bond that Will Smith did share with the Beckhams—and with Cruise and Holmes—was their representation by the Creative Artists Agency. CAA was the most respected and feared talent agency in Hollywood, with clients that included Brad Pitt, Oprah Winfrey, Sean Penn, Julia Roberts, and George Clooney, among dozens of other A-listers. In large part due to its relationship with Simon Fuller, it was crucial for CAA to ensure that the Beckhams made as big a splash as possible upon their arrival in the United States. On July 16, CAA had hosted a welcoming bash for David at its new Century City headquarters, an eight-floor, $400 million building that people in the movie business had nicknamed The Death Star. (CAA employees were reportedly instructed beforehand to line the staircase and clap for Beckham upon his arrival.) And while it was fun to imagine that Holmes and the Smiths had made all the arrangements for the following week's party as cohosts, CAA had in fact organized the event and handled all the preparations, including the gold-embossed invitations.

When you're the most powerful agency in Hollywood, there are no limits to how much you can orchestrate when it comes to hosting a party for David and Victoria Beckham—most of all the celebrity guest list, which was almost entirely CAA-affiliated talent. It was glitz by association, a classic case study on how to package foreign stars as A-list

American celebrities. Yet when U.S. viewers saw breathless coverage of the party leading off the following night's editions of *Entertainment Tonight* and *Access Hollywood*, the word "CAA" was never mentioned. What they saw was "the party to end all parties, welcoming the Beckhams to the upper stratosphere of Hollywood," highlighted by the money shot: David and Victoria posing with Tom Cruise, Katie Holmes, and Will and Jada Pinkett Smith.

Somewhere, Simon Fuller smiled.

Not that it wasn't a hell of a party. It was. Inside the Geffen Contemporary gallery, where thousands of flowers, a booming sound system, and concert-quality lighting had transformed the trendy warehouse space, guests could munch on catered comfort food like burgers and fries from In-N-Out and British bangers and mash (both David's favorites). But more than anything else, the night was about pure, unbridled dancing. Celebrity deejay Samantha Ronson blasted a playlist featuring Amy Winehouse's "Rehab," John Mellencamp's "Jack and Diane," and the Spice Girls' classic "Wannabe." Then Doug E. Fresh laid the beat while Stevie Wonder sang a fifteen-minute a cappella set that included his hit "Signed, Sealed, Delivered." But the highlight of the night was Will Smith's impromptu session, in which the former Fresh Prince performed "Summertime," splitting the dance floor into two sections, asking which side was having more fun, and demanding that each side scream louder. Acting like a man who forgot he was wearing a designer suit, Smith even did the splits, bringing the house down.

Beckham's Galaxy teammates appreciated that he had invited all of them to the party—even the developmental-roster guys making less than $20,000 a year—and that Beckham had taken the time to greet them, say hello to their significant others, and mention the Galaxy players during his onstage toast. "I'd like to thank my teammates for coming out here," Beckham said, raising his glass, "and I hope we have a great season." Nearly all the Galaxy players had a fun story from their night with the Hollywood stars. Forward Gavin Glinton talked with one of his favorite rappers, Common, about his new CD. Defender Kyle Veris spoke with Tom Cruise, and Katie Holmes complimented his girlfriend on her dress. Meanwhile, defender Ante Jazic and goalkeeper Lance Friesz did all the guys proud, sharing a lengthy conversation with the former *Spin City* actress Jennifer Esposito. (Hey, nobody ever said that soccer players were lacking in the looks department.)

"That was probably the best party I've ever been to," said Chris Klein. "You have this perception of Hollywood that either everyone's on drugs or all they do is party because that's all they have to do, but this was pure fun and entertainment. No one was falling over drunk. And the way David acted toward his teammates, he was just a genuine guy, a great host."

From a celebrity-positioning perspective, the party couldn't have gone any better. On Monday night, in a typical show of restraint, *Entertainment Tonight* treated the event as nothing less than an epochal Hollywood moment. ("They are the It couple right now, and we are your Posh and Becks source!") If you flipped the channel, *Access Hollywood* was doing its own story on the Beckham bob, Victoria's new haircut, which it said had become America's most requested style of the summer.

But just as some television stars had a hard time extending their appeal to the big screen of the movies, the Beckhams struggled to translate their newfound popularity from short-attention-span celebrity shows, magazine items, and YouTube highlight clips to the longer-term appointment viewing of one- and two-hour TV broadcasts. Victoria's 19-produced reality-show special ran in prime time on NBC that night, and it was predictably awful. David made only a token appearance, and while Victoria tried to send up her image ("I don't want to be seen smiling, having fun, or eating!"), she never came across as a fish out of water, the supposed conceit, but rather as one more mindless Hollywood wife. "It's exhausting being fabulous," Victoria proclaimed, but it was even more exhausting watching the show. "There must be a reason NBC chose to lavish an hour of prime time on *Victoria Beckham: Coming to America*," wrote the TV critic of the *New York Times*. "But conspiracy theorists will be hard put to connect the dots."

It wasn't that complicated, really. Months earlier, Fuller had negotiated a deal with NBC in which the network would broadcast six half-hour episodes of Victoria's show. But NBC's interest cooled, and it decided to shift the episodes to the lower-profile Bravo cable network. Fuller was irate, and he and NBC reached a compromise: The show would air as a one-hour, stand-alone broadcast on NBC. If *Coming to America* had drawn world-beating ratings, network executives would have forgiven the fact that it was terrible. But while the show won its time slot, earning a 2.2 rating, the tepid numbers weren't high enough to leave NBC clamoring for more. Victoria would end up making occasional TV guest appearances—she played herself in one on ABC's *Ugly Betty*—but Posh's prospects as a small-screen star were bleak.

For his part, David had an advantage over his wife: Most of his Galaxy games would continue to be broadcast on national television. But you get only one chance to make a first impression, and the megahyped Chelsea match was a huge missed opportunity for Beckham to sell soccer to Americans, earn an eye-popping television rating, and position himself as an athlete, not just celebrity eye candy. Although the Cruise-hosted party had been a hit, Beckham's injury-shortened appearance in his own made-for-TV event had upset the delicate sports/celebrity balance that powered the Beckham sweet spot. What's more, now that the initial wave of publicity was over, would it even be possible for the soccer side to catch up with the celebrity side? If Beckham was going to make any inroads in the project that mattered most to him—he was here for the soccer, remember—he needed to get back on the field ASAP. And so, in a move that went unpublicized at the time, Beckham hired a physical therapist outside the Galaxy medical staff to spend hour after hour with him at his house in Beverly Hills.

Who was the guy that Beckham had trusted to recommend the new therapist? Tom Cruise.

"LET HIM BE THE CAPTAIN, YOU BE THE STAR"

The summit meeting took place at Mastro's, a high-class steak house in Beverly Hills just off Rodeo Drive. On July 25, three days after the Hollywood party to end all parties, David and Victoria Beckham joined Landon Donovan and his wife, Bianca Kajlich, for a get-to-know-you meal at one of the trendiest meateries in Los Angeles. At the Home Depot Center, the ten-foot-high profiles of Beckham and Donovan stared at each other like separated Mount Rushmore heads across the south side of the stadium on gigantic banners bearing their names and numbers. Now, for the first time, the Galaxy's two biggest stars were facing each other across the dinner table.

Nearly everywhere else in the world, Donovan's achievements would have made him a household name in his own country, a fixture on the covers of sports magazines and (considering that his wife starred in the CBS sitcom *Rules of Engagement*) the celebrity rags, too. As a twenty-year-old at the 2002 World Cup, Donovan had scored the goal that sealed the most important victory in U.S. men's soccer history, a 2–0 second-round defeat of archrival Mexico. Now twenty-five, he had already won three MLS championships and a record three awards as his national team's Player of the Year. Yet Donovan had the fate, equal parts fortune and curse, of being born in the United States. Which is to say that the posse of three dozen paparazzi outside was not there for him.

In the Galaxy's pre-Beckham world, though, Donovan had been a giant, the captain of the team, the U.S. scoring star who was committed to raising the sport's profile in America. Beckham's arrival changed

everything for Donovan—most of all his status as the main attraction—
and if the Beckham Experiment was going to work, Donovan needed to
be happy. Beckham knew it. Donovan knew it. And so did Frank Yallop,
the Galaxy's mild-mannered second-year coach, who had left nothing to
chance. Yallop put Beckham's locker next to Donovan's at the HDC, the
better to encourage their interaction. The coach had also arranged this
dinner, bringing along his wife, Karen, in the hope there would be less
pressure on the two couples if it was a table for six.

A forty-three-year-old Canadian who had played in England for Ipswich and finished his career as a defender with the Tampa Bay Mutiny,
Yallop had won MLS championships with Donovan in 2001 and 2003
while coaching the San Jose Earthquakes. He enjoyed a reputation as a
players' coach who presided over a harmonious locker room, but Yallop
also faced doubts that his personality was big enough to handle the
media glare that surrounded any team with David Beckham. He knew
as well as anyone that Beckham had played for six coaches in four years
at Real Madrid, and it hardly helped that Yallop's Galaxy had missed the
'06 MLS playoffs and gotten off to its 3–5–4 league start in '07. Yallop
needed wins. He needed Donovan to be on board with the Beckham Experiment. "Landon is an important part of the equation," said Alexi
Lalas. "So Frank's trying to put out any fires before they start."

As they looked over their menus, Donovan had a lot on his mind,
not all of it related to soccer. Would Bianca and Victoria connect? Victoria was the grande diva of England's WAGs—the wives and girlfriends
of famous soccer players—and Donovan wondered if she and Bianca
might set up a western WAG outpost in Los Angeles. (Bianca had already appeared in a Beckham story on *Entertainment Tonight*.) The
Tom Cruise–hosted party had gone well (Bianca had been "a dancing
fool," Donovan said), and the two players' wives could find common
ground swapping tales about life in L.A. and the entertainment industry. But Landon and Bianca had also talked about the astonishing magnitude of the Beckhams' fame, and he could sense from Bianca's
questions beforehand that she was nervous about the dinner. *What's it
going to be like? Do I talk to her like a normal player's wife?*

But Victoria wasn't a normal player's wife, Donovan knew, and
David wasn't a normal MLS soccer player. Donovan couldn't help but

laugh as forty-year-old men in business suits sidled over to their table and asked Beckham for autographs (*Mr. Beckham, I'm a big fan . . .*), ignoring the best player in America. Nor could Donovan avoid noticing the gawking by patrons at other tables when they realized that Posh and Becks were there in the flesh. As the wives chatted among themselves and Yallop got the conversation going by asking David questions about his playing days in Europe, Donovan kept in the back of his mind the stinging memory of two conversations that had taken place just the week before.

On successive days, both Yallop and Alexi Lalas had met privately with Donovan and explained that "people above me"—meaning Tim Leiweke—thought Beckham should eventually be the Galaxy's captain. Both men leavened the blow with the sugarcoated spin you might expect. "They want David to come in and make an impact," Yallop told Donovan. "I don't really look at who has the armband. You're a leader to me, a great player. It would just be great if you could have a relationship with David and you pass it on to him." For his part, Lalas issued Donovan a challenge: "Let him be the captain, you be the star."

What Yallop and Lalas *didn't* tell Donovan—and what the Galaxy's most famous American still didn't know—was that the request to give up his captaincy to Beckham originated not with Leiweke but rather with Beckham's own handlers. The topic had come up when Yallop and Lalas visited Beckham and Terry Byrne (his best friend and personal manager) in Madrid the previous spring. After a lunch at Beckham's house, Beckham stayed inside as Byrne walked Yallop and Lalas out onto the porch. "What are you doing about the captaincy?" asked Byrne, who felt Beckham should be wearing the armband as soon as he joined the team. Neither Yallop nor Lalas felt comfortable reaching a resolution at that point, and so the men agreed to table the idea for the time being. But in the subsequent months before Beckham's arrival, Lalas said, Byrne had made his best friend's wishes explicit more than once to Lalas and Leiweke. "It was made very clear to me that David wanted to be captain—not directly from him, but either from Terry to me or Terry to Tim to me," Lalas would say later. "This was something that was important to David." (Beckham's side confirmed that Byrne had brought up the captaincy issue in Madrid, but denied that it was coming from

Beckham and that Byrne had continued bringing up the topic with Galaxy officials before Beckham's arrival.)

In soccer more than in any other professional sport (except perhaps ice hockey), the players regard wearing the captain's armband as an honor worthy of surpassing respect. Although Beckham had never been the captain at Manchester United (where Roy Keane wore the armband) or at Real Madrid (where Raúl had the role), Beckham considered his five-plus years as the captain of England to be his greatest achievement as a soccer player. Beckham choked back tears at the 2006 press conference announcing he was giving up England's captaincy, and afterward, he said, he threw up. "It may look on the surface like high-school bull-shit," Lalas said, "but in a professional sports environment you'd be surprised to know the gravity with which it's seen and how important it ends up being."

Donovan's first reaction to his bosses' request was a human one. *That's pretty shitty*, he thought to himself. It wasn't so much that he had a problem with someone else being captain, least of all a player with Beckham's credentials, but Donovan did have an acute sense for what he perceived as disrespect. He also enjoyed his role as captain, encouraging and chiding the younger players when necessary, representing the team's views to the coaching staff, being responsible for something bigger than himself. And so Donovan decided not to act immediately. Yallop and Lalas might sweat a bit ("If Landon doesn't want to do it, then I've got a fight on my hands," Yallop would say), but Donovan wanted to get to know Beckham first before he'd consider giving up the armband. The fastest way to bond with a new teammate is by playing games and training with him every day, but Beckham's injury hadn't allowed that to happen yet.

Tonight was Donovan's first real chance. Here at Mastro's, over thick steaks and fine red wine, he was going to pick Beckham's brain and see what he found out. "It's hard," Donovan said, "because there's always this perception of people, so you're just trying to get behind that, get behind the outer wall and see what they're like."

But Donovan also wondered: Would David Beckham let him in?

———

In time, if Beckham and Donovan developed a friendship, there were plenty of common experiences they could share with each other. For starters, both players had grown up in cash-strapped homes surrounded—and heavily influenced—by women. Beckham was raised in the East End of London by his father, Ted, a gas engineer who worked long hours, and his mother, Sandra, a haircutter who did most of the traditional work around the house while keeping an eye on David, his older sister, Lynne, and his younger sister, Joanne. David's high-pitched Essex accent was hardly the patois of the moneyed classes, and while the family wasn't destitute, they made just enough to get by. Ted Beckham, a former Sunday-league soccer player, introduced David to the sport and spent countless hours teaching him its finer points, but David felt closer in personality to Sandra Beckham, crying easily, showing the sort of emotion that his gruff father would never display in the privacy of their home, much less in public. Soccer was David's passion, but he also liked going shopping with the women of the family.

Donovan grew up much the same way in Ontario, California: His parents divorced when he and his twin sister, Tristan, were two years old, and their mother, Donna Kenney, raised them by herself on her meager income as a special-education teacher. The phrase Landon used to describe their circumstances was "American poor": not poor by world standards, but certainly so in the United States. For years they lived on Spam, hot dogs, condensed milk, ramen noodles, macaroni and cheese, and canned vegetables and fruits. "Going to Taco Bell was a big treat for us," Landon said. The family couldn't afford cable television or many indoor toys, so Landon was encouraged to play different sports outside: basketball, baseball, American football, tennis, soccer. Even as an adult, Landon called himself the Ultimate American Sports Fan.

His father, Tim, a former semipro ice hockey player, was an enigma. Landon and Tristan enjoyed spending time with Tim Donovan whenever they got the chance, but they would sometimes go six months or a year without seeing him, and his child-support checks often failed to arrive. "When it was convenient for my dad he would be a father, and when it wasn't he'd be a single man doing whatever he wanted to do," Donovan said. "For a kid, that's hard, because you need your parent there." Tim's absence pushed Landon even closer to his sister and mother (who remarried when Landon was ten and moved the family to Redlands, California), and his devotion to them was unconditional. He felt like he shared a sixth sense with his twin, an impulse that told them whenever they needed to talk to each other. And he would be forever grateful to his mother for giving him the freedom to discover what he loved (soccer) and making the hard financial sacrifices to let him play. If Landon was a mama's boy—he famously brought a teddy bear to the Under-17 World Cup in 1999—then he was proud of it.

Both Beckham and Donovan were careful to acknowledge their fathers' influences. Beckham appreciated his father's love for soccer, even if he wished Ted Beckham had been quicker to praise his only son. And Donovan credited his dad for teaching him to avoid using painkillers for injuries, to tough it out and listen to your body's pain. But both players had grown distant from their fathers as adults. Beckham blamed his dad for the 2002 divorce of his parents, and David nearly cut off the relationship for good when Ted released a book that included embarrassing details of his life and rise to fame. For his part, Donovan was keenly aware of how much more time Tim Donovan started spending with him after it became clear that Donovan had a bright future as a pro soccer player. During the 2000 Olympics, Tim embarrassed his son by writing a series of critical Internet message-board posts about U.S. coach Clive Charles, and as the years passed Landon thought more deeply about his largely fatherless childhood. By the summer of 2007, he hadn't spoken to his dad in nearly two years. "I've had a lot of time and a lot of therapy, and you get on with it," Donovan said. "I don't hate him, but at the same time that's not someone I want in my life."

In the traditionally macho world of professional male team sports, Beckham and Donovan weren't from Mars, they were from Venus. Beckham was, by his own account, "shy," "really emotional," and "a lot softer, a lot more affectionate" than his father, who was "sort of a man's man." He talked constantly of being in touch with "my feminine side." Donovan went a step further, saying his priority as a soccer player wasn't so much to brag about his list of career accomplishments, like so many other players, but rather to earn goodwill and respect. "What I care about is the relationships I make, what my teammates think of me," he said, "and that kind of grooming I got from my mom." Their shared sensitivity certainly made Beckham and Donovan more enlightened and well-rounded as *people*, but it might also create tensions in the locker room if they allowed their emotions and resentments to fester.

Beckham and Donovan both had interests in fashion as well, to say nothing of participating in fashion shoots. Granted, few humans could match Beckham in the looks department. The editor of the celebrity magazine *Us Weekly*, Janice Min, called Beckham "one of the few men who can reasonably claim to be better-looking than Brad Pitt," and she presumably couldn't pick out Landon Donovan in a police lineup. But Donovan was a handsome guy: His admirers overlooked his slowly receding hairline and focused instead on his piercing eyes, his welcoming smile, and his chiseled facial features, which called to mind the drumskin-tight cheekbones of an elite cyclist like Lance Armstrong. Donovan had posed for plenty of fashion spreads over the years, including *Tiger Beat*–style layouts for teens and a particularly provocative close-up of him in a $480 Tom Ford shirt using an outdoor drinking fountain in the *New York Times Magazine*. David Beckham wasn't the only soccer player who could appeal to both the gay and hetero communities.

As Beckham and Donovan grew apart from their own fathers, it was striking how many men had served as their father figures. Beckham himself used the phrase to describe his up-and-down relationship with Manchester United coach Sir Alex Ferguson, and the media often characterized Tony Stephens, the agent who guided Becks to superstardom, in the same way. Beckham dropped Stephens for Simon Fuller in 2003, and Fuller had cast himself in news articles as (surprise) "the father figure" during the early stages of David and Victoria's relationship, a pairing that he'd ignited by introducing them to each other. Donovan's experience was similar. His father figures included agent Richard Motzkin, who had advised him since his early teens, and two coaches: Yallop, who'd won Donovan's trust during their MLS championship runs in San Jose, and Bruce Arena, who'd coached Donovan for six years on the U.S. national team.

Yet by far the biggest influences in the lives of Beckham and Donovan were the women sitting at their table that night at Mastro's. Victoria's role in engineering David's "transition to a different person," as Ferguson put it, was well documented. Meanwhile, Bianca had sparked

Landon's own transformation in how he viewed his soccer career. From the day they had met—July 4, 2002, as Donovan could tell you in a heartbeat—Kajlich had struggled to make it as an actress in Hollywood, and only now was she starting to enjoy real success with her role on CBS's *Rules of Engagement*. "She's had to fight so hard, and there's a constant reminder there that's good for me," said Donovan, who'd had a reputation for coasting on his talent. "I'm starting to really cherish my career and taking it seriously every day. As cheesy as it sounds, there are a lot of people that would kill to do it, and you only get one career."

If Beckham and Donovan weren't close enough yet to talk about their childhoods or their fathers or the highs and lows of their wives' careers, they could always discuss their shared passion for soccer. Both players had an unslakable thirst for the sport, for watching it on TV, for breaking down the tactics, for hearing stories about famous teams and players. Beckham had been much more successful on the European club stage, but Donovan had gone just as far in the World Cup—the quarterfinals—as Beckham had. When the U.S. defeated Mexico to clinch a quarterfinal berth against Germany in 2002, the twenty-year-old Donovan appeared on the cover of *Sports Illustrated*, beating out a murderers' row of competition that week: the NBA champion Los Angeles Lakers, Tiger Woods's U.S. Open triumph, and the Detroit Red Wings' Stanley Cup victory.

World Cup '02 was a life-changing experience for Donovan and Beckham—who finally exorcised his demons by scoring to beat Argentina—but both players' 2006 World Cup campaigns fell to earth with a crashing thud. Under the captaincy of Beckham, who had a mediocre tournament, England played poorly and endured yet another disappointing quarterfinal exit (on penalty kicks to Portugal). As for Donovan, he was the face of a U.S. team that came in with high expectations (and an overinflated No. 5 world ranking), only to manage a total of four shots on goal in two losses (to the Czech Republic and Ghana) and a tie (against Italy). "I thought about things too much and never got focused on the games, and it showed," Donovan said of his lowest moment. "You always want to look in the mirror and say, 'Did I do enough?' And I was like, 'Not even close.'"

Aside from the relative sizes of their fame and wealth, Beckham and

Donovan had some other major differences, of course. Beckham was seven years older than his teammate—in a different stage of life, really—and the Beckhams had three children, while Donovan and Kajlich so far had none. There would be no playdates for little Beckhams and Donovans to attend with their parents. Regular socializing between the couples would also be difficult since they lived so far apart in the traffic-choked phantasmagoria of Los Angeles, the Beckhams in Beverly Hills and Donovan and Kajlich twenty miles to the south in Manhattan Beach.

From a soccer perspective, the biggest difference between Beckham and Donovan wasn't just that Beckham had achieved at the highest levels of the European club game while Donovan had not. There was another dimension to it: When both men had faced their European crucibles, their fight-or-flight moments of truth, Beckham had fought and Donovan had flown. In the fall of 1998, when post–World Cup death threats could have forced the twenty-three-year-old Beckham out of England to a club on the Continent, he stayed with Manchester United, kept his mouth shut, and helped lead the Red Devils to their historic Treble that season. But when the twenty-three-year-old Donovan returned to Germany's Bayer Leverkusen in the winter of 2005, his stay lasted all of two and a half months. He fought homesickness, struggled to earn regular playing time, and allowed his keen sense for perceived slights to take over. The turning point came in a 3–1 Champions League loss to Liverpool, in which Donovan played badly and was removed by coach Klaus Augenthaler eight minutes into the second half. "Just sub me at halftime if you think I'm playing poorly. Don't bring me off five minutes in," Donovan said. "But clearly he wanted to embarrass me. At that point I just said, 'I don't want to deal with this.' That was pretty immature of me to feel that way, because that's the way it goes around the world and you just have to wait your turn and fight your way back in." Instead, Donovan arranged for a return to MLS, joining the Galaxy, and he staged a one-man *tour de force* in guiding L.A. to the 2005 MLS championship.

The question about Donovan wasn't whether he had the talent to succeed in Europe. He did. The question was whether he had the desire and the maturity. The most fascinating aspect of Donovan's personality was his tendency to whipsaw from self-aware sage to childish diva, sometimes in the same conversation. At one extreme, Donovan had been the key figure in solving a 2005 labor dispute between the players and the U.S. Soccer Federation, one that threatened to cause a walkout for World Cup qualifying games. He was the most active player among the leaders of the MLS Players Union, and he rarely missed a chance to pick up the check when he was out to dinner with his Galaxy teammates. But then there was the other extreme: Donovan's thin skin, his occasional habit of disappearing during games, and his constant assurances that he needed to be "comfortable" in his living circumstances (read: beach, L.A., no German winters) to succeed on the soccer field. "I like Landon a lot, but Landon is also still young," said one MLS executive who knew Donovan well. But was twenty-five *young* anymore? "That's exactly my point. I think Landon desperately wants, in his mind, to be older."

It was possible that Donovan's full maturation was now finally in the process of happening. He was clearly *aware* that his behavior in Germany had revealed his immaturity, and he was convincing now when he spoke of getting only one career, of treating soccer more seriously, and even of being ready, perhaps, to take one more crack at Europe. But deep down, did Donovan really believe it himself? And how would he respond now that the pressures of Europe—in the form of the Beckham circus—had come to him? "Listen, as much money as we're paying David, we're paying a lot of money to Landon," said Lalas. "He has a responsibility. In a certain sense we've exploded this nice controlled cocoon that he ran to here in the States, and some of what maybe we perceive that he has run from is right back in his lap again. And we'll see how he reacts."

Let him be the captain. You be the star. Lalas's challenge to Donovan was sincere, even if Lalas neglected to mention that the impetus for the captain switch was coming from Beckham's own handlers. But what if Donovan *did* become the star? What if he—and not Beckham—ended up being the Galaxy's best player? One of the cardinal rules of professional sports is this: Never bring in a new player on a higher salary than your best player if the new guy isn't better himself. It's a recipe for resentment in the locker room. And while Donovan made sure to acknowledge Beckham's lengthy credentials and the special circumstances of American soccer—Beckham could fill stadiums and sell 250,000 jerseys; Donovan couldn't—there was no guarantee that Beckham would be the Galaxy's best player. "I would like to think that I can be up there with the best players [in the league], but who knows?" Beckham said. "We'll have to wait and see. That's what I'll be hoping for: not just to be the best player in the league but to be one of the best teams in the league." Already, though, reasonable minds in the Galaxy locker room disagreed. "At the end of the day, David is the best player in the league," said Peter Vagenas before Beckham had played an MLS game. Chris Klein, however, had different ideas: "A rested Landon is by far the best player in our league."

In Alexi Lalas's perfect world, Beckham and Donovan would connect for dozens of goals, the Galaxy would win championships, Beckham would be an ideal captain, the jersey sales and attendances and TV ratings would all be high, and everyone would be happy. But if those things didn't happen, and if Beckham was the captain while Donovan was the star? Then Lalas might want to be careful what he wished for.

For now, though, Donovan wanted only a few things from the teammate who was sitting across from him at Mastro's. He wanted Beckham's respect. ("I think David respects me. I know Frank does.") He wanted Beckham to work hard, once he returned from injury, and to be a good teammate. And he wanted Beckham to pick up a few dinner checks with the players and perhaps even spread some of the wealth in the locker room. When Donovan had been quoted in *Sports Illustrated* saying it would be nice if Beckham "splashed the locker room with cash for some of the younger guys," he was referring to the American pro sports tradition in which NFL quarterbacks like Tom Brady sent their linemen on Caribbean vacations or Kobe Bryant bought $9,000 Rolex watches for his Los Angeles Lakers teammates after he won the Most Valuable Player Award. But it was a sticky subject. Maybe Beckham didn't know how little some of his new teammates were making. Maybe Beckham didn't know about U.S. locker-room customs. And maybe Donovan was off-base. Maybe those customs didn't fit this situation anyway. Didn't those beach vacations and Swiss watches come as thanks *after* a season or *after* an award was won? Besides, while Donovan picked up dinner checks, it wasn't like he had been Santa Claus in the Galaxy locker room, doling out expensive gifts left and right.

Still, though, Alan Gordon admitted that he'd hoped he might find a Beckham-gifted Rolex in his locker one morning. But none came. Beckham's response to Donovan's *SI* quote had taken place instead the previous week on the AEG private jet returning from the All-Star Game in Denver.

"Landon?" said Beckham.

"Yeah?" Donovan replied.

"I've bought some speakers for the locker room. Would it be okay if I brought them in?"

"Really? Yeah, that would be great."

"I just felt like it wasn't a great vibe in the locker room all the time."

Donovan felt comfortable enough to take a playful jab. "That's pretty interesting that you're such a busy guy but you had time to buy speakers."

"Yeah, well, I had somebody go get 'em for me."

"Yeah, I think the guys would love that, man."

The next day, two Bose speaker systems with iPod docks had magically appeared, one in the Galaxy locker room and one in the treatment room. Music was now playing constantly, Donovan noticed, and while it wasn't a batch of Rolexes, he was impressed with Beckham's gesture nonetheless.

By the time their dinner at Mastro's was over, Donovan considered the evening with the Beckhams and the Yallops a success. Bianca was thrilled. She had spent the whole time gabbing like old friends with Victoria. "Bianca loves her," Donovan said. "Victoria is always *on*, all bright and bubbly, but you have to think at the end of the day she's a normal person, at least to some extent." Meanwhile, Landon's interactions with David couldn't have gone much better. Frank Yallop knew all the arcane details of Beckham's career and kept the conversation flowing, but Landon felt like he'd been able to get behind David's "outer wall"—at least a little bit—with a few questions of his own. Among other things, Beckham explained that he'd made up his mind to come to Los Angeles more than a year before he signed the Galaxy contract, a revelation that surprised Donovan.

When it came down to it, Donovan thought, everything about the Beckham Experiment was a little surreal. On the night the Beckhams had landed at LAX Airport, Donovan watched slack-jawed in his living room as ESPN's *SportsCenter* cut to "Breaking News" and showed the horde of photographers smothering the new British arrivals. Donovan's response that night (*Are you kidding me?*) was a lot like the one he had at Mastro's after dinner. David and Victoria left through the restaurant's back door to avoid the paparazzi, and the rest of the group waited for five minutes at the table. Outside, the livid shooters were screaming at the Beckhams as their security detail positioned their cars so that they sped away without offering a clear shot.

"Go back to England, you motherfucker!"

"Nobody cares about soccer here!"

"Your wife has no talent!"

Donovan shook his head. Unbelievable. When the remaining four-some left through the front door of Mastro's ten minutes later, the scene was a ghost town. The three dozen paparazzi were gone. The circus had moved on for the night.

The sooner Beckham got on the field, Donovan reasoned, the sooner things would get closer to normal in the Galaxy locker room—whatever *normal* meant anymore. But his firsthand impressions encouraged Donovan: Beckham's welcome of the Galaxy players at the Cruise party, his focus watching videotape of games he hadn't even played in, his genuine-guy demeanor at Mastro's. Three nights later, after the Galaxy's 1–0 loss to CD Guadalajara in a Superliga group game at the L.A. Coliseum, Donovan was waiting in the drive-thru lane at In-N-Out Burger when he saw a customized black Cadillac Escalade pull into the lot. He text-messaged Beckham, who'd watched from the bench that night.

Ru at INO?

Yep. You?

Donovan spied one of Beckham's suited security guards carrying out a monster to-go order, and after Donovan was done paying he rolled up alongside the Escalade and lowered his window to address the hopeless In-N-Out junkie inside.

"You fat fucker!" Donovan yelled.

Beckham laughed. "I couldn't resist."

CHAPTER 6

VELVET ROPES, FRIED CHICKEN, AND ALLIGATOR ARMS

I f you stood inside the velvet-roped VIP section in Toronto's Ultra Supper Club just before midnight on August 5, 2007, you would have thought you'd stepped into a time warp back to 1977, to the days when the New York Cosmos of Pelé and Giorgio Chinaglia partied with Andy Warhol and Bianca Jagger and the gang at Studio 54 in Manhattan. For the Galaxy players, that night in the Supper Club—the hottest nightclub in downtown Toronto—was the first time they felt like a SuperClub. On the team's opening road trip with David Beckham, L.A. (now 3–5–5) had tied Toronto FC 0–0 earlier in the evening, an ugly game that was now being redeemed by the packs of pretty young things packing the open-air dance floor, waiting in block-long lines outside the club, and flashing eye-popping amounts of skin at the Galaxy players, all in the hope of being invited with one crook of an index finger inside the velvet rope.

Joe Cannon took a sip of his drink and surveyed the scene. For nine years the Galaxy's All-Pro goalkeeper had waited for this, waited for MLS to feel like the spectacle of the NBA and the NFL, waited for gorgeous women in skintight sequined tops to flash come-hither looks his way just because of the team he played on. Cannon *knew* this would happen once Beckham arrived. Wasn't that what he'd said at Cobi Jones's birthday party in June when one of the players' girlfriends had asked if Cannon was dating anyone?

"Nah," he replied. "I'm kind of waiting for David to get here."

"What does that mean?" Alan Gordon asked.

"You know, all the girls."

Gordon couldn't take it. "Joe, what do you think is going to change?" he asked. "Seriously. You're still the same person. Like a girl is going to want to get with you just because David Beckham is on the team. What are you gonna do, pull a little Beckham out of your pocket and say, 'See, look! Here I am!' *No, dude.*"

Now look. For one night, at least, Cannon had sweet vindication. Who knew if it would happen again? This was a team function, after all, and Beckham was obligated to be here. But for now Cannon couldn't let go of the thought: *Everyone wants to be inside this VIP section because we are the Los Angeles Galaxy.* It was an intoxicating feeling, due only partly to the free bottles of Patrón and Grey Goose being passed around like water jugs on the practice field. For it wasn't just the women who were trying to get in, lying to bouncers and snatching VIP passes. Men were pleading with Galaxy players too. *I know Ante! I know Joe! Can you get me up there?*

Yet Cannon was also fully aware that none of this—the VIP section, the free drinks, the women—would be happening if it weren't for one individual, the global icon who was talking quietly with some team-mates at a corner table behind the velvet rope. Every once in a while, Beckham's hulking bodyguard Shane, who everyone said was once an Ultimate Fighter, would let in a fan for an autograph or a picture. As the music thumped and the VIP section filled and the clock struck 1 A.M., Galaxy midfielder Peter Vagenas tried to wrap his mind around the strangeness of it all. How does Beckham deal with it, he wondered, the notion that if he were to get up and walk to the other side of this club, everyone else would suddenly migrate to that section as well? How would the other players deal with it too? For his part, Gavin Glinton wanted to keep things in perspective ("We know *why* it's that scene, you know what I mean?"), but the dreadlocked reserve forward was too busy chatting up some runway-model types to worry about what was going on in everyone else's heads.

If these were the perks that came with being David Beckham's teammates, then playing the real-life versions of Turtle from HBO's *Entourage* wasn't so bad a deal. The road trip had plenty of other benefits, too. All the players had been given new Hugo Boss suits for official events, courtesy of an agreement the team had made with the clothing designer for the rest of the season. Instead of staying in the usual MLS-mandated (read: mediocre) hotel, the Galaxy was using one of its two exceptions for the season to lodge at the fancy Le Meridien King Edward downtown. What's more, the hotel stay was free, the result of a deal the Galaxy had reached with a Toronto promoter. As part of the pact, the Galaxy players also got a free shopping spree at the Roots clothing store and free meals and drinks at the Ultra Supper Club. In return, those outfits publicized their connection to David Beckham and the suddenly sexy L.A. Galaxy, leading to the mob scene at the dance club. "We were riding David's coattails," Lalas said. "The welcome mat was laid out wherever we went."

Perhaps, but Beckham's handlers were hardly thrilled that he was being used so nakedly for free hotel stays and shopping sprees; they made sure no such "local promoter deals" ever happened again. Even Lalas was uncomfortable with what he had witnessed from the Galaxy's players in Toronto, most of all the 0–0 result against a terrible expansion team. "You guys have to understand," Lalas announced to the team at dinner one night. "All of this comes with a price. And don't for a second think that if this guy"—he pointed to Beckham—"wasn't on our team that we'd be getting this. It's all because of him. Thank you, David, it's been wonderful. But at least David understands this comes with a price, and you pay that price on the field."

Beckham had opened an entirely new world for the Galaxy. For the first time in its history, the team was flying charters instead of using commercial airlines on this ten-day, three-city road trip to Toronto, Washington, D.C., and New England. MLS had always forbidden charter flights, claiming they provided a competitive advantage, although the players reasoned that the ban was the result of the league's cheaper owners not wanting to be pressured into an arms race. ("Don't you *want* to have a competitive advantage in everything that you do?" Donovan asked.) MLS had relented somewhat upon Beckham's arrival, allowing the Galaxy to charter on his first road trip due to security concerns, and AEG had sprung for the expense. For most of the players the flight from LAX to Toronto was their first noncommercial trip. When the flight attendant came to offer Alan Gordon a pretakeoff cocktail, he looked around at the first-class leather seating, the lie-flat beds, and the fully stocked bar up front.

"Let me tell you something, ma'am," Gordon said, turning on the charm. "This is nicer than my apartment."

The flight attendant laughed.

"No," he replied. "I'm serious."

When you examined the list of Galaxy salaries, you could understand why Gordon wasn't necessarily joking. MLS's $2.1-million-per-team salary cap meant that if a team signed a Designated Player exception like Beckham, the difference between its top and bottom wage-earners was extreme (see table on p. 89).

To the new Galaxy fans who were following the team solely because of Beckham, his supporting cast (aside from Donovan) might have seemed like a bunch of faceless drones. But soccer is much more of a team sport than, say, basketball, in which one player can take over a game. Beckham, in particular, was not a Brazilian-style ball magician, and he would need his teammates to perform for the Galaxy to win. There was an elemental purity in playing a sport for the love of the game, which had to be the case for some Galaxy players, most of them college graduates, who could have earned more money as management trainees or insurance salesmen or data-entry operators. Galaxy fans may not have known or cared, but the players they watched (and sometimes booed) were often more like them than any athlete in the big-time American professional sports.

Bit by bit, Beckham himself would learn more about his new teammates, some of whom had stories unlike any of the players on Beckham's previous teams:

ALAN GORDON
Position: Forward. Age: 25. Birthplace: Long Beach, California. College: Oregon State. Years Pro: 4. Salary: $30,870.

When Sandi Epperson, Gordon's girlfriend, first visited the three-bedroom Redondo Beach apartment he shared with teammates Gavin Glinton and Kyle Veris in the middle of 2007, her initial thought was an unwelcome flashback: *Oh, God, I'm in a college dorm room.* A life-size

THE 2007 LOS ANGELES GALAXY

POSITION	NAME	COUNTRY	SALARY
M	David Beckham	England	$6,500,000
F	Landon Donovan	United States	$900,000
GK	Joe Cannon	United States	$192,000
D	Chris Klein	United States	$187,250
D	Abel Xavier	Portugal	$156,000
F	Edson Buddle	United States	$150,000
D	Chris Albright	United States	$142,500*
F	Carlos Pavón	Honduras	$141,500
M	Peter Vagenas	United States	$131,875
D	Ante Jazic	Canada	$114,250
M	Quavas Kirk	United States	$111,500
M	Cobi Jones	United States	$95,000
M	Kelly Gray	United States	$85,000
F	Israel Sesay	United States	$57,083
M	Kyle Martino	United States	$55,297
F	Gavin Glinton	United States	$50,000
GK	Steve Cronin	United States	$42,229
M	Kevin Harmse	Canada	$40,800
F	Alan Gordon	United States	$30,870
D	Troy Roberts	United States	$30,000
D	Ty Harden	United States	$30,000
M	Josh Tudela	United States	$17,700
D	Mike Randolph	United States	$17,700
D	Kyle Veris	United States	$17,700
M	Mike Caso	United States	$12,900
GK	Lance Friesz	United States	$12,900

*Out for season with injury

poster of Bob Marley greeted visitors to Gordon's room, and the dingy walls of the common area were as bare as a prison cell. The smell of sweaty clothes and overflowing kitchen garbage hung in the air, and the carpet was filthy—the roommates had never bought a vacuum. Gordon liked Glinton and Veris personally, but they were also "the messiest, dirtiest people in the world," he said. They never cooked for themselves, and their cartons of days-old, half-eaten takeout piled up on the kitchen counter.

Gordon had begun dating Epperson, an attractive blond nurse five years his senior, in April 2007. A common friend introduced them, but Gordon had to be persistent, calling her every day for a week before she reluctantly agreed to go out with him. "I mean, it's not a huge pickup line saying you're an MLS player," Gordon cracked. Like most Americans, Epperson didn't watch soccer and had no idea who Gordon was. But they hit it off on their date—Gordon had a way of winning people over—and not even the shock of visiting his apartment for the first time had sent her running in the other direction. "Once I saw the dorm room and the two roommates, it's not rocket science to say he doesn't make millions of dollars," she said. "But it didn't matter. It wasn't an issue, not for me, anyway."

Yet his meager paycheck was a daily struggle for Gordon. More than three-fourths of his income was going straight to paying bills, such as his $845 monthly share of the rent. The cost of living in the L.A. area was among the highest in the country, and so were the gas prices for all the miles he was driving. For nearly four years he had made the exact same annual salary with the Galaxy: $30,870 on a four-year contract in which MLS had all the leverage, retaining the right to drop him after every season. (Fully guaranteed contracts were extremely rare in MLS, a fact of life that could send a player's world into turmoil if, say, a new coach decided to cut him before the midseason freeze-date.) Gordon's MLS deal had no incentives, no bonuses, no mandated increases. He had no 401(k), and he was not saving a dime. "It's stressful," he said. "There's more month than there is money. It'll be the eighth, and you're getting close to being dry and you've gotta go to the fifteenth until you get another paycheck."

Gordon was also thinking about firing his agent. The more he talked to other players, the more he realized his contract should at least have had some incentives. What's more, younger players were coming into the league with résumés much thinner than his—Gordon had won

Rookie of the Year in the A-League, the U.S. second tier—and earning more money. To make matters worse, Gordon said, his agent, Patrick McCabe, had called him "probably four times in three years." Now that they were growing closer, Sandi was pushing Gordon to hire a new agent who might be able to negotiate the best possible contract if Gordon succeeded in 2007, the last year of his four-year deal.

Sometimes, Gordon felt, the pressures facing him seemed overwhelming. Most professional athletes need to worry only about performing on the field—a big enough challenge as it is—but like many players in MLS, Gordon had a second job to supplement his income. For the past three years he had coached the same girls' youth team in North Huntington Beach, south of Los Angeles. On Mondays and Wednesdays after Galaxy practices, he would drive an hour in heavy traffic, lead a ninety-minute training session, and drive a half hour back home, exhausted. Gordon coached the team's games on Saturdays or Sundays, unless he was on the road with the Galaxy, in which case one of the girls' sisters would take over, receiving the lineups from Gordon over the phone.

When it came to playing for the Galaxy, Gordon was in excruciating pain nearly every day. He had only recently returned to the field after recovering from surgery on a broken metatarsal in his left foot—the Chelsea game was his first start of the season—but now he had developed an inflamed trapped nerve, called Morton's neuroma, in the same foot. Most players would sit out with such a painful condition, but Gordon knew it was his contract year, and so (against the advice of some friends) he was getting cortisone injections before every game to numb that part of his foot. "Anytime you shoot up your foot that many times, there's some obvious risk," Gordon said. During daily practices he went injection-free, simply trying to fight through the searing charge running up his foot and leg.

Remarkably, though, Gordon had turned into a goal-scoring machine of late, keying the Galaxy's surprise run to the Superliga semifinals with a gorgeous goal in L.A.'s 2–1 win over Pachuca, the Mexican league champion, and two more in a wild 6–5 victory a week later at FC Dallas. "Alan could be a good player in this league," said Lalas, "but he just has to be consistent and stay healthy." Watching from the sidelines while injured, Beckham was impressed with the heart of Gordon, the player who'd had the guts to ask him his name that first day in the Galaxy locker room. Although Beckham's salary was 210 times greater than Gordon's, the two men were becoming friends, exchanging daily banter in the locker room. When Beckham agreed to meet one of Gordon's youth-team players, who was undergoing chemotherapy for a melanoma, Gordon thought Beckham might pose for a quick picture and sign an autograph. But Beckham gave sixteen-year-old Allison Whalen much more: a signed game-worn jersey. "He made her year," Gordon said.

Things were going well, too, with Sandi, who bought a vacuum for Gordon's three-man apartment and even spent some time cleaning the place herself. It still looked like a dorm room, but at least it was a more presentable dorm room. Gordon was amazed by what Sandi would put up with: the bass thump from Veris's stereo would sometimes shake the walls until 3:30 A.M., even though Sandi had to get up at 5 A.M. to attend classes for her master's program in nursing. As much as he liked Veris and Glinton, Gordon wanted to move out. He just didn't know how he could possibly afford it.

CHRIS KLEIN
Position: Midfielder/Defender. Age: 31. Birthplace: St. Louis, Missouri. College: Indiana. Years Pro: 10. Salary: $187,250.

When David Beckham signed with MLS in January 2007, Chris Klein was a member of Real Salt Lake, the team in Utah somewhat goofily named after Real Madrid and the other "royal" clubs in Spain. Yet even on another team, Klein viewed Beckham's signing as a watershed moment for MLS. Klein, one of the league's top right-sided midfielders, was a Beckham fan. He had read *White Angels*, John Carlin's chronicle of Beckham's first season at Real Madrid, and he had bought a Beckham jersey for his son, Carson, now five, during a trip to Madrid. Klein thought that Beckham, in a way unlike any other soccer player in the world, could connect with millions of mainstream American sports fans. "This is an opportunity for us to showcase our game like we've been begging for for ten years," Klein said. "If people come to see one guy and end up being impressed by five others or by the experience of an MLS game, that can only benefit us moving forward." He hoped that in twenty years the Beckham Experiment would be regarded as the start of the boom of Major League Soccer in the United States.

Married to his college sweetheart, Angela, and the father of a young son and daughter, Klein was a devout Christian who asked for guidance from God when he was traded to the Galaxy three weeks before Beckham's arrival: *Where are you leading me in all this?* The answer, Klein concluded, was simple. His purpose was to go to a team that was attracting global attention, play hard, be a good teammate, and perhaps offer helpful advice to the younger players. For Alexi Lalas, trading away two good young prospects for Klein had been a risky move. But Lalas thought Klein could provide important leadership, experience, and an attacking verve as either a right midfielder or a right back.

Klein may have been earning more money than Gordon, but like nearly every MLS player, he knew he would have to find a regular job after his playing days. And so, putting his business degree from Indiana to work, Klein had presented a business plan to a company in Minneapolis. His idea: to work as a financial adviser for soccer players, providing everything from estate planning to a comprehensive investment strategy. In February 2007, Klein earned his Series 7 and Series 66 certifications, and he was now speaking three to four times a week with his mentor in Minneapolis. "I don't really have any desire to be a coach or a GM," Klein said. "But I want to be involved in the game, settle my family, and start to build a business." Sure enough, he was already picking up some clients.

All things considered, Klein had more in common with Beckham than did any other Galaxy player. They were at similar stages of their lives, both family men with children, and they had made their bones as right-sided players who ran their tails off. If Beckham was the king of epic career comebacks, then Klein was his American brother in arms, having twice been named the MLS Comeback Player of the Year after returning from serious knee injuries. Affable and easygoing, Klein wasn't even bothered when his son chose to wear a No. 23 Beckham Galaxy jersey to the games instead of one with his dad's name on it. In fact, the jersey was part of Klein's favorite Beckham story. Before a game one night at the HDC, Klein introduced his son to Beckham, who was being treated on the training table. Carson Klein's eyes lit up when Beckham asked him some questions, and the Kleins returned to the locker room. But ten minutes later, Carson asked his father if Beckham could sign his jersey. Back in the training room, Beckham not only signed the jersey, but he personalized it: *To Carson.*

"*He remembered his name,*" Klein said. "David's got people coming in and out, all these requests, he's got an injury and all this pressure. But he meets my son, ten minutes go by, and he didn't even have to ask his name again. From then on he's always calling him over and talking to him. These are the things that you can never see and never know about somebody unless you're involved with them one-on-one."

ABEL XAVIER
Position: Defender. Age: 34. Birthplace: Nampula, Mozambique. College: None. Years Pro: 17. Salary: $156,000.

PETER VAGENAS
Position: Midfielder. Age: 29. Birthplace: Pasadena, California. College: UCLA. Years Pro: 8. Salary: $131,875.

On the day after the invitations to Tom Cruise's party appeared on the Galaxy players' chairs, nearly identical red copies materialized in the locker room. The gold script of these invitations was the same, but the content was, oh, slightly different. This party was to be thrown in honor of Abel Xavier, the recently signed defender whose signature look—his bleach-blond hair and goatee—made him appear like a psychedelic soccer version of the god Neptune. This event, the invitation said, would be held at "the castle for wizardry and sorcery." Food would be served, including "the live chickens that Abel prefers." The guests, it continued, should come dressed the way Xavier hit the party circuit—covered head to toe in white.

The little piece of locker-room genius was conceived and executed by Peter Vagenas, the droll veteran midfielder whose unique brand of humor had already won over Beckham (whose locker was next to his) and Xavier (his roommate on the road). "It was a complete riot," said defender Chris Albright. "Obviously, David felt a little uncomfortable about the [Cruise party] invitations being on our chairs, and he wasn't sure how we'd react. Then the next day Pete shows David what he made for Abel, and he's just shaking his head going, 'Holy fuck.' David was new, so it was a good ice-breaker to pull him in—and a bit of a shot at him, in a sense, but with the right tone."

For his part, Abel Xavier (pronounced ay-BELL egg-ZAHV-i-er) was the most globally recognizable Galaxy player aside from Beckham. A former fixture on the Portuguese national team, Xavier had logged time in no fewer than seven leagues—in Spain, England, Italy, the Netherlands, Portugal, Turkey, and Germany—before deciding to sign with the Galaxy. "I'm not coming here for the money, as you can imagine," said Xavier. "But sometimes you must challenge the unknown. Because if you don't, you're going to get a very comfortable view of life, and I hate that. For that reason, when a big challenge came, I was very open." Xavier's career included many colorful chapters, and not just in a literal sense. In the Euro 2000 semifinals, he became the Bill Buckner of Portugal, committing a last-second handball penalty that led to France's 2–1 victory. Five years later, Xavier was suspended for a year in England after testing positive for the performance-enhancing drug Dianabol.

Yet Xavier had loads of experience, and his Galaxy teammates said he had a European-bred professionalism that belied his freak-show appearance. (Xavier's catchall phrase for something that failed to meet his standards, on or off the field, was: "This is not correct!") The question was whether Xavier still had any legs. One MLS executive said his team had passed on Xavier after calling around Europe and learning he couldn't run anymore. But Lalas had taken a chance on him, going so far as to sign Xavier to a rare (in MLS) fully guaranteed two-year contract. As for Xavier and Vagenas, they might have seemed like the Odd Couple, but it took Vagenas to provide the perfect description of his road roomie. "If you were able to morph people together," Vagenas explained, "you would need a splash of Michael Jackson during the *Thriller* years, a splash of Peter Pan, a splash of the neighborhood fortune-teller gypsy person, topped off with Dennis Rodman. But then splash in an intellectual figure like Nietzsche. That would pretty much cover Abel Xavier."

Beckham participated in his first training session with the Galaxy in Washington, D.C., on August 7, two days before L.A.'s nationally televised game against D.C. United. It was only for twenty minutes ("In a perfect world he's not even with us right now, he's at home rehabbing," Lalas said), but an excitement was pulsating through the team, one that only continued that night when Beckham helped organize a dinner with ten other players (including Donovan, Cannon, Xavier, and Vagenas) at Morton's steak house in Crystal City, Virginia, a short walk from the team hotel. Beckham had enjoyed the players-only meals at Real Madrid, which were paid for by the club, and if he was going to be just one of the lads inside the Galaxy locker room, things needed to get off on the right foot.

It was a night of surprises for everyone. Not long after they took their table at Morton's, the waiter asked if anyone wanted wine. They all raised their hands.

"Okay," the waiter said. "I need to see some IDs."

He checked Donovan's driver's license, then Kelly Gray's and Kyle Martino's, and then he came to Beckham.

"I don't have my ID with me," Beckham said.

"No ID, no wine!" the waiter announced, theatrically snatching Beckham's wineglass from the table.

Beckham thought it was a put-on. "Is this guy taking the piss?" he asked. But the waiter was serious. When Xavier couldn't produce an ID either, his wineglass disappeared too. "What is this?" the thirty-four-year-old Xavier thundered. "Do you know how old I am? I have *a kid* who can drink." The other players were laughing hysterically now, partly because the waiter hadn't recognized the world's most famous athlete, and partly because Beckham and Xavier were so used to being mobbed in Europe that they didn't bother carrying any identification. Welcome to soccer in America, guys.

Shane the Bodyguard pulled the waiter aside to explain. Soon the restaurant's maître d' came over. "I don't care *who* they are!" the players heard the waiter say to his boss. Finally, the maître d' relented, and Beckham and Xavier got their wineglasses back in time to join their teammates in a toast. Crisis averted.

The Galaxy had pulled out all the stops to introduce the Beckhams to the players' families, hosting a team barbecue at the Home Depot Center's tennis pavilion a week after the Cruise party. All the players brought their wives and girlfriends, as well as their kids, who wolfed down hot dogs and hamburgers, had their balloons twisted into dogs, and played with the Beckhams' children on an inflatable bouncy castle. But the Morton's dinner was the first time Beckham had held center stage at a players-only meal, and he came out of his shell, answering questions and telling stories about his days with England and Real Madrid and Manchester United. "I'm a fan of soccer first," said Vagenas, "and David and Abel have great stories about guys that we've watched who to them are the same that Landon is to me. Except it's Roy Keane or Luis Figo or Ronaldo. I could listen to those all night long."

Most of all, the vibe was comfortable. There was no weirdness, no awkward self-consciousness with Beckham. "You can break his balls," said Chris Albright, "and he'll break your balls right back." Martino was stunned that night that Beckham could be such a regular-acting guy.

And then the check came.

It was a profoundly odd moment. David Beckham was earning a $6.5 million salary that ballooned to an income of $48.2 million in 2007 when you added endorsements. The player sitting next to him, Kyle Martino, was making a base salary of $55,297—before taxes—and living in one of the U.S.'s most expensive cities. Nearly everyone at the table was thinking about it—*Is Beckham going to pick up the check?*—but nobody said anything. For his part, Beckham had never been in this situation before. The players on his other teams had always been millionaires, and Real Madrid paid for all the team meals anyway. The Galaxy provided nothing more than a $45 per diem on the road. What would Beckham do? What *should* he do?

Donovan eyed the bill from his seat at the table. He'd paid for teammates' dinners in the past, and he'd made his position perfectly clear even before Beckham's arrival. "He'd better be picking up meals and shit, too," Donovan had said, "or else I'll call him out on it." This wasn't like giving your teammates Rolexes, Donovan thought. This was the simple gesture of the superstar player buying them a meal. But Donovan's opinion was by no means unanimous. Chris Klein, one of Donovan's best friends on the team, had a different viewpoint. "If you're out to dinner with the guys and you pick up a check here or there, then fine," Klein said. "But if you start to feel like you're being used, these aren't your friends anymore. These are *leeches*. You can look at it two ways: Here's this guy that's making a lot of money, and maybe he should pick up the tab. But the other side of it is, maybe he's trying so hard to be one of the guys, if you're paying for everything then you're not one of the guys anymore."

Beckham didn't pick up the check. The players ended up splitting the bill, Beckham putting in a few dollars to cover his share and passing it along. It would end up being standard operating procedure at similar meals as the season progressed. "We just split it all the time," Kelly Gray, one of Beckham's frequent dinner companions, would say. "None of us care. It's just nice to go out to dinner." Donovan, conspicuously, didn't call Beckham out at Morton's, but he could never get over Beckham's alligator arms when the bill arrived. Nobody would have believed it, he thought. David Beckham is a cheapskate.

As he had done with his gift of the locker-room stereo speakers, Beckham did make a smaller gesture on the road trip: He instructed the team to give his $45 per diem to the developmental-roster players who were making as little as $12,900. "Hey, dude, thanks for the money!" third-string goalkeeper Lance Friesz said to Beckham near the hotel lobby one night. It wasn't big bucks, but at least it was something.

Though Beckham didn't really share his immense wealth, the Galaxy players noted that he never flaunted it much, either. The only exception was a big one: his cars. Beckham's Escalade was his usual choice for driving to Galaxy practices and games, but he also had a black Porsche 911 and a $400,000 black Rolls-Royce Phantom, among other automobiles. His Galaxy teammates couldn't help but see Beckham's car every day, since he was allowed to park it near the locker-room entrance downstairs inside the HDC. Lalas made a rule that any player whose car was worth more than $100,000 could park next to Beckham's wheels inside every day, but that group was so far limited to one: Abel Xavier, who acquired a white convertible Bentley to match his all-white outfits.

The rest of the players were allowed to park downstairs on game nights, but on practice days they were forced to use the public lots outside the HDC. If the lot near the building's entrance was full, as it often was, they had to park in the next lot down the hill and walk nearly 300 yards to the facility, only to see Beckham and Xavier's rides fifteen steps from the locker room. It was a daily reminder to everyone (including Donovan) that Beckham was different—a status that was reinforced whenever Beckham was given his own hotel room and the other players (except for elder statesman Cobi Jones) had to double up.

The money issue would never go away, not as long as MLS mandated that bottom-rung players could earn barely more than $1,000 a month *before* taxes. Raising the league's minimum salary was going to be a major item on the Players Union's wish list when negotiations started for the next collective bargaining agreement in 2009. "I love that David's making $6.5 million a year. He deserves it," said Klein, who sat on the union's executive board. "But I think these guys [at the low end] deserve more, especially if the league is beginning to make money." When pressed on the issue, MLS commissioner Don Garber argued there was a clear disparity between a world-class player like Beckham and a developmental-roster player just breaking into his first few games. "Look at the difference between A-Rod and a guy on the Yankees who gets called up on a minor-league contract," Garber said. "It's apples and oranges." But that was missing the point. The Yankees player on the minor-league contract was at least earning enough to cover basic living expenses in New York City without taking on a roommate, a second job, or the need to ask his parents for money.

Up in the ESPN2 booth, Eric Wynalda sighed. Not again. He'd been following David Beckham across North America for the past three weeks, from Los Angeles to Toronto and now to Washington, D.C.'s RFK Stadium, where 46,686 fans (nearly three times the average crowd) had gathered on a Thursday night to see Beckham . . . start the game on the bench again. Wynalda, a three-time World Cup participant, was still the U.S.'s all-time leading scorer (at least until Landon Donovan bagged a couple more goals), and his national television broadcasts of the Beckham Experiment had turned into a cruel twist on the old *Seinfeld* description: a show about nothing.

"In television terms it's a disaster," Wynalda said before the game.

"We would love to be covering his every move. Literally. And what has happened now is we are guilty of our own arrogance. Because we have the ability and the access, we are covering nothing. *He tied his shoe. He pulled his sock down. He thought about putting his shin guard on. He touched his hair. He almost picked his nose.* It's stupid. We have a Beckham Cam. And you want to live in a fishbowl? The sad thing about David is the normal player who's hurt gets to sit on the bench, try to heal, and be a good teammate. And when they do pick their nose, we edit that out. The world can't wait for this guy to pick his nose! And it's so unfair. If he decides to grimace a little bit and squeeze out a fart like a normal athlete on the bench, we're gonna know. And that's horrible. I don't think anybody wants to be put in this kind of shitbox. This is no fun for him."

The Beckham backlash had begun. The back page of *ESPN The Magazine* featured a full-page photo illustration of a youth soccer game in which seven kids in Beckham jerseys were sitting on the sideline under the headline BENCH IT LIKE BECKHAM. In Dallas, where ticket buyers had paid up to twice the normal price, fans held up critical signs after Beckham skipped the trip entirely (on doctor's orders, he said): DAVID, WELCOME TO AMERICA/WHERE PEOPLE LIKE YOU GET PAID TO DO NOTHING. "We've had billboards all over Dallas for months saying he's coming to play for the Galaxy, and then he's not here. What a letdown," said Kari Hampton, a twenty-eight-year-old dental hygienist from Dallas whose sign read (under the heading ENGLISH EXPORTS): 20 MILLION COPIES OF HARRY POTTER = PRICELESS/$250 MILLION FOOTBALL PLAYER = WORTHLESS.

The signs at RFK Stadium were a bit more creative, such as the gigantic one in the raucous Barra Brava/Screaming Eagles fan section: WE SING BETTER THAN YOUR WIFE. But the potential for disappointment was still there. The parents of the twenty-two youth players who escorted the Galaxy and United starters onto the field had paid $230 each for the chance to have their child hold Beckham's hand, only for nobody to win the honor in the end. At his press conferences Beckham was running out of ways to talk about his bum ankle. "I can't really apologize for being injured," he said. "It's just a part of life in any sportsman's career. But I must say it's so frustrating for myself to not be out there on the pitch—more frustrating probably than for people waiting for me to step on the pitch."

It didn't help that MLS had insisted on a diabolical schedule for the Galaxy upon Beckham's arrival: 26 games in 13 weeks in 15 cities, in order to let each MLS team reap the windfall of a Beckham visit during his first half-season in the league. "Sometimes you have a crazy schedule in MLS for two weeks," said Yallop. "We've got it for two months." The barnstorming tour was the result of a trade-off. In order to persuade MLS owners to pass the Beckham Rule, Tim Leiweke had promised that every team would receive a piece of the Beckham bonanza. But the plans didn't account for an injury. Even if Beckham had been healthy, the overloaded schedule was yet another example in which the financial concerns of the moneymen outweighed common sense from a soccer perspective. By the time this mammoth road trip was over, the Galaxy's already-thin roster would be missing seven players (including Beckham and four other starters) to injury. Meanwhile, MLS teams had leveraged Beckham's arrival as much as possible, in some cases doubling ticket prices or forcing customers to buy multigame ticket packages if they wanted to attend the Galaxy date. Ultimately, Beckham's injury combined with the profiteering and all the road dates to spread the PR damage over a wide area. The publicity hit, in turn, put enormous pressure on Beckham to play on a bad ankle. "Everybody is feeding off of this," Lalas said, "and we have to be careful that we're not just left with a carcass."

Yet there was reason for optimism at RFK Stadium. Beckham was in uniform tonight, and the game was being played on natural grass, unlike the ankle-jarring artificial turf in Toronto or New England three days later. What's more, England coach Steve McClaren was watching in a luxury box, hoping to see firsthand if Beckham might be ready for a friendly against Germany in two weeks. Late in the first half, just after Luciano Emilio had put D.C. United up 1–0, a visibly agitated Beckham rose from the bench and started warming up, drawing a roar from the nearly full stadium. It was a false alarm. But the crowd got its wish in the seventy-second minute, when Beckham pulled off his warm-up top (he never missed a bare-chested moment), donned a new white No. 23 jersey, and entered his first competitive MLS game. A biblical rainstorm was falling, but the fans hadn't left their seats. A volley of camera flashes lit up the stadium.

Despite two months of rust, Beckham made a difference instantly. He hit a long free kick that Carlos Pavón should have finished for the equalizer but butchered instead. Then in the final minutes Beckham served a perfectly weighted through-ball into Donovan's path, only for onrushing United goalkeeper Troy Perkins to break up the play at the last possible moment, sending Donovan airborne. "There was tenderness, there was hesitation," Beckham said afterward, but even at 70 percent he was one of the best players on the field. The Galaxy lost 1–0, bringing its record to 3–6–5, yet the mood in the locker room wasn't entirely gloomy. Donovan, for one, appreciated the chance to talk at last with Beckham about shared soccer experiences and how they could have done things better. "That helps big-time," Donovan said, "because he's a good player. You can see it. He knows what he's doing when he gets the ball, and he makes things happen, so it's going to help us a lot."

ESPN was modestly encouraged, too. The broadcast averaged a 0.4 rating, hardly earth-shattering—the Scrabble All-Star Championship earned a 0.5 on ESPN that weekend—but still double its normal rating for MLS games. Even more strikingly, the rating for the fifteen-minute period from 8:45 P.M. to 9 P.M., when Beckham was on the field, shot up to 0.8. Clearly, Beckham was the only MLS player who moved the needle for ESPN. But the broadcast had been so embarrassingly Beckham-centric, with so many Beckham Cam bench shots, that MLS commissioner Don Garber called ESPN's on-site producer during the game to complain. "It was disappointing to have cameras focused on David on the bench as the game was going on," Garber said. "Fortunately, ESPN agreed and changed their perspective."

A pattern was starting to emerge. From national television's point of view, the Beckham Experiment was sparking lukewarm excitement (at best) about his soccer. But when it came to seeing Beckham in person, the Spice Boy was a hit. That night Washington, D.C., caught a raging case of Beckham Mania, and not just during the game. In the wee hours at RFK Stadium, the United equipment manager nabbed three young men trying to steal Beckham's game-worn jersey from the Galaxy laundry, the *Washington Post* reported. D.C. nightclubs hosted no fewer than three heavily promoted after-game parties: one at the club Lima sponsored by United defender Bobby Boswell, one at Indebleu in Chinatown, and a third, guest-list-only affair at Play. Around 1 A.M., Beckham entered Play through a side door with a group that included Cobi Jones, Chris Klein, and Abel Xavier. As if someone had pressed a magic button, the dance floor cleared and partygoers climbed atop their chairs to get a look at the baseball-capped figure in the VIP section. When Beckham was escorted across the club to the bathroom, he smiled and shook hands like a head of state, the most popular foreign emissary to visit Washington in many, many years.

The Sheraton Hotel in Braintree, Massachusetts, south of Boston, may just be the worst Sheraton in America. Located hard by an Interstate 93 exit ramp, bathed in car-exhaust fumes, the hotel shares a parking lot with a TGI Friday's chain restaurant across the street from a charmless, seen-better-days shopping mall. For some reason, never explained, the Sheraton Braintree is designed to look like a castle, with turrets, flags, and a notch-top façade. Inside, the small, poorly lit lobby is paneled in the cheap-looking wood that you might have seen on the side of a 1970s station wagon. It is the kind of hotel that serves cubicle-dwellers from Syracuse in dandruff-speckled sport coats on a five-day, five-city New England business trip. The classy Ritz-Carlton and Four Seasons overlooking Boston Common are ten miles to the north, but they might as well be a universe away.

The Sheraton Braintree also happened to be the league-mandated hotel for visiting MLS teams in town to play the New England Revolution. When the Los Angeles Galaxy arrived to check in on August 10, David Beckham and Abel Xavier—European pros used to the finest of accommodations—did an exaggerated double take, looking first at each other, then "looking at us like it was an episode of *Punk'd* with Ashton Kutcher," as Kyle Martino put it. But it wasn't a joke. The common perception in Europe may have been that the Galaxy was the Manchester United of MLS, the gold-plated backer of "David Beckham's $250 million contract," but the reality was that the team stayed in the same depressing road hotels as every other MLS outfit. Most league hotels were the equivalent of Soviet-era toilet paper, the topic of shared-misery wisecracks among the players, but Beckham and Xavier did not appreciate being the source of unintentional comedy. The final straw was the Sheraton Braintree's pregame meal, which was (no lie) plates of greasy fried chicken. "This is not correct!" Xavier bellowed, his righteous anger threatening to explode the bleach-blond hair right off the top of his head.

Before he joined the Galaxy, Beckham had said all the right things about needing to adapt to the quirks of MLS. "Things in the U.S. will definitely be different," he told me. "It might even be frustrating at times. But that's part of why I'm going over there: to experience it and to enjoy it." Now that Beckham was experiencing his first Galaxy road trip, however, there were several aspects of MLS life that he did not enjoy at all. Leaving aside the skill level of his teammates, the travel accommodations were, as Beckham would privately tell associates, "shocking." At the Doubletree in Crystal City—a concrete jungle of dreary hotels near Washington's National Airport—some joker had pulled the fire alarm during the players' game-day nap, forcing Beckham and his teammates to spend twenty minutes standing in the 100-degree sun. And so far Beckham had visited only three MLS cities. Every player had horror stories of MLS road hotels. Martino told one about the time in Chicago when the hotel burned the marinara sauce for the pregame pasta meal. "It tasted like charcoal," he said. "So no one could eat. It was that bad." For his part, Donovan recalled the time in 2003 when his San Jose Earthquakes stayed at the MLS hotel in Carson before a game against the Galaxy. "The night before, there had been a fatal shooting in the parking lot of the hotel," he said. "We were just like, 'Come on.' You at least want to be safe."

But for Beckham, the most strident of soccer purists, no affront got his blood boiling more than MLS's artificial-turf playing surfaces, many of them irreparably scarred by the presence of lines for American football. To Beckham, who had played in the cathedrals of Manchester United's Old Trafford and Real Madrid's Estadio Bernabéu, the field was supposed to be sacrosanct, a perfectly manicured carpet of natural grass. Not a glorified living-room carpet. In New England, as the Galaxy players started watching a game on TV from Giants Stadium, the site of their next league match against the New York Red Bulls, Beckham just about lost his mind. "What the hell are all those lines all over the field?" he asked. His teammates didn't know whether to laugh or be embarrassed. *David Beckham playing on artificial turf in New York with gridiron lines?* "It's like Eric Clapton showing up and playing a Fisher-Price guitar," said Martino. "You just don't do that."

Five of MLS's thirteen teams in 2007 had fake-grass fields, but Beckham was seeing three of them in his first four league games. The reviews of Toronto's FieldTurf surface had been withering. Xavier sounded like Clapton singing "Layla" (*You've got me on my knees!*), arguing that his knees couldn't handle the pounding. "It's dangerous to play on this kind of surface," said Xavier, who was so adamant that he never played on artificial turf again. Once the Galaxy had arrived in Washington, D.C., Donovan and Xavier convinced Beckham the problem was big enough that he should go public with it. They knew full well that anything Beckham said would carry far more weight than any complaints coming from the other players on the team. And so, when I asked an innocuous question at Beckham's press conference (*What have you learned so far about this league from the games you've seen?*), Beckham pounced on the opportunity.

"I think there's many things that can change, and I'm sure in time will change," Beckham said. "I think there's one major thing that should actually change. I don't know whether I'm being too controversial, but I think the fact that, you know, there's four or five teams with FieldTurf. As professional athletes you can't play a game like soccer on that sort of field. We play on it three or four times a season, maybe more. The reaction of the players and what it does to your body, as a soccer player you're in bits for two or three days after that. So I can't imagine what it's like for the Toronto players, who play week in and week out and train every day on it. So that's one thing I personally think should change about the league. Every team should have grass, without a doubt. You can't ask any soccer athlete to perform at a high level on FieldTurf."

For the normally anodyne Beckham to issue such a public rant without consulting his management team was stunning. What's more, he hadn't realized that FieldTurf was an actual company, not a generic name for artificial grass. Just as Beckham's endorsement could bring millions to a company, his criticism could be crippling. Within an hour, a rep from FieldTurf was on the phone with an MLS executive. As it turned out, not only had the David Beckham Academy in London installed FieldTurf playing surfaces, but the branch in Los Angeles was planning to order more—at a significant discount. Beckham made sure to apologize to FieldTurf at his press conference the next night, but the damage had been done. The discount was gone. "Your question," I was told, "potentially cost David millions."

With the worlds of European and American soccer colliding head-on, the frustrations of Beckham and Xavier came to a head at the Sheraton Braintree. As they fumed over the fried chicken, a players protest was taking shape—with the almost gleeful instigation of the long-suffering American players. Beckham couldn't change the fact that the following week's league game would be played on artificial turf in Giants Stadium, but he might have an impact on the Galaxy's accommodations. The team had plans to stay at the MLS hotel in Secaucus, New Jersey, a town best known as the place where mobsters dumped dead bodies in *The Sopranos*. If so many others were cashing in on the Beckham Experiment, Beckham and his teammates reasoned, the least the Galaxy could do was to put them up at a nice hotel in Manhattan. And so, after a long discussion with Beckham about the team's concerns, Donovan and Xavier wrote down a wish list of things the players would have in an ideal world, including better hotels and meals on the road. They gave it to Yallop, who passed it up the ladder to Lalas.

Of course, it went without saying that the Galaxy also needed a win. Badly. MLS is a forgiving league. Unlike most of its counterparts around the world, which crown their champions based on their record over the entirety of the season, MLS has American-style playoffs. In 2007, eight of the league's thirteen teams would qualify for the playoffs, a four-weekend-long tournament that would determine the MLS Cup champion. As long as you finished the regular season in the top eight, you could still raise the trophy—as the Galaxy had done in 2005, winning the MLS title after squeaking into the postseason as the eighth-best playoff team based on its regular-season record. If the Galaxy didn't start winning some games, though, it was in danger of missing the playoffs entirely, which would be a catastrophe for MLS, to say nothing of any team that had David Beckham and Landon Donovan.

But that elusive win didn't come in New England. Before a crowd of 35,402, more than double the Revolution's average, the Galaxy took the field without five injured starters—including Beckham, who was dressed in a Hugo Boss suit on the bench. His ankle had flared up after the game in Washington, and there was no way he'd risk playing on Gillette Stadium's artificial turf. Yet Beckham's playing status was never announced to the New England fans, many of whom had been forced to buy four-game ticket packages just to see Beckham and the Galaxy. When Gillette's giant video board showed a close-up of Beckham's face late in the game, Beckham tried to smile, only for a chorus of boos to echo through the stadium. The Galaxy's play was no better: It went down 1–0 midway through the second half, and an exhausted Donovan botched a sitter in the final minutes to seal the defeat. The longest single road trip in MLS history had been a disaster for Los Angeles: three games, two losses, one tie, no goals, and a mere eighteen minutes of Beckham on the field. The Galaxy was now 3–7–5.

The glimmer of optimism in Washington had melted in a puddle of fried-chicken grease, and not even a cocktail or three on the charter back to Los Angeles made anyone feel better. The Galaxy needed something good to happen. It needed David Beckham on the field.

CHAPTER 7

NEW YORK TO LONDON TO LOS ANGELES (IN FIVE DAYS)

Most of the Galaxy players had already left the locker room after practice on August 14 when Landon Donovan spotted his most famous teammate, took a deep breath, and decided to make his move. Following the global icon out the door after he finished his lengthy daily treatment session for his ankle, Donovan intercepted David Beckham just as he reached his black Cadillac Escalade. Donovan didn't want to risk having this conversation with anyone else around: trainers, coaches, or especially teammates. The Galaxy's American star wasn't stupid—that's why he was standing here right now, after all—but he wasn't a glutton for public self-emasculation, either.

"David?" he said.

Beckham turned around. "Yeah?"

"Can I talk to you for a second?"

Donovan's initial response to the requests from Alexi Lalas and Frank Yallop that he give up his captaincy had been that it was a "pretty shitty" thing to do. But the more Donovan thought about it, the more he realized he had only two options. He could dig in his heels, force Yallop to make the change himself, and create palpable tension with Beckham in the locker room. Or he could just accept that he was boxed into a corner, give up the armband, and hear public praise from Beckham and Yallop hailing a selfless act of Donovan's own volition for the good of the team. Of course, nobody—including Donovan—would tell the media the whole story: that the switch had been instigated by a host of actors, including Yallop, Lalas, and Terry Byrne.

For that matter, Donovan wasn't aware of the whole story either, but he told Beckham what he knew: that Yallop and Lalas had approached him a few weeks earlier on the topic, and that Donovan now thought giving Beckham the captaincy was the right thing to do. "I want you to take the armband," Donovan said. "I think it would help the team, assuming you're ready and willing to do it." Beckham may have had no desire to be a Hollywood actor, but he knew what the script called for him to say. "I'd be honored to wear the armband, but it doesn't have to be that way," he replied. "I don't want to step on any toes, and I don't want you feeling like you have to do this. I'm fine wearing it or not wearing it."

But Donovan insisted. When Beckham led the L.A. starting XI out of the tunnel the next night for the team's Superliga semifinal against D.C. United, there was mild surprise among his teammates that he was taking over as captain so soon—even superstars usually need to earn the armband on the field with their new team, and it was Beckham's first Galaxy start—but it was entirely plausible that Beckham would have ascended to the position before long. His playing history spoke for itself, and nobody questioned whether he'd be a good leader in the locker room. Hadn't he worn the armband for five years as the captain of England? "I've never had a problem speaking up in locker rooms," said Beckham, "and if that's needed in this team . . . I will still do that."

In the long term, the sub-rosa machinations that led to the captain switch would set the tone for the Beckham Experiment on a number of levels. Galaxy executives and coaches would continue bending over backward to accommodate (and even anticipate) the wishes of Beckham and his handlers, rarely saying or doing anything they feared might offend their meal ticket. For their part, Beckham's handlers would exert more and more influence behind the scenes, almost always using Beckham surrogates—Terry Byrne, mainly—to avoid leaving any of Beckham's own fingerprints. Meanwhile, Donovan's resentment would build as he slowly began understanding that outside forces were taking over the team. In hindsight, there was no need for Yallop and Lalas (and everyone else) to force Donovan's hand on the captain switch. Donovan was smart enough that it would have happened in time organically, and it would have been *his* decision alone.

But that was in the long term. In the short term, as the Galaxy learned that night, switching captains looked like a stroke of genius.

Time for a set piece: Carson, California. August 15, 2007. Superliga semifinal. Los Angeles Galaxy versus D.C. United.

This is David Beckham's signature moment, the chance for one of his classic free kicks to erase four weeks of existential frustration. A Galaxy player has been fouled in the twenty-sixth minute of a scoreless game just outside the penalty box, to the left of the United goal. A hush falls over the 17,223 fans at the Home Depot Center, then morphs into a pulsating, expectant thrum. "As soon as a free kick is given and it's any-where near the box, I get excited," Beckham says, his eyes closed as he imagines a scene he's experienced hundreds of times. "The crowd lifts theirself, and there's a buzz around the stadium. I know it's my turn for everyone to watch me."

The charged tableau packs even more drama than usual. This is Beckham's first Galaxy start, his first game wearing the captain's arm-band, his first free kick on goal—in practices or matches—since the fi-nale of the Spanish-league season in Madrid eight weeks ago. America is starting to write off Beckham as a high-priced fraud, a marketing tool who has duped gullible sports fans and the U.S. media into devoting their dollars and attention to a bench-warming British gimp who pals around with Tom Cruise. Why, just today, the ABC news program *Nightline* interviewed Alexi Lalas for a story asking whether Americans have been sold a bill of goods with Beckham.

Beckham places the ball gently, as if he's laying a wreath on a loved one's grave, then takes six steps backward and to his left. He sucks in two quick, deep breaths. Two human barriers loom before him. United's goalkeeper, Troy Perkins, crouches twenty-six yards away, his 6'2" frame coiled in the goalmouth's right-hand side. Lined up ten yards away is a seven-man United wall, its purpose to block the goal's left-hand side. "I don't really concentrate much on what side the keeper is on," Beckham says, "because I always think that if I catch it as well as I can, then I can beat him whichever way he goes." And the wall? "I do see them. Some walls, they jump, so some players hit it under the wall. But that's sort of lazy. I like doing it the hard way."

Standing in the wall, United defender Greg Vanney turns to defender Chris Klein. "So is this going to be what everyone expects it to be?"

Klein nods. "I'm afraid so."

Beckham springs forward. At the moment before impact, he is a picture of serenity and balance, his legs splayed, his right arm pointing straight down, his left arm extended like a traffic cop's. All angles and energy, he looks like a Keith Haring drawing come to life. Physicists from Europe to Japan have spent hundreds of hours studying his free kicks, the perfectly calibrated mix of forces—angle, speed, spin, and direction—that conspire, as one researcher puts it, to achieve "optimal turbulent-laminar transition trajectory." Or, as Beckham says, he knows precisely how "to get as much whip on it as possible," to strike the side of the ball with his right instep, sending it screaming over the wall, then dipping, improbably, thrillingly, under the crossbar, past the helpless keeper's outstretched hands.

A million little things can go wrong, of course. "If you don't catch it right, it can end up in row zed," Beckham says. "It's happened to me a couple times, when my boots or my standing foot give way. That's pretty embarrassing."

This is not one of those times. "As soon as I hit the ball, I know it's in," Beckham says, a smile cleaving his face. "I know it's in. Even before it reaches the wall." The wall jumps, only to get buzzed by a Becks flyby. Poor Perkins is doomed. In a flash the ball is droppingdroppingdropping . . . *in*.

Who needs practice sessions when you've got the muscle memory of the world's greatest free-kick taker? Beckham turns and celebrates, his tongue hanging out like that of another No. 23, Michael Jordan, until his Galaxy teammates swarm him at midfield, the team's collective angst of the last month escaping in one seismic release. Abel Xavier smothers Beckham in an embrace. Even Joe Cannon races all the way from his goal to join the gang pile. Later, the Galaxy players will struggle for words to describe the moment. "Like a fairy tale," says Kyle Martino. "Like a movie," says Landon Donovan, who'll seal the 2–0 victory—and a berth in the Cup final against Mexican champion Pachuca—with a second-half goal from a Beckham assist.

The Spanish-language announcers broadcasting the game on Tele-Futura nearly cough up a lung in their excitement: *"Gol! Gol! Gol! Gooooool!"* Within a half hour, it's the lead highlight on ESPN's *Sports-Center*. By the next evening, a clip of Beckham's free kick will have been viewed more than 500,000 times around the world, making it the most popular video of the day on YouTube.

Things you learn while standing behind David Beckham in the TSA security line at LAX Airport: There is no super-secret VIP line for Hollywood celebrities and sports stars. Beckham ties his shoes deliberately, placing his feet on the counter, one after the other, like a sprinter frozen in midstride. He doesn't carry a laptop computer but does travel with a DVD viewer. He likes DVDs of the show *Friends*. He is kind of slow. Painfully slow, actually. *Hey, pal, move it! You don't need to take your belt off in this country!*

Statistics showed that 2007 was the second-worst year for U.S. commercial air travel in history. Flight delays, lost luggage, cramped seating, terrible customer service: No matter how you measured it, passengers had more reasons to be angry than ever before. But MLS had its rules—charter flights were a "competitive advantage"—and so, a few hours after Beckham's glorious free kick, the Galaxy players arrived at LAX for the first commercial flight of the Beckham Experiment. "Everyone has to stay in line!" the Continental Airlines agent announced at check-in. "You have to be here ninety minutes prior to departure time!" (Beckham, it should be noted, checked in at 10:17 A.M., ninety-six minutes before the 11:53 A.M. departure of Continental flight 90 to Newark, New Jersey. The guy was never, *ever* late for an appointment.)

For months, the Galaxy and Beckham's handlers had planned the details of this flight with the precision of the Secret Service arranging a presidential motorcade. "The toughest part is getting him through

LAX," said Lalas. "Once we put him in the airport lounge and get him on the plane, it shouldn't be a problem." One by one, Beckham and his teammates, all dressed in their Hugo Boss suits, disappeared into the Continental lounge across from Gate 62. Starstruck travelers barely had enough time to pull out their camera phones before Beckham was gone. But then, slowly, a crowd started gathering outside the door to the Continental lounge. One man, Fernando González, a thirty-year-old American Airlines ramp worker from Inglewood, was holding an official Beckham Galaxy jersey with the tags still on. "My wife got it for me yesterday for my birthday," he said. A relative who worked at LAX had tipped him off ahead of time, and he was going to get the jersey signed and framed. "I thought he'd have his own private jet," González added, "but it's pretty cool that he's actually flying with the team. The only thing that surprised me yesterday was they had him as captain right away. I don't think that's right, because Donovan is the captain."

At 11:51 A.M., the lounge doors opened, Beckham emerged, and, after signing some autographs (including one for González), he was whisked through Gate 62 onto the Boeing 757. If Beckham had to fly commercial, the 757 was at least an ideal plane design, since coach-class passengers didn't go through first class on the way to their seats. Just in case, though, Shane the Ultimate Fighter Bodyguard stood sentry next to the flight attendant as everyone boarded the plane, the better to prevent any autograph-seeking interlopers from turning to the left instead of to the right.

The Galaxy had purchased five first-class seats, which created yet another staging ground for an elaborate display of the team's pecking order. The seating arrangement was Yallop's call, and his choices—made just as carefully as the eleven men he would put on the field for a game—reflected his rep as a players' coach. Beckham and selected veterans (including Donovan and Cannon) sat in first class, players from the next step down the pay scale (Peter Vagenas, Edson Buddle, Ante Jazic) took exit-row or bulkhead seats in coach, and the rest (Alan Gordon, etc.) filled in wherever they could. Yallop himself sat in coach. Halfway through the flight, Donovan and Cannon ventured back into coach for a quick visit, as if they were almost embarrassed to be up front. "Nice exit row," Cannon told me. "You must have some clout."

"If I had some clout," came the reply, "I'd be sitting where you are."

"You could have sat next to Beckham," Cannon said. "Some random guy took the seat next to him."

Beckham stayed in first class the whole time. Everyone else, it seemed, had their feet in two colliding worlds: the Wal-Mart world of MLS and the Giorgio Armani world of David Beckham. Most of the Galaxy players still traveled with nylon backpacks bearing the team's logo, which made them look like prep-school kids when carrying the backpacks over the shoulders of their designer suits. Then again, nobody was complaining after the coach bus that picked up the team in New Jersey bypassed the exit for the Secaucus Sheraton, descended into the Lincoln Tunnel, and deposited the Galaxy at the door of the historic Waldorf-Astoria Hotel in midtown Manhattan.

The players' protest had succeeded. Within hours of returning from Boston and the horror show of the Sheraton Braintree, Yallop had passed the players' wish list on to Lalas, who in turn had spoken to Tim Leiweke. "I knew from the moment I talked to our staff and our players that something needed to be done, and it needed to be done quick," said Lalas. "That means upgrading the travel, the hotels, the meals. David's involvement obviously facilitated it, but this was about explaining to Tim what these guys are going through and recognizing that this is such an unusual situation." When Beckham spoke, the Galaxy listened. Leiweke signed off on the upgrades, all of them coming at AEG's significant expense.

Beckham and Xavier had zero problems with the Waldorf, naturally, and for the Galaxy players who'd dealt with burned pasta sauce, greasy fried chicken, and murderous hotel parking lots, the switch from *Sopranos*-land to Manhattan was a godsend. "It's a scenario where we're all used to one thing and they're used to another," Martino said one night in the Waldorf's palatial, tastefully upholstered lobby. "Now flip the tables, and we're here where they feel comfortable and we're all smiles. Normally, you can't wait to skip the team meal to go out and eat dinner, but everyone's in the team meal loving dinner. These are the best meals we've ever had."

———

Truth be told, for all his celebrity, Beckham has always seemed like more of a New York City guy than a Los Angeles guy, more comfortable in the streets of SoHo than on the freeways of SoCal. His personal preferences—his clothing, his music, his work ethic—run more to the gritty East Coast hip-hop style than to laid-back West Coast cool. When given a choice of reading *Sports Illustrated* or *Slam*, the hip-hop basketball magazine, Beckham would always opt for the latter, flipping to the pages showing off the latest in street-level hoops fashion. Why, the man named his first son Brooklyn—after the borough he and Victoria had visited soon after learning they were having a child.

"What's great about New York, and you don't get it in many cities in the world, is there's a lot of positivity, a lot of energy," Beckham said, "and if someone doesn't like you they'll come up to your face and say, 'I don't like you.'" What exactly that had to do with "positivity" was anyone's guess, except that perhaps Beckham was referring to New York's authenticity, an honesty (sometimes brutal) that is rarely associated with, say, Los Angeles. Clearly, though, Beckham was in his element on the afternoon of August 17, when he held a clinic for forty girls and boys on an artificial-turf soccer field at 138th Street and Amsterdam Avenue in Harlem. For nearly an hour, Beckham led the seven- to eleven-year-olds in drills and scrimmages alongside teammate Ty Harden and New York Red Bulls stars Juan Pablo Ángel and Jozy Altidore. At one point, Beckham was signing autographs when one of the neighborhood boys who had gathered outside the soccer field's chain-link fence started calling out to him.

"Hey, David! Come out here and see the real Harlem!"

Sometimes it's good to abandon the script. And so, as soon as he was done signing, Beckham raced outside the fence (flustering his security detail), leaped atop a bicycle rack, and threw his right arm around his primary heckler. Later, when another boy asked him for his shoes, Beckham went so far as to literally pull off his shoes and hand them over. It was, to put it mildly, a command performance. "Today," he said at a packed news conference in midtown Manhattan, "has been one of the best days I've had since I arrived in America."

The Beckham Experiment had been gaining momentum all week,

but its apotheosis came the following night, when 66,237 fans saw the Galaxy and Red Bulls play one of the most memorable games in the history of Giants Stadium. In Beckham's first MLS match on artificial turf—the American football lines had been painted over in green—he acted as though he had been playing on the surface for years. After Ángel's fourth-minute free kick had given New York a 1–0 lead, Beckham responded two minutes later by serving a perfect corner kick onto the head of Carlos Pavón for the equalizer. (On cue, Beckham theatrically turned and shushed the crowd.) Two minutes later Beckham struck again, bending a free kick onto the head of Pavón for *another* Galaxy goal. Eight minutes, three goals. There was an electricity in the stadium that nobody had felt for soccer since the 1994 World Cup and the days of Pelé, Chinaglia, and Beckenbauer with the Cosmos.

There was more to come. New York tied the score 2–2 just before halftime (on a stunning volley by Clint Mathis) and took a 4–2 lead on a pair of strikes by the seventeen-year-old Altidore in the forty-ninth and seventy-first minutes. Yet just as the Red Bulls were thinking they had sealed the win, Donovan raced downfield on the ensuing kickoff and pulled one back: 4–3. By now, Beckham was bordering on exhaustion in the end-to-end game, and his ankle was flaring up, too. Players on the New York bench heard him yelling obscenities every time he stopped on his left foot. What's more, Beckham's free kicks on goal were now a constant source of frustration. Like a golfer trying to hit range balls on a mats-only day, he scuffed four straight free kicks into the Red Bulls wall. But Beckham had one piece of inspiration left. In the eighty-second minute, he drove a corner kick toward the cornrows of the 6'4" Kyle Veris.

This was Veris's chance: to become known for something other than his $17,700 salary, to score his first Galaxy goal, to make a statement that he had a future on this team, to play a starring role in what for years had seemed like an oxymoron, an MLS instant classic. He had already planned his goal celebration for the moment it finally happened, and he had studied Beckham's free kicks, the way they dipped suddenly at the last second before impact. Veris caught it flush with his forehead, snapping the ball toward the goal. It slammed off the crossbar—*thwack!*—and onto the foot of Edson Buddle, who bundled in the equalizer: 4–4. Beckham thrust his fist into the New Jersey night sky.

If it had ended there, if L.A. had throttled down and played for a hard-earned tie, the stirring two-goal comeback might have been the turning point of the Galaxy's season. But the game had been such a continuous blast of attacking energy that you knew, deep down, that neither side would pull back. Someone was going to score again. It happened to be Ángel, the ruthless Colombian maestro, who beat Cannon from a ridiculously acute angle in the eighty-eighth minute to put New York ahead 5–4. When the final whistle blew, the Giants Stadium crowd gave both teams a deserved standing ovation. Beckham returned the favor, applauding the fans. It may not have been the most technically proficient performance—both sides made mistakes—but for pure entertainment value the game was a gem, a spectacle of images and emotions to be treasured.

"That was one of the best sports experiences I've ever attended, and I've been on the field at countless Super Bowls," said MLS commissioner Don Garber, a former NFL executive.

"If the fans tonight didn't enjoy that, then they know nothing about soccer and they have no idea what they're looking at," said Yallop.

When it came to Beckham, meanwhile, "every ball he touched was a piece of magic," said Ángel.

Even in defeat, Beckham couldn't help but marvel at the epic swings of momentum. "I haven't been involved in a game like that since I was nine or ten years old," he said. "There were so many goals, and the play changed so much in ninety minutes. But it's great for the fans, great for the people who've turned out tonight. You've seen the stadium and the amount of fans who've turned up. It's pretty incredible, and it's great for the league and great for both teams to play in an atmosphere like that."

All true. But it was also another league loss, L.A.'s third straight. The Galaxy was 3–8–5.

––––––––

Alexi Lalas was picking at the remnants of his quesadillas over lunch at the Home Depot Center the following Thursday when his cell phone rang. It was his boss, Tim Leiweke, who no doubt had Lalas at the top of his Verizon friends list.

"Hey, Tim," Lalas said. "Landon got in twenty minutes ago. David's flight was delayed forty minutes."

The voice on the other end sounded pleased. "If those guys play tonight, they'll be my heroes," Leiweke told him.

Heroic might be one word to describe what Leiweke wanted Beckham and Donovan to do that night. *Stupid* would be another. Less than twenty-four hours earlier, Donovan had played in most of the U.S.'s 1–0 friendly loss against Sweden in Göteborg. An hour later, the Galaxy coaching staff had watched the television in growing horror as Beckham stayed on the field for all ninety minutes of England's 2–1 friendly loss against Germany at Wembley Stadium in London. Now, *on the very next day in Los Angeles*, they were going to play for the Galaxy against intracity archrival Chivas USA in a must-win MLS game broadcast nationally on ESPN2.

Most soccer players run about six miles in a typical game. Beckham was about to play his third game in six days on two continents—on an ankle that had not yet fully healed. "Under normal circumstances it would be insane," Lalas admitted. "But we have passed normal circumstances a long time ago and moved on to a point where because of our current position in the standings, because of the lack of depth that exists in the league as a whole, we have to seriously think about finding a way to play guys that have flown 6,000 miles and played sixty and ninety minutes in games the day before. It's the reality of the league and of our particular position right now."

Reality was the term that Lalas often used to describe only-in-MLS moments that flew in the face of common sense. In this case, a perfect storm of circumstances was conspiring to put Beckham and Donovan in a risky, even dangerous situation. For starters, MLS was one of the only leagues in the world that scheduled games during FIFA-mandated "blackout" periods for national-team matches on the international soccer calendar. (MLS argued that it couldn't afford to lose money by going dark on so many weekends each year.) For its part, ESPN had given MLS a Thursday-night time slot and wanted as many Beckham games as possible to drive ratings. When the network and MLS made the schedule, they either didn't know or didn't care that Beckham and Donovan might have played in Europe the day before.

Beckham was driven by his own incentives to attempt such madness. He had a burning desire to show he could still compete at an elite level for England while playing his club ball in America. "Everybody knows that I want to play as many games as possible for England," he said. He knew that the Galaxy was desperate for points in the league, and that a 50 percent Beckham was preferable to a 100 percent Josh Tudela. And he knew that watching another Galaxy game from the bench on ESPN2 would be bad PR in front of a sold-out stadium in L.A.'s first home league match in six weeks. If Beckham could physically be present at the HDC, there was no way he would beg off taking the field.

The only person who could stop Beckham from playing was Frank Yallop, whose very job it was to do so. But Yallop was hardly in a position of commanding authority, since another loss would put his coaching future in serious jeopardy. What it really came down to was this: Did Frank Yallop have the guts to say no to David Beckham, even if the decision was for Beckham's own good? For all the benefits that came with being a "players' coach," there was a downside as well. It hadn't escaped anyone's notice that Yallop was still partying during the wee hours alongside the players at the Ultra Supper Club in Toronto. (Would Sir Alex Ferguson have ever been caught doing that?) And when you asked Lalas about Yallop's relationship with Beckham, his response was revealing: "I will say that the wide-eyed effect is not limited to players."

Yallop was in an awful spot. The man who had played in nearly 400 games for Ipswich and fifty-two times for Canada had never experienced anything like this during his two-championship tenure in San Jose. "You could argue that Frank is the best coach in the history of this league," said New York coach Bruce Arena, who called the Galaxy's schedule during the Beckham's first two months "a no-win situation. I don't think one coach in this league would look at that schedule and say we can deal with it. Everybody would be throwing their arms up saying this is impossible. Yet Frank has taken the high road, and he goes about it and does his job."

When Beckham arrived at the stadium—less than four hours after his plane from London had landed—he visited Yallop in the coach's office. "I want to give it a go," Beckham said. "I've probably got forty-five minutes in me."

"We might get murdered for what we're doing," Yallop replied, but they decided Beckham would start and see how long he could go. (Donovan, who was carrying a strained right calf, would come on as a second-half sub.)

Once the whistle blew, it was nothing short of a nationally televised fiasco. As early as the twenty-first minute, Beckham was running over to the sideline near the Galaxy bench to rehydrate with a sports drink. (Dehydration, of course, is one result of transatlantic plane flights.) Furiously working his jaws on some chewing gum—the first time many observers had ever witnessed him doing so—Beckham told Yallop he felt dizzy. But Beckham stayed in the game. Just before halftime, with the score still 0–0, Chivas midfielder Jesse Marsch caught Beckham with a rash kick to his stomach. Enraged, Beckham flew after Marsch, sparking a melee that resulted in red cards for the Galaxy's Kevin Harmse and Chivas's Alex Zotinca. Playing a wide-open game of ten-versus-ten meant that surely the fatigued Beckham would come off for the second half, but there he was, back on the field.

An ugly game got uglier. In the fifty-ninth minute, Kyle Veris muffed an easy clearance, gift-wrapping a goal for Maykel Galindo to put Chivas ahead 1–0. The Cuban defector scored again ten minutes later, taking advantage of a miscommunication between Kyle Martino and Carlos Pavón, and the boos of the home fans starting raining down on the Galaxy. "They really should be booing," said Eric Wynalda on the ESPN2 broadcast. "These fans have to start booing these guys. This is just outright *bad*. The people around [Beckham] just aren't good enough." By the time Chivas made it 3–0 in the final minutes, Beckham was hobbling in the center circle, unable to run, a proud athlete reduced to a shadow of himself.

It wasn't heroic. It was just sad. Nobody had shown the good sense to stop the Beckham feeding frenzy—not the Galaxy, not MLS, not Beckham himself—and now the carcass that Lalas had warned of was limping around, hands on his hips, in the center circle of the Home Depot Center.

CHAPTER 8

$18,465 PER MINUTE

If Alexi Lalas wasn't the president and general manager of the Los Angeles Galaxy, you would have looked at him and thought he was one of three things: the deflanneled former lead singer of a moderately successful 1990s Seattle grunge band; the popular assistant professor of American studies at UCLA who published papers on the historical significance of 1980s hair-metal groups; or the onetime hippie who had cleaned up, gotten married, and found a real job (only to keep writing beat poetry in his spare time). Lalas liked to conduct interviews at the Hangar Bar, a gloriously seedy dive on Aviation Boulevard in Manhattan Beach where the old-fashioned jukebox played everything from the Ramones to mariachi music. He drove a slightly beat-up 1994 teal Mercedes sedan. And he still wrote and recorded songs in the studio of the Manhattan Beach house he shared with his wife, Anne, and their one-year-old daughter, Sophie—the legacy of a performer who had four albums to his name and was the opening act on the 1998 European tour of Hootie and the Blowfish.

On the afternoon of August 29, as he welcomed a visitor to his windowless corner office at the Home Depot Center, Lalas was sporting a look that might be called Vagrant Chic: a four-day-old scruffy red beard, a white V-neck T-shirt untucked at the waist, and the bemused expression of a man who had just been assailed on national television. Only a few minutes earlier, the panelists on ESPN's *Around the Horn* had ripped Lalas for complaining about the Galaxy's overloaded schedule after its latest defeat: a 3–0 loss at Colorado three days after the Chivas debacle for which the exhausted Beckham and Donovan hadn't even made the trip. "I guarantee you I'm the first MLS GM ever to be called out on national television," Lalas cracked. "I think it's awesome.

It's what we need. It's part of the evolution of this sport. But listen, my responsibility is to protect—and, if need be, divert. To protect Frank and the players from external forces that might further harm our chance of having success."

By now, the words *success* and *Galaxy* were rarely being used in the same sentence. In the wake of the Galaxy's fifth straight league loss, Yallop, for one, realized that his job might depend on the result of that night's Superliga final against Pachuca. "I would think so," Yallop said. "I mean, I'd be a fool if I'm sitting there going, 'Well, if we lose I'll be fine.' Because results are results, no matter what the circumstances."

Lalas's job was in jeopardy, too. The Galaxy was now 3–10–5 in MLS, and the Beckham Experiment was starting to look like an on-field disaster. L.A. had missed the playoffs in 2006, Lalas's first season as president and GM, and was staring at the prospect of missing them again despite having Beckham and Donovan. Nor was *Around the Horn* the only source of voices criticizing Lalas. On Bigsoccer.com, the American soccer equivalent of talk radio, Galaxy fans had posted altered pictures of Lalas as Baghdad Bob, the delusional press secretary for Saddam Hussein, and of Lalas, Yallop, and Leiweke replacing the heads of the Three Stooges. But while Yallop was wearing a thousand-yard-stare these days, Lalas was defiant, even smiling. "What's the worst thing that could happen?" he said. "Tim walks into this office and says, 'Thanks for your time, you're on your way.' All right, I've had a good ride, and I'll go off and do something else. But until that day comes, fuck everybody! All right? I love this job. Even at its most challenging point, it's better than 99.9 percent of the things I could think of doing out there."

If Lalas's dimly lit office seemed surprisingly cramped, it was because the walls were literally closing in: He had downsized to give more space to his assistant, Director of Administration Martha Romero. Aside from the guitar with the Galaxy logo on its stand next to Lalas's desk, there wasn't room for much else: a television, a chair for guests, jars of Red Vines and granola bars. On the walls, Lalas kept Polaroid pictures of front-office staff (he could be bad with names and faces), a copy of the Galaxy's 2007 schedule ("This is our crazy fucked-up schedule, Mr. Commissioner!"), and a color-coded bar chart of the season's results: green for wins, yellow for ties, red for losses. (There was a lot of red lately.) Hanging on the door were his shirt and suit coat for that night's game.

Lalas's job description included several duties. He was responsible for signing off on, and often initiating, player-personnel moves. He was responsible for hiring and firing coaches. He was responsible for overseeing the Galaxy's business side and ticket-sales operations. And, as one of the most recognizable personalities in American soccer, he was responsible for being "the captain of the ship," as he put it, the public face of Galaxy management who spoke constantly to the domestic and international media about the team. (Although Leiweke had done all the work on the Beckham signing, he had far too many other tasks in the entertainment world as AEG's CEO to manage the Galaxy on a daily basis.) Part of Lalas's role as the Galaxy's public face, he believed, was to be accessible to ordinary fans, whose e-mails would go straight to his account. It often required a thick skin. "Want to hear one?" asked Lalas, who pulled one up on his laptop and began to read:

> **Hey Lalas, why are you and Yallop not fired yet? Your firings are way overdue. Do you have naked pictures of your boss with another woman? Good job on trying to injure Beckham for life. Keep it up. Good job on negotiating reduced playing time for Beckham with both Beckham and that clown McClaren. Good job on playing him 90 minutes vs. Chivas. Go into the broadcasting booth, Lalas. There's hope for you there. Quit Lalas! Quit before the entire world knows you're a clown. May be too late for that, huh? Fire Yallop and then resign yourself. Do it, Lalas! Do it!**

Lalas sighed. "So that's what happens," he said. He kept the e-mails in a file called "Fan Folder." Lalas liked it when angry fans included their names and phone numbers. He would often call them and be amazed by their change in tone when "that bum Alexi Lalas" was a live voice on the line. "But some of them, to their credit, stand behind their assertions about me and my mother," Lalas said. Others had even gone so far as to wish Lalas bodily harm. "Not 'I am going to kill you,' but 'You should just die,'" he said. "Whatever. It's part of the deal. It sucks for my wife and kid, but I'm not going to sit here and whine. Behind it all, as demented as it may be, is a love and a caring for this team."

In that regard, at least, Lalas thought, they were no different from him. Nobody questioned whether Lalas had a passion for his work or for the Galaxy, the team he had helped lead to its first MLS Cup championship as a player in 2002. He put in long hours. He watched every single MLS game on the weekends, the better to keep on top of the players around the league. And he was constantly on the phone—with agents, coaches, and general managers—proposing deals that could bring in players who might handle the media glare of the Beckham Experiment.

No, people never doubted Lalas's effort—or, for that matter, his sense of humor or his engaging disposition. They just wondered if he was any good at his job.

Two weeks before the start of the 1994 World Cup, Lalas sat next to an elderly woman on a plane flight. He was a twenty-four-year-old, Uncle Sam–bearded defender on the U.S. national team that would soon play in the world's biggest sporting event, which was being hosted on home soil for the first time. The younger man and the older lady exchanged the usual small talk of airplanes.

"What do you do?" she asked.

"I play soccer," he said.

"Oh, really? Who do you play for?"

"I actually play for our national team right now."

"All right. But what do you do *for a living*? How do you make your money?"

A few weeks later, Lalas was a Madison Avenue sensation, signing endorsement deals and landing on the late-night talk shows after his U.S. team had upset Colombia, qualified for the second round, and scared the *samba* out of eventual champion Brazil on the Fourth of July before giving up a late goal to lose 1–0. Using himself as an example, Lalas would tell young players all the time: *You have these moments of opportunity. It has nothing to do with how good you are, but everybody's given them, and you either take them or you don't.* "I'd like to think I maximized it as much as possible and parlayed it into a halfway decent career and the honor of leaving a bit of a skid mark on the face of

American soccer," Lalas said. "Because of the way I looked and the power of a World Cup, every single day I knew from the moment I left my house people were going to recognize me, even if it was to say, 'Isn't that *that soccer player*?'"

Lalas treasured his two years in Italy's Serie A with Padova, learning Italian and competing against the world's best players, but he returned to the U.S. in 1996 for the start of the new first-division professional league, Major League Soccer. After some loss-filled seasons with the New England Revolution, New York/New Jersey MetroStars, and Kansas City Wizards—and a brutal 1998 World Cup, in which he didn't play a minute for a U.S. team that collapsed in turmoil—Lalas abruptly retired after the 1999 season. He spent a year recording music, touring with his band, and doing television commentary for soccer games. On a night off from working at the 2000 Olympics in Australia, he and Anne returned from an evening on the town to their hotel room.

"I'm doing it," Lalas said. "I'm shaving the beard."

"Well, okay," said Anne, a television filmmaker who grew up near Lalas in suburban Detroit. "But first, if you're doing it, I'm going to tape it. And second, don't you dare ever blame this on me!"

The beard had been Lalas's calling card, the universal symbol that drew knowing smiles and autograph requests from Detroit to Dar es Salaam. "It had become a part of who I was," he said. "I'm not naïve that it helped me out tremendously over those ten years." But losing the beard was also a rebirth of sorts. Lalas returned to soccer, joining the Galaxy, a team that had come one step from the MLS title on three different occasions without ever winning. Peter Vagenas, who would become one of Lalas's closest friends, believed Lalas was the missing ingredient that put L.A. over the hump on its way to the 2002 championship.

Lalas retired for good after the 2003 season. Galaxy coach Sigi Schmid told him he had no plans to bring him back in '04, and only a few days later—after Lalas had mentioned in a newspaper article that it was important for his generation of players to be involved on soccer's business side—he got a call from Tim Leiweke asking to meet him at the Palm restaurant downtown. Leiweke offered Lalas the job as general manager of the San Jose Earthquakes, an AEG-owned team. Granted,

Lalas didn't have the traditional background of most MLS general managers, whose main tasks are selling tickets and sponsorships and inching their teams toward profitability. For one thing, he had never graduated from Rutgers, leaving college to start his pro soccer career in 1991. When he met his new staff in San Jose, Lalas was honest: "Listen, you all have much more of an education than I do. But I'd like to think you can teach me a tremendous amount from your knowledge and background, and I can also give you a unique perspective from mine."

Indeed, few people had done more than Lalas had over the years to sell and promote soccer in America. Along the way he had developed some bedrock philosophies that would shape him as an executive, none more important than this: Soccer players had to realize they were more than just athletes, they were *entertainers* with an obligation not just to win games but to be interesting while doing so. "We love to encourage personality on the field, but we stifle the personality off the field," Lalas said. "When a player actually says something interesting or fun or creative, or we actually catch a glimpse of them as human beings, we're startled. *Oh my goodness.* It's ridiculous. But think about your favorite sports teams. It always comes back to these personalities: what they're doing, what they said, who they're dating, all this other crap that I guess the sports purist says is not what it's really all about. Well, yeah, that is what it's all about—for me."

Of course, Lalas cautioned, if you didn't back it up with performance—paying the price on the field—you were a clown. It was like the scene from *Bull Durham* with Crash Davis and Nuke LaLoosh: If you have fungus on your shower shoes and you win twenty games in the major leagues, then you're *colorful.* If you don't pitch well, then you're just a slob.

Lalas changed addresses frequently. He spent one year in San Jose, trying in vain to placate fans when everyone knew the team was about to move to Houston. Then he relocated to the New York City area and oversaw a tumultuous year as the GM of the MetroStars, another AEG-owned team. The fans forgave Lalas for the time he flipped off the home crowd during his days as a MetroStars player, but his decision to fire coach Bob Bradley was a controversial one, not least because Bradley would go on to be named the U.S. national-team coach less than two years later. When the energy-drink company Red Bull bought the team from AEG, Lalas stayed on briefly, until it became clear that he didn't have a future there under the new ownership.

That was when Leiweke called again. "When the phone rings and it's Tim, there's something exciting going on," said Lalas, "and usually it involves me packing my suitcase." Five weeks earlier, Galaxy president Doug Hamilton had died tragically of a heart attack on a flight back from a game in Costa Rica. Lalas had been close friends with Hamilton, whom he considered a mentor, but enough time had passed that the Galaxy needed to move forward with a full-time replacement. "We're bringing you home," Leiweke told Lalas.

For all the spinning he could do, Lalas often showed a candor that was refreshing in the boilerplate world of professional sports. "A lot of my job, fortunately or unfortunately, has been kind of winging it and trying to do the best that I can," he said. In the fifteen months since Lalas had been on the Galaxy job, the most surprising aspect of his performance was that he had enjoyed far more success on the business side (for which he had no formal training) than on the player-personnel side (which was supposed to be his area of expertise). Even before Beckham had signed, the Galaxy was the most financially stable team in MLS, leading the league in attendance and turning a small profit thanks to AEG's ownership of the Home Depot Center. Beckham's arrival, of course, had caused the sales of sponsorships, season tickets, and luxury boxes to skyrocket. Lalas's biggest personal success had been his oversight of the team's rebranding process, developing a new logo, new uniforms, and new colors that were now ubiquitous on the Beckham Galaxy jerseys being sold around the globe.

Yet even Lalas admitted that his results on the soccer side had been "a mixed bag," which was probably a charitable analysis. Failing to reach the MLS playoffs in 2006 (or advance beyond the first round in his other two seasons as an executive) spoke for itself. What's more, the same emotion that made Lalas so passionate about his job sometimes prevented him from reaching clear-eyed personnel decisions. The list of players Lalas had lost patience with, only for them to go on and succeed elsewhere, was a long one—Nate Jaqua, Robbie Findley, and Joseph Ng-wenya from his Galaxy tenure alone—that Lalas couldn't just dismiss by saying they failed to handle the L.A. media glare. Lalas also refused to trade his close friend Peter Vagenas, even though Vagenas's skills had declined and Yallop had wanted to ship Vagenas and a draft pick to Colorado for midfielder Kyle Beckerman, a younger player with a brighter future. "I know I'm biased: I have a soft spot for Pete," Lalas said. "Having said that, trading Pete is not something we need to do from a cultural perspective. It's important to have people in the locker room who understand where the Galaxy came from."

In Lalas's defense, his decision to hire Yallop in June 2006 was regarded as a smart move, at least until the Beckham signing changed the equation. Lalas also continued to be a master when it came to delivering provocative quotes to the media, and he never went into hiding, even when the losses started piling up. Most of all, Beckham's injury and the Galaxy's death-march schedule made it hard to know how good (or bad) the team really was.

Lalas and Yallop also faced a situation unlike any other in MLS. When Alan Gordon shanked a sitter in front of 66,000 fans against New York, how angry could you really get at a guy who was on a $30,000 salary? "If he's making a million dollars a year and he misses that sitter, you go, 'What the fuck?'" Lalas said. "But the problem is we are asking these guys to perform in what normally would be associated with a SuperClub situation—like the Yankees or Real Madrid—and yet we don't compensate them as such. I can only appeal to their sense of honor and class, as opposed to their wallet. There's something kind of disingenuous about the whole thing."

Ultimately, the biggest concern about Lalas wasn't his two-for-one trades or his willingness to give up young prospects for older players, but rather his handling of the Galaxy's salary budget. MLS was the ultimate *Moneyball* league: Every team had the same $2.1-million-per-team salary cap to work with, and it was up to Lalas and Yallop to field the best roster possible outside the cap space that Beckham and Donovan accounted for. Under Lalas, the Galaxy was always pushing right up against the cap, which forced him to trade or waive players the team wanted to keep when their salaries increased or when the team wanted to acquire a new player like Xavier or Pavón. It didn't have to be that way, though. "One thing we've never had to do is make a trade for cap reasons," said a rival MLS executive. "We manage our budget, and theirs has been badly mismanaged."

While Lalas may have lacked the financial acumen associated with, say, a business-school graduate, he did have a larger-than-life presence in the Galaxy front office that earned fierce loyalty from the staffers who worked under him. But his full-throttle emotions carried both positives and negatives. On the one hand, you found yourself nodding when Lalas went into his kids-these-days rant about the current crop of American soccer players. "We have raised a generation of boys as opposed to men in U.S. Soccer, and it is coming back to haunt us," Lalas argued. "In our desire to identify the most talented players, we forgot the other part of the equation, which is a passion, a heart, a personality that combined with even mediocre ability can allow you to do some good things." Lalas wanted his players to care as much as he did, and yet his zeal sometimes led to cartoonish emotional outbursts. After the Galaxy's 6–5 Superliga win at Dallas, in which L.A. nearly squandered a 4–0 lead, Lalas walked into the locker room as Yallop was finishing his talk with the players. "Frank, I need to see you and your staff in the coaches' office," Lalas said. "Immediately."

Fully aware that the players were only a few feet away and could hear everything, Lalas slammed the door and started screaming like a madman at Yallop and his assistants: "This is not a FUCKING game! Get your fucking shit together! Fuck me!!!"

And this was after a victory. "Frank and I are fine," Lalas said afterward. "There's some theater to it, without a doubt. Sometimes you have to use some creative ways to get the message across. Maybe if they feel that their coach, who many of them adore, is being unfairly blamed for their performance, that wouldn't be a bad thing."

Some of the younger players were clearly scared afterward, but not all of them. "It's like, we won the game, dude," Donovan said. "What the fuck are you yelling about?"

The Galaxy players didn't always know what to make of Lalas.

Sometimes he engaged them in conversation; sometimes he stared right past them. And when he spoke about the team in public, Lalas instructed his players not always to believe it. "The first thing I tell all my teams is: Take what I say in the paper with a grain of salt," Lalas said. "You need to ignore it. If I have a problem with you or want to pat you on the back, I'll look you in the eye and tell you that. That's just the recognition that this is *entertainment*. This is The Show." Lalas certainly had a talent for issuing controversial statements that drew headlines, such as his claim to the British press that you could put a bunch of MLS players in a helicopter, drop them into the Premier League, and not notice any drop in quality. But some of his players wondered: If Lalas himself tells us not to believe what he says in the media, then how credible is he? How is that any different from, say, pro wrestling? And at what point does he become little more than an attention-seeking buffoon?

Donovan, for one, thought Lalas was "in over his head" and "trying to do too much" as the team's president and general manager. But Donovan had come around on one thing: the soccer-as-entertainment mantra. When he first got to know Lalas during 2004 in San Jose, Donovan said, he couldn't understand why Lalas came in telling a championship team that it had to be more entertaining. Wasn't winning enough? But now that Donovan was older, he realized that fans were paying hard-earned money to be entertained—and that they had plenty of other options, especially in Los Angeles. "If you're watching a 0–0 or 1–0 boring game, then what am I wasting my time for?" Donovan said. "I'll go to the beach or go watch the Lakers because Kobe's bringing it every night. That's one thing I actually like about Alexi. A lot of players don't like or respect that, but I really do."

How Beckham would respond to Lalas remained to be seen. In some ways, Beckham was the perfect example of Lalas's philosophy: a player whose appeal transcended the soccer field (and sports itself) in the biggest way possible. But Beckham also went out of his way *not* to say anything provocative—he didn't need to do that to draw attention—and it was easy to imagine Beckham shaking his head at some of Lalas's more outlandish public pronouncements. Obviously, Lalas wanted to get along with Beckham, but he didn't really speak to him often. It wasn't as though Lalas spent much time in the Galaxy locker room. And besides, Beckham's relationship with Galaxy management was with Lei-weke, not Lalas. If Beckham or his people ever had a problem with Lalas, they could go right above him to his boss.

Of course, if the Galaxy kept losing, Lalas wouldn't have to worry about his relationship with Beckham—because he wouldn't have a job. Winning the Superliga title that night would go a long way toward qui-eting all the Galaxy critics on television and the Internet, and the chance to see Beckham raise a championship trophy in front of the home fans was reason enough for Lalas to call the Superliga final "one of the most important games in our club's history." Beckham was rested. Donovan was rested. Lalas felt good. "It would be a great message to counteract the negative stuff that's been out and continues to be out," he said. "If we are fortunate enough to win tonight, we'll celebrate it as we should, and it's also a moment to be able to write some history. Because many years from now, people would talk about the Galaxy winning Superliga, and this MLS portion would kind of fade away."

At least that's what Lalas was hoping for.

A full moon rose over the east roof of the Home Depot Center that night, a not-so-subtle suggestion that strange events might be afoot in David Beckham's first Cup final with the Los Angeles Galaxy. It was easy for cynics to lampoon the Superliga, an eight-team made-for-TV event that had zero tradition. But the games in the tournament's first edition had been surprisingly entertaining—the highlight was Beckham's mar-velous free-kick goal against D.C. United—and both the Galaxy and Pachuca were taking the final seriously, not least because the Superliga organizers were appealing to the players' wallets. The champion would receive a $1 million prize, nearly half the size of a typical MLS team's en-tire salary budget for a year.

Money was never a simple issue in MLS, though, and Superliga was just one more example. Although MLS and the Spanish-language net-work TeleFutura constantly publicized the $1 million prize, MLS had ruled the Galaxy players' share would be only $150,000 if they won the game. The rest would go to the team's ownership. MLS argued that it didn't want the Superliga-winning player pool to exceed the player pool that went to the MLS Cup winners, which was $165,000. The Galaxy players thought the decision was outrageous, yet another instance of the league sticking it to the players, and their indignation only increased when the Pachuca players told the media their share would be $350,000 if they won the game.

Even so, a portion of $150,000 would be a welcome bonus for the Galaxy players who were earning $20,000 or $30,000 a year. And there was plenty more at stake, too. The players knew that Yallop's job was in danger, and they remained devoted to the mild-mannered Canadian, who they felt was bearing far too much blame for the team's schedule-induced struggles. Beating Pachuca again (L.A. had won their group-stage game 2–1) would also give the Galaxy bragging rights against the reigning Mexican and continental champion. What's more, now that reaching the MLS playoffs seemed like a pipe dream, the Superliga final was the Galaxy's best opportunity to win a trophy in 2007. "This is a chance to salvage something," Donovan said. "And I don't care what anyone says, if we can beat Pachuca twice and win a tournament with the four best teams from the U.S. and the four best teams from Mexico, then that's pretty damn good."

From the opening whistle, Pachuca showed why it was the best team in North America. *Los Tuzos*, as they were known, had held out eight starters from their Mexican-league game the previous weekend, the better to be at full-strength against the Galaxy. It showed: Their passes were crisp, their movements quick and sure. Pachuca almost never made mistakes, and it dominated possession early on. Los Angeles, by contrast, struggled to mount a credible attack. Beckham was playing as a right-sided midfielder for the first time with the Galaxy, and his replacement in the center, Peter Vagenas, kept giving the ball away. Vagenas's night only got worse when he knocked in an own-goal in the twenty-eighth minute to give Pachuca a 1–0 lead.

Beckham, meanwhile, was charging all over the field with reckless abandon, especially after Pachuca's goal. The impulse came from a good place, but it was a Beckham habit—trying to do too much to make things right instantly—that was not always a positive one. If Beckham ever lost the ball, he had a tendency to rush back at the opposing player with such ferocity that he would clatter into him, running the risk of drawing a yellow or red card. As for Beckham's forays all over the field, they were admirable in some ways—*look how much he wants to win!*— but they also reflected Beckham's lack of trust in his teammates (even if it was sometimes deserved) and left L.A. open to counterattacks as the Galaxy players scrambled to cover the space that Beckham had vacated. Beckham was always one of the best players on the field, but if he was retreating deep into his own end to demand the ball, then he wasn't in a position downfield to serve the deadly crosses that the Galaxy needed.

All of which may explain why Beckham the right-sided midfielder was on the far *left* side of the field two minutes after Pachuca had taken the lead when Donovan, running at full speed, reached the ball and flicked it back toward Beckham to save it from going out of play. Beckham ran in hard, but his right foot met the ball at the exact same moment as the right foot of Pachuca's Fernando Salazar. Both men fell in a heap. It was a freak play, the kind of thing you could go months without seeing, but within seconds it was clear that Beckham had suffered a significant injury. Again. Beckham pounded the field-level signboards in frustration, limped to the Galaxy bench, and held his head in his hands as trainer Ivan Pierra examined his right knee. Within minutes, Alan Gordon took his place on the field. When the halftime whistle blew, Beckham hobbled to the tunnel alone, his head down, his right sock pulled down to the ankle. He was holding a plain white towel, which seemed appropriate. Maybe it was time, after seven weeks of pain— seven weeks of hell, really—to wave the white flag of surrender.

But then something strange happened in the second half. The Galaxy rallied, creating more chances, playing better even though Beckham was receiving treatment in the locker room. Yet L.A. couldn't find a way to finish. It was still 1–0 in the second minute of injury time when Donovan, now wearing the captain's armband, sent a Hail Mary free kick downfield from his own end. Left wing Mike Randolph—the same Mike Randolph who was making $17,700 and living with his parents— pinged a header like a BB off the crossbar. Pachuca was desperate now, its defenders flailing wildly, and when one of them headed the ball straight up into the air, Chris Klein had enough time to peer skyward and realize: *It's coming to me.*

The bicycle kick is the most dynamic play in soccer, a move so unlike any other on the field that its appearance is almost always startling, even for regular observers. It requires such exquisite timing and coordination that the smallest of errors can make a player look silly, leaving his feet to shank a ball into the thirtieth row or to kick an unwitting foe square in the face. But when the bicycle kick works—when a player with his back to the goal somehow shoots the ball into the net—it is one of the aesthetically perfect moments in sports. In the ninety-second minute of the Superliga final, with his team trailing 1–0, Klein thrust his body backward like a diver performing a backflip, scissored his right leg through the air, and fired a shot so sweet and true that even the Pachuca players wore looks of amazement as it flew inside the right post.

1–1.

The stadium roared. Cannon ran the length of the field to join in the celebration. Beckham shot up from the treatment table in the locker room to put on a suit and rejoin his teammates on the bench. Klein, for his part, couldn't believe what he had just pulled off. "I don't even know if I could do one of those on my bed," he would say.

Thirty minutes of scoreless extra time followed. The title would be decided in a penalty-kick shoot-out, the diabolical soccer tiebreaker that vexes the psyches of players and fans alike. *Los Tuzos* took a 1–0 lead, and Vagenas made his horrible night even worse by sending his spot kick off the diving arms of Pachuca's do-ragged goalkeeper, Miguel Calero. The Galaxy connected on its next three penalties, however, through Cobi Jones, Klein, and Edson Buddle, and Cannon's kick save in the third round brought L.A. even again. When Pachuca's Marvin Cabrera slammed his shot off the crossbar in Round 5, Cannon pumped his fist in the air and exhorted the crowd to join him.

All that remained was for Donovan to finish off Pachuca and let the celebration begin. *It's over*, Cannon thought. All year long, Donovan had converted important penalty kicks for the U.S. national team and for the Galaxy. His teammates and Yallop watched from midfield as one, their arms wrapped around one another's shoulders, including Beckham in the same gray Burberry suit that he'd worn at his Galaxy introduction seven weeks earlier. Donovan turned his back to Calero, crouched low, and went through his lengthy prekick ritual, kissing his wrists for good luck. (It looked ridiculous, but hey, whatever works.) He stood up. The referee blew his whistle.

Donovan delivered his spot kick head-high to the left side of the goal.

And Calero saved it.

It was a gut-punch moment: for Galaxy fans, for Donovan, and for his teammates, whose shoulders sagged at midfield. You didn't have to be a human-behavior expert to predict what happened next. Pachuca's Carlos Rodríguez beat Cannon with his penalty kick, and Abel Xavier— a defender not known for his shooting poise—airmailed his shot completely wide of the goal. Game over.

The Galaxy players fell to their knees. Their fans went silent. The PA system played Gnarls Barkley's song "Crazy." It seemed like the right choice. When the Pachuca players accepted the championship trophy, the same confetti cannons that heralded Beckham's arrival seven weeks earlier blasted away again, only now the mood—of the Galaxy, of Beckham—was mired at the opposite extreme. Everyone responded in his own way. Donovan apologized to the team in the locker room. "I told myself I wasn't going to get caught up in everything," he said of his penalty kick. "Usually, I slow myself down and take a look at the goalie. But at that moment I just panicked a little bit. That's the worst place I could have put it."

A teary-eyed Cannon was barely audible. "This was the one game this year that we could really make up for such a frustrating and disappointing season," he whispered. "We win this game, and even if we don't make the playoffs, at least we put a trophy in the case. That's what you play for. That's why it's so devastating." He called it the most painful defeat in his ten years as a professional.

Seated next to Beckham on the dais at the postgame press conference, Yallop finally released two months of pent-up frustrations like the pressurized contents of a fire extinguisher. All it took was one question about the Galaxy's slow starts. "I could go on about why we came out flat, why we look like we're not interested, but guys are fuckin' knackered, to be honest," he said. "That's the truth. But I'll tell you what: They kept going, and that makes me proud. They're fucked. . . . All the crap that we've been fuckin' through, I'm telling you, has been difficult to fuckin' deal with—sorry to swear—but it's been hard. And they kept going, and that makes me proud. And that's all I can say."

As for Beckham, his eyes were moist and red. For five weeks—ever since his debut against Chelsea—he had tried to play on an injured ankle, abandoning common sense in an effort to satisfy the demands and pressures of American commerce. The smiles and bonhomie that usually marked his press events were gone. An MRI the next day would reveal that Beckham had strained the medial collateral ligament of his right knee. His left ankle had never fully healed, and now he was saddled with additional damage that might even be worse. "It's just gone from one thing to another thing," he said. "So maybe it's a sign for me to just say I need the rest and get it right and don't come back until it's right."

The doctors said Beckham would be out for six to eight weeks—essentially the remainder of the Galaxy's woeful season. Beckham disappeared from public view in the days after the injury, surfacing to speak not to the *Los Angeles Times* but rather on the radio show of Ryan Seacrest—the *American Idol* host and fellow associate of Simon Fuller. "I shouldn't have played so soon," Beckham said. "I rushed back too early." But now it was too late. All that remained was for the Galaxy to limp to the end of its MLS campaign.

With Real Salt Lake's win that week, the Galaxy now had the worst record in the league.

Seven weeks later, on a windy October day in Bridgeview, Illinois, David Beckham stood over a ninetieth-minute free kick with the most unlikely of opportunities: if the Galaxy could break a 0–0 deadlock and win the final game of the regular season against the Chicago Fire, it would complete a remarkable rise from the dead to reach the MLS playoffs. The twin recoveries—Beckham's and the Galaxy's—had been equally stunning. Thought to be out for the season, Beckham had flung himself into his injury rehab, returning to the field for the first time three nights earlier against New York and coming off the bench in the fifty-eighth minute against Chicago. The Galaxy, meanwhile, had bottomed out in mid-September, falling to 4–13–5, but a five-game winning streak had put L.A. (now 9–13–7) into contention for the eighth and final playoff spot in MLS's all-too-forgiving postseason format.

By now, it wasn't lost on anyone that the Galaxy (starting against Pachuca and continuing ever since) somehow fared better when Beckham wasn't on the field. Since Beckham's arrival, L.A. was 8–6–2 (a winning percentage of .563) in the sixteen games Beckham *hadn't* played, while it was 1–3–2 (.333) in the games in which he *had* taken the field. The disparity wasn't a reflection of talent—only a fool would suggest that Beckham's skills hurt the team—but it was a clear indication that the Galaxy players couldn't handle the attention that surrounded him. "He's not around for five or six games, and nobody cares about us and we do well," said Donovan. "Then he comes back, and the circus is back and we struggle. I'm not saying *it's because he's back*. It's just everything around it."

Donovan had another theory, too. He thought the Galaxy was succeeding now that Frank Yallop was no longer dealing with as much of what Donovan considered to be the constant meddling of Lalas. Yallop had managed to avoid being fired after the Pachuca loss, and his standing had improved thanks to the Galaxy's resurgence, which Donovan called "the one point during the year when Frank was given the chance to be himself and make his own decisions." How much truth there was to Donovan's assertions about Lalas was up for debate. Yallop was closer to Donovan than to any other player, and the coach often vented privately to Donovan over his frustrations with Lalas, whether they included Lalas's disagreements about player evaluations or his vetos of the proposed Peter Vagenas trade and potential acquisitions from other teams (such as Arturo Álvarez and Jeff Cunningham).

Lalas dismissed the notion that he was "this puppet master constantly manipulating behind the scenes," arguing that it was too easy for Donovan or the fans to blame "the big red-headed guy who likes to shoot his mouth off." Still, Donovan wasn't inventing stories about the tensions between Lalas and Yallop. When asked later about Donovan's claims, Yallop acknowledged his desire for more control. "Alexi likes to be hands-on," Yallop said. "Sometimes we agree, sometimes we don't. I just feel in this league the coach gets fired in the end if you don't win games, so you'd like to think he has more say in players coming in and out, and how he values them."

Despite the Galaxy's late-season turnaround, Yallop's chances of returning in 2008 were almost certainly depending on the result of the game against Chicago. Missing the playoffs is missing the playoffs, after all, and everyone knew the expansion team starting in San Jose would be an ideal fit for Yallop, an opportunity to return to the site of his greatest coaching success. As Beckham stood over his ninetieth-minute free kick and the sellout crowd screamed as one to distract him, it was amazing that the Galaxy had a chance to win the game at all. Chicago had dominated, outshooting L.A. 22–5, but a series of saves by Cannon had given the Galaxy a lifeline. Beckham's free kick was too far out to shoot directly on goal, but how many times had everyone seen a Beckham set piece produce belief-defying magic in the dying minutes of a big game?

Hands on his hips in a pose known the world over, Beckham took two quick breaths, approached the ball, and delivered a long, swerving cross toward the head of Carlos Pavón. On two occasions in New York, Pavón's noggin had turned Beckham's inch-perfect passes into goals. But this was not an inch-perfect pass. Chicago defender Wilman Conde beat Pavón to the ball and cleared it out of danger. A few moments later, Beckham's errant pass sparked a Fire counterattack, and John Thorrington's goal gave the home team a 1–0 victory, sealing Chicago's own playoff berth in the winner-take-all game. The Galaxy's season was over.

Beckham skipped the postgame press conference, but for the first time all year he answered questions in the locker room, just like any other player. There was none of the red-eyed emotion that characterized his response to the Pachuca loss; in fact, you suspected he found it absurd that the Galaxy was even in contention for the playoffs despite its 9–14–7 record. But there was a palpable sense of emptiness, of a missed opportunity during the hype-filled summer of 2007 that might not come his way again. "I've never had so many injuries in such a short space of time," Beckham said. "I'm happy to be an ambassador of the MLS, I'm happy to be the face of the league, but I need to be playing out there. That's the biggest thing for me."

Beckham's final Galaxy totals for 2007 told the story: 352 minutes played, seven competitive games, one goal. Or, put another way, the Galaxy had paid him $18,465 per minute, $928,571 per game, and $6,500,000 per goal.

It was never a good sign when a player's salary was being calculated by the minute, or when all those new Galaxy season-ticket holders got to see Beckham play in a grand total of two MLS home games. When Beckham was asked on *60 Minutes* to describe his first season in America, he spoke for everyone connected to the Los Angeles Galaxy: "It was a nightmare, to be honest."

Landon Donovan had finally had it. It was bad enough that he had been forced to give up his captaincy, watch his beloved coach be thrust into an impossible situation, see Beckham refuse to pick up the dinner checks, and (not least) lose game after game during a miserable Galaxy season. But Donovan was damned if he was going to let Alexi Lalas reach into his wallet and steal $25,000 of *his* money. And so, a few hours after the Galaxy's season-ending loss to Chicago, Donovan rode the elevator to the revolving bar atop the W Hotel on Lake Shore Drive (a rare MLS-allowed upgrade), tracked down Lalas, and tapped the Galaxy president and general manager on the shoulder.

"Could we go talk where it's quiet?" Donovan asked. "I want to ask you about something."

A week earlier, before the Galaxy's home game against Toronto, the team had presented its annual player awards. Donovan won the Humanitarian Award (for his work with the Galaxy Foundation) and the Golden Boot Award (for his eight goals), but when it came time to present the Galaxy's Most Valuable Player Award, it had gone instead to Chris Klein.

Soon afterward, a couple of media members mentioned to Donovan that nobody they had talked to had voted for Klein. That week, Donovan poked around the Galaxy offices and learned that the media balloting hadn't even been close: He had received all of the votes except one. Donovan was good friends with Klein, his roommate on road trips, and if Donovan's concern had been only about public recognition he wouldn't have taken the matter any further. But Donovan's contract promised him a $25,000 bonus if he was named the Galaxy's team MVP for the season, so he approached Galaxy public-relations director Patrick Donnelly. "What happened here?" Donovan asked.

"Well, what's happened in the past," Donnelly replied, "is the media all vote, and then when Doug [Hamilton] was here, he would have input on it and a decision was made."

"So what happened this time?"

"Well, the votes were all gathered, Alexi had an input, and then a decision was made."

"Does that mean Alexi could have changed it?"

Donnelly paused. "Um, yeah."

Donovan could feel his anger burning, the resentment from a season's worth of slights piling one on top of the other. His acute sense for disrespect was in DEFCON mode, and now Lalas—the target of that anger—was standing in front of him at the hotel bar in Chicago.

Donovan got to the point. "Who was the MVP of the team this year?" he asked.

"Chris Klein," Lalas replied.

"Are you sure?"

"Yeah."

"Well, I know what's going on here, and I'm fully aware of it. Don't bullshit me. I know what happened. I know the media voted for me, and somehow I didn't get it."

"Well, first of all, in my opinion, Chris Klein has been the MVP of the team this year. I just think for what you make and what you should be doing for this team that you weren't the MVP."

"Whatever's your opinion is fine. I don't care. But if the media gets to vote, then why am I not the MVP?"

"Well, it is the media, but then the GM has a vote, and then it's decided who's the MVP."

"Then why even give the media a vote? You're not only insulting me, you're insulting them by saying they don't know what they're talking about. I can go tell them you're basically telling them to fuck off and we don't care what you think."

"No, that's not the way it went."

"That's bullshit, Alexi. I'm so fuckin' pissed right now. I have a bonus for this. You're taking money from me. It's completely unfair."

"It's nothing personal. It's just the way it was done."

"Well, it's wrong. It's completely wrong."

"What do you want me to do about it? Pull you both on the field and say you're co-MVPs?"

"I don't care what you do or don't do publicly. I just want what's right to be right."

"Okay, let me think about it."

"All right."

Donovan walked away, but the issue wasn't over. A few days later, Donovan called Tim Leiweke and explained the situation. Leiweke said he would look into it. The Galaxy never announced anything—Klein is still listed as the 2007 team MVP—but Donovan got his $25,000.

Lalas was his usual defiant self when asked about the incident. "My PR guy sent me an e-mail and said, 'Who do you want to win? Because ultimately you get to decide,'" Lalas said. "I said Chris Klein. Should I have clarified it with the parties involved? Maybe. But look, if it's my decision, it's Chris Klein. Landon got his money because he cried, but I still looked him in the eye and said: 'I don't personally believe you're the MVP.' And that burned the shit out of him."

Two weeks later, in a move that surprised almost nobody, Frank Yallop announced he was resigning as the Galaxy coach and taking over the San Jose Earthquakes. Tim Leiweke had told associates that Yallop was going to be fired if he didn't resign, and the expansion team starting in the Bay Area provided a soft landing for the coach. In San Jose, Yallop could build a team from scratch in an environment where he was wanted, where the emphasis was on the soccer, not the circus that surrounded the Beckham Experiment. In the final analysis, the Beckham-era Galaxy and Yallop just weren't a good match. "I felt like the focus wasn't on the actual game, it was on David," Yallop said. "That's nobody's fault, not his or the club's. It's just the way it goes."

The coach's departure was one more stinging blow for Donovan, who couldn't believe that Yallop was leaving his Galaxy position while Lalas was staying in his. That week Donovan and Lalas met for two hours in a clear-the-air session in Vancouver, where the Galaxy was playing a money-generating friendly against the second-tier Vancouver Whitecaps. Donovan told Lalas how he felt about everything: the tensions between Lalas and Yallop; his lingering anger over the team MVP vote; his concerns that the Galaxy's thriving business operation appeared far more important to the team's management than winning soccer games. Lalas responded that Donovan's perceptions of what happened behind the scenes might not necessarily match the reality. They agreed to disagree on several topics, though Lalas added that he wanted Donovan to stay with the Galaxy, which he thought was a significantly better team with the U.S. star's involvement. (Donovan had a no-trade clause in his contract, so it wasn't as though Lalas could ship him to another team, anyway.) Lalas also reemphasized that winning games mattered to him more than Donovan could know. "The fact that we haven't made the playoffs in two years—and that I've been in charge both years—is no source of pride, believe me," Lalas said. "I take it very personally that this has happened on my watch to a team that I love."

And they left it at that. Donovan didn't know what more he could do. Lalas wasn't going anywhere, was still his boss, but it didn't mean they had to be friends. "I know who he is, I know what he is, and I know what he does," said Donovan. "I've got him pegged perfectly. But whether I like it or not, he's running the ship."

Maybe so, but Lalas's authority over David Beckham's team was about to change in a big way.

CHAPTER 9

THE 19 TAKEOVER

With his manic energy, his calling-card hair, and his masterly talents for theater, promotion, and spin, Alexi Lalas was often the sports equivalent of the 1980s magician Doug Henning. But Lalas knew the trick facing him at the Galaxy's standing-room-only news conference on November 9, 2007, was going to be as hard to pull off as any of Henning's signature stunts. Nearly a hundred members of the international media had assembled in the television studio at the Home Depot Center in front of a dais that included Lalas; AEG chief executive Tim Leiweke; new Galaxy assistant coach Cobi Jones; and new Galaxy head coach Ruud Gullit, the Dutch former World Player of the Year who had just signed a three-year, $6 million contract to become the highest-paid coach in the history of Major League Soccer.

Lalas knew his tasks that day would have tested the skills of the most brilliant illusionists. How do you feign rousing support for a coach whom everyone thinks you hired, when in fact you had nothing to do with it? How do you sing the praises of a great soccer mind when, in fact, you counseled your boss against him? Yet the most challenging trick of all for Lalas was this one: How do you make a team president who has been cut off at the knees appear whole again?

As he sat before the media flashing his most convincing fake smile, Lalas couldn't stop thinking of the horrible scene from earlier that day in the Galaxy locker room. In an introduction that he had orchestrated for maximum effect, Lalas brought Gullit in front of all the Galaxy players, held out his right arm, and announced to the team: "Guys, this is your new coach, Ruud Gullit." Gullit said a few words, and then, out of nowhere, another man suddenly stepped forward and took over the proceedings, stealing Lalas's thunder and speaking to the team as if *he* was in charge. Most of the players were confused. Who was this British guy who looked like the comedian Ricky Gervais? Who was this person whom nobody had bothered to introduce? When Landon Donovan asked a question—about whether the players would need to change their Thanksgiving plans—it was *this guy*, not Lalas or Gullit, who answered him. "That was weird for me," said Chris Klein. "Alexi Lalas is the general manager of this team, and then here's this other guy presenting our new coach. If Tim Leiweke was in there talking, I would understand that because he is the top guy, then you have Alexi and then the coach. But I was like, *What is going on here?*"

The mysterious figure was Terry Byrne, David Beckham's best friend and personal manager—and a business associate of Simon Fuller's 19 Entertainment. Even though Beckham was in the room, he remained oddly silent. Nobody would ever bother explaining to the players (or the public) what had happened: that Leiweke had hired Byrne as a paid consultant to the Galaxy, that Byrne (not Lalas) had conducted the coaching search, recommended Gullit, and made the first phone calls in the negotiating process, and that Byrne would now be a regularly participating member of the Galaxy's management team, along with Lalas and the coaching staff. Lalas left the locker room that morning shaking his head. It was inappropriate for Byrne to be there, he felt, and even more so to have spoken. "I walked out," Lalas would say, "feeling the team I had been in charge of was no longer mine."

In the wee hours of November 1, more than a week earlier, Lalas had sent an angst-ridden e-mail to Byrne (soon forwarded to Leiweke) detailing his reservations about Gullit, whose track record as a coach was marked by short-term stays, up-and-down results, and tensions with players and club officials. "There's no chance in hell I would ever hire this guy," Lalas would say months later. (His preference had been for U.S. Olympic coach Peter Nowak, who had won the 2004 MLS Cup with D.C. United.) Byrne and Leiweke disregarded Lalas's e-mail and pressed ahead anyway. Lalas had only a few options now, none of them good. With his authority irretrievably diminished, he could resign, but Lalas loved the Galaxy, had a growing family to consider, and still had one year left on his contract. He could stay on and announce he'd had nothing to do with Gullit's hiring, removing himself from accountability, but

Lalas's pride was too deep for such public embarrassment. Or he could grin and bear it, working with a coach he didn't hire, a coach who didn't report to him, but rather to Leiweke. "What are you going to do?" Lalas would say. "If your boss makes a decision, you can go in and say, 'You're a stupid motherfucker, what the hell are you doing?' Or you can go in and say, 'Okay, it's going to be great,' and give two thumbs up. Or you can do what I did and say, 'I'll make the best of it and try to figure out how to work with it.'"

For Lalas, who was now gritting his teeth through Gullit's press conference, making the best of it meant swallowing his pride, putting on a positive front, selling the illusion of his unqualified support for Gullit with the skill of the finest magician. "For what we're trying to do, he's kind of the perfect candidate," Lalas argued publicly, echoing Leiweke's equally glowing comments. Leiweke would later call Lalas's performance "being a good soldier," an odd choice of words for the president and general manager of a sports franchise. Even though they weren't on stage that day, the shadow of David Beckham and his handlers hung over the proceedings. If you looked closely at the news conference announcing Gullit's appointment, the logo of 19 Entertainment was plastered all over the backdrop. Beckham's handlers had successfully taken over the Los Angeles Galaxy, snatched away Lalas's power, and installed their man as coach. Simon Fuller, master string-puller, had seized control again.

Tim Leiweke had always swooned for European soccer stars, to say nothing of the culture surrounding the European game and, in particular, the English Premier League. You could tell by the way Leiweke, a St. Louis native, used the British word *pitch* all the time instead of the American term *field*. ("I want everyone in the league to be envious of us, on and off the pitch.") You could tell by his adoration of Jürgen Klinsmann, the former German superstar who lived in Southern California. ("Whatever vision we have today, Jürgen Klinsmann had a lot to do with it.") And you could tell most of all by listening to Leiweke talk about that vision, which would someday result in MLS becoming one of the world's top soccer leagues and in the United States winning the World Cup.

"What we ought to be doing is taking the best young American kids and shipping them over to Europe to learn how to play against the best players," said Leiweke, who included Landon Donovan in that group. "Until they learn how to compete, we will not win a World Cup. And then you take the great European players who are through their cycle there and have them come to MLS and turn on the fans to the greatest game in the world. We need to get to a day and time when all the best [American] players *should* stay here, because we're good enough to create an environment on a club basis where you're playing against the other best players in the world. I don't know if we're five, ten, or fifteen years away, but we're not there yet."

The Leiweke/Klinsmann vision was a controversial philosophy in MLS circles: The commissioner and most of the owners thought MLS should be trying to *keep* top young Americans in the league, not send them overseas. But Leiweke's love for the magic dust of European star power (e.g., Beckham) extended to his desire to land a big-name European coach for the Beckham-era Galaxy. To Leiweke, the hiring of Gullit (and of Terry Byrne as a paid consultant) was the result of a logical thought process. He didn't think there was another coach in MLS or in the U.S. national-team program that had the stature to take over the Galaxy. He knew the Galaxy couldn't bring in another star European *player* due to MLS's salary cap, but there was no limit on how much it could spend on a European *coach*.

Klinsmann, Leiweke's ideal choice, said he wasn't interested. But there were other candidates. "What we can do is get a coach that creates that brand that we were trying to create and at the same time is used to the circus," Leiweke would say. "We've gotta find a guy that has been under far greater pressure than anything he's going to see here, a guy that's as big a name and as big a personality as anyone else in the locker room. Terry [Byrne] had the better idea of who on the world stage was the right guy for that. When we made the decision to go international, I think Alexi was not the right guy at the end of the day to go out and make that decision."

That didn't make total sense. Even if you agreed that hiring a big-name foreign coach was the best decision—a dubious proposition given the history of MLS—Lalas had global contacts from his days as a soccer player on the world stage, while Byrne had coaching contacts from his days as . . . a physical therapist and equipment manager for Chelsea and England (and a short stint as director at second-tier Watford). Ultimately, three of the Chelsea coaches Byrne had worked for (Gullit, Glenn Hoddle, and Gianluca Vialli) were on the list of candidates he gave to Leiweke. (Other coaches on the list included recently fired Chelsea coach José Mourinho, former Chelsea player Gianfranco Zola, and Beckham's former Real Madrid manager Fabio Capello.) Unwilling to spend $5 million a year on a coach, Leiweke asked Byrne to call Gullit, who was on vacation in the Dominican Republic, and they set up appointments for Gullit to meet with Byrne (and Simon Fuller) in London and soon Leiweke himself. It wasn't a long search process, but Leiweke trusted the opinion of Byrne, not least because he knew Byrne would represent Beckham's interests.

In the end, at least Leiweke was honest about one thing that Beckham and his handlers refused to admit: By the end of 2007, David Beckham and 19 Entertainment were the biggest influence—the *only* influence, really—over the most important decisions shaping the future of the Galaxy. "When Wayne Gretzky was with the Kings, Wayne had a lot of input on the Kings' direction player personnel–wise. It's just a fact," Leiweke would say. "You had a dominant guy that was the franchise. When Magic Johnson was with the Lakers, Magic had a lot of input about where they were going and the direction they were headed. So does Kobe [Bryant] today. I mean, obviously, as Kobe proved this year, when Kobe speaks, people listen.

"When David or his people spoke, we obviously listened."

There was a major difference, however, that Leiweke didn't acknowledge. Gretzky, Magic, and Kobe never had their best friend and personal manager put in paid management positions exerting significant influence over their teams, paid management positions that were never spelled out to the public—or even to the players on the team.

Beckham did.

Who *was* Terry Byrne? "He is really David's confidant," said Frank Yallop, who had spoken to Byrne regularly in the months before Beckham's arrival. "David needs someone like that he can really trust." In some ways, the Beckham Experiment had begun on the day in 2002 when Leiweke met Byrne in London and they started talking about Beckham's interest in putting his name on soccer academies for boys and girls. "I started with Terry on this whole thing a long time ago," said Leiweke. "And Terry's been my partner from day one, someone I loved."

19 Entertainment said Byrne never did media interviews—in that regard, he was even harder to reach than Simon Fuller—and that only added to the mystery surrounding him. Yet Byrne's path from cabdriver to David Beckham's best friend was a remarkable journey. Byrne had driven the cab after his brief and unremarkable career as a soccer player, which included trials at lower-level Leyton Orient and Cambridge United in England. In 1993 Byrne joined Chelsea as its physical therapist and equipment manager, and he started performing the same roles for England when Chelsea coach Glenn Hoddle took over the national team in 1996. (Byrne continued his work at Chelsea for Hoddle's replacement, Ruud Gullit.)

The watershed moments of Byrne and Beckham's relationship came during the 1998 World Cup, when Byrne served as Beckham's listening post during the ups and downs of his first major international tournament: his benching for the opening game against Tunisia, his marvelous free-kick goal against Colombia, and, of course, his red-card ejection against Argentina. In Beckham's autobiography, he wrote that part of him had wanted to run by the England bench after scoring against Colombia, and not just to say *I told you so* to Hoddle. "It was a pity I didn't," Beckham wrote, "because on the way to the dugout I might have remembered to do what I'd promised before the game: to go and hug Terry Byrne and Steve Slattery, the England masseurs, if I scored. Terry and Slatts had talked to me—and listened to me—through all the highs and lows so far. They'd been great company. The right company: They'd say what they thought, not just what they thought I wanted to hear. And they'd listen for as long as I had something to say. Terry has become a really close friend over the years."

While Beckham got the cold shoulder from Hoddle and most of his teammates after his red card against Argentina, it was Byrne who ran over from the bench, put an arm around Beckham, and walked the distraught twenty-three-year-old to the locker room. Beckham would never forget Byrne's gesture on the worst night of his career. "I remember walking off and being in the dressing room with Terry, my best mate who was England masseur at the time," Beckham said at a 2008 gala dinner in London. "I said, 'Why me?' He said he didn't know. But a year ago, Terry said he knew why I had to go through that: 'It was because with everything that has been thrown at you in the last ten years, it's put you in a good position to handle it.'"

From that night in '98 forward, Byrne became Beckham's Zelig, his Forrest Gump, the unidentified figure who was almost always in Beckham's immediate orbit. When Beckham served as the captain of England under the regime of Sven-Göran Eriksson, Byrne continued his previous roles with the national team. In 2001, Byrne took on his first job in soccer management, joining second-tier Watford as its general manager and then director of soccer. But two years later, after Beckham had moved to Real Madrid and switched his representation from Tony Stephens to 19's Simon Fuller, Byrne left Watford to become Beckham's full-time personal manager. If it seemed strange that Beckham's best friend was also his employee, that didn't appear to be a point of concern for them. Byrne and his wife, Jennie, were godparents to the Beckhams' children, along with Sir Elton John and his partner, David Furnish. And when Beckham left England's World Cup headquarters in 2006 after his emotional speech giving up the national-team captaincy, it was Byrne who wrapped him in a tight embrace.

Conflicts of interest were nothing new in the world of MLS and U.S. Soccer, in part because the sport didn't generate enough money in America to attract many off-the-field actors (agents, executives, owners, etc.) who made soccer their livelihood or their vanity project. And so you had one agent, Richard Motzkin, who represented players (Landon Donovan), team officials (Alexi Lalas), and coaches (Frank Yallop, Bruce Arena). You had an owner (Phil Anschutz) who at one point owned six MLS teams. And you had a president of the U.S. Soccer Federation (Sunil Gulati) who wore several hats, including president of Kraft Soc-

More than 700 media members and 5,000 fans attended the ceremony presenting David Beckham as a Los Angeles Galaxy player on July 13, 2007. Adidas sold in excess of 300,000 Beckham Galaxy jerseys in 2007, making it the most popular athletic jersey in the world. *(WireImage)*

Victoria Beckham arrived in her fuchsia finest at her husband's introductory event at the Home Depot Center. The former Posh Spice's bob hairstyle was all the rage among American women in the summer of 2007. *(FilmMagic)*

ABOVE: The moguls who engineered the Beckham Experiment: 19 Entertainment chief Simon Fuller (far left) and Tim Leiweke (far right), the CEO of the Galaxy's ownership group. Joining them at the 2005 launch party for the David Beckham Academy were (from left) David and Victoria Beckham, CAA agent Jeff Frasco, and British pop star Robbie Williams. *(Getty Images)*

LEFT: Alexi Lalas, the Galaxy's president and general manager, clashed with most of the Galaxy's major figures during his tenure with the team. *(Getty Images)*

A media frenzy greeted Beckham at his first Galaxy game, a made-for-TV exhibition against Chelsea FC on July 21, 2007. *(Getty Images)*

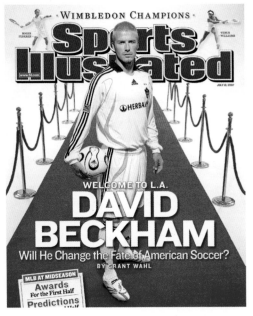

ABOVE: Victoria and David Beckham were the guests of honor at a star-studded party thrown on July 22, 2007, by Tom Cruise, Katie Holmes, and Will and Jada Pinkett Smith. *(Getty Images)*

LEFT: Galaxy star forward Landon Donovan and his wife, the television actress Bianca Kajlich, at the party. Under pressure from Galaxy executives at the urging of Beckham's handlers, Donovan gave up the team captaincy to Beckham in August 2007. *(WireImage)*

Beckham appeared on the cover of the July 16, 2007, issue of *Sports Illustrated*, becoming the first player in a Major League Soccer uniform ever to do so. *(Simon Bruty/ Sports Illustrated)*

Displaying his gift for theater, Beckham scored on a trademark bending free kick on August 15, 2007, in his first start, his first game wearing the captain's armband, and his first free kick on goal—in practices or matches—for the Galaxy. *(MLS)*

Already playing on an injured left ankle, Beckham sprained a ligament in his right knee on August 29, 2007, causing him to miss seven of the last eight weeks of the 2007 season. Asked to describe his debut campaign in MLS, Beckham was succinct: "It was a nightmare, to be honest." *(Getty Images)*

The Galaxy named former World Player of the Year Ruud Gullit as its coach in November 2007, making the Dutchman the highest-paid coach in MLS history (with a $2 million annual salary). The presence of the logo for 19 Entertainment at the announcement of Gullit's hiring stunned several Galaxy players. "*Bizarre* isn't even the right word," said one. "It was just so *crooked*." *(Getty Images)*

Terry Byrne (far right), Beckham's best friend and personal manager, became a paid consultant to the Galaxy in 2007. Byrne conducted the coaching search for Ruud Gullit, irretrievably diminishing the power of Galaxy president Alexi Lalas (far left). *(AFP/Getty Images)*

Beckham celebrates with Landon Donovan after providing the assist on Donovan's goal in a 2–0 victory over San Jose in the second game of the 2008 season. *(MLS)*

ABOVE: A veteran of seven European leagues, former Portuguese national-team defender Abel Xavier was the Galaxy's most globally recognized player other than Beckham. *(WireImage)*

LEFT: Despite earning a salary of only $30,870 in 2007, Galaxy forward Alan Gordon (shown here after scoring against Chivas USA) became one of Beckham's best friends on the team. *(MLS via Getty Images)*

Beckham, shown with his oldest son, Brooklyn, joined Jack Nicholson as a courtside celebrity fixture at Los Angeles Lakers games. "I love basketball," Beckham said. "I'm hooked by it, and I love the Lakers." *(AFP/ Getty Images)*

Beckham's advertising campaign for Emporio Armani underwear turned heads around the globe—and appeared in giant form on the side of this building in San Francisco. *(Getty Images)*

Despite his status as one of the world's top dead-ball specialists, Beckham scored only twice on free kicks in thirty-two games over his first two MLS seasons. *(Getty Images)*

Beckham joined Italian giant AC Milan on loan in January 2009, and he sparked a global media saga a month later by announcing that he wanted to leave the Galaxy for Milan indefinitely. The teams reached an agreement that allowed Beckham to finish the Serie A season with Milan and return to the Galaxy in July 2009. *(AFP/Getty Images)*

cer, the brains behind MLS's New England Revolution. None of those circumstances would have been allowed in an established American sports league like the NFL.

But 19's shadow takeover of the Galaxy took American soccer's conflicts of interest to new heights—probably not what Beckham had in mind when he spoke of "raising the level" of MLS. "You can't have a personal manager of one of the players on the team being involved in the management of the team," Lalas would say. "He could be the smartest person in the world, but you can't have that." Nor was Lalas naïve to the fact that AEG (Leiweke) needed to be on the best of terms with 19 (Simon Fuller) for reasons that had nothing to do with soccer, since AEG made tens of millions of dollars promoting 19's talent stable on joint deals in the concert business—including, of course, the 2007–08 global reunion tour of the Spice Girls (with Victoria Beckham). "Everybody sleeps with everyone," Lalas would say. "I understand the bigger picture and how much money concerts and entertainment and music make. But when your soccer decisions are being dictated by relationships within the concert business or the entertainment business, then you're going to have a problem. You're going to have a *big* problem."

Lalas was hardly the only figure inside the Galaxy who was troubled by 19's influence. American soccer players aren't stupid, and the Galaxy players started connecting the dots: Terry Byrne's strange locker-room performance (several players called Lalas to find out who he was), the 19 logos at Gullit's news conference, the press-release quote from *Simon Fuller*, of all people, saying he was "proud to have played my part in bringing [Gullit] to L.A. Galaxy." Fuller hadn't done nearly as much as Byrne, in fact, but there was no way the Galaxy would have publicized Byrne's new role with the team. "It's so ridiculous, it almost makes me sick," one player said. "Like with 19 Entertainment's logo being on the backdrop for the press conference. It was so bizarre."

Byrne's role as the Galaxy's paid consultant was multifaceted. His first major task was a review of the Galaxy's soccer operations, from scouting to conditioning to youth development. His second was the coaching search, taking over what used to be one of Lalas's most important jobs. To Leiweke, Beckham's best friend had a better idea "on the world stage . . . who might be players that we could fill in" and of "how we set ourselves up so that we were more of a Premier League kind of club on structure, on conditioning, on training." Byrne signed up Chris Neville, the Galaxy's new conditioning coach, bringing him over from England, where he (like Byrne) had worked in the national-team program. Yet Byrne also had an influence on the Galaxy's player-personnel decisions. A few days after Gullit took over as coach, the Galaxy had to submit a list of twelve protected players who couldn't be taken in the MLS expansion draft. A Beckham associate confirmed that Byrne gave his own opinions on protecting certain players when asked by the Galaxy coaching staff, based on what he and presumably Beckham had seen in 2007. Byrne also played a role in the pursuit of Celestine Babayaro, a former longtime Chelsea player who would join the Galaxy in the 2008 preseason as a much-hyped solution to the Galaxy's left-sided weaknesses.

Under orders from Leiweke, Lalas began including Byrne on all e-mails, conference calls, and other correspondence with the Galaxy coaching staff on the direction of the team. "It was relayed to me through my boss that Terry would be a part of the Galaxy in a consulting capacity," Lalas said, "and that I was to include him in what we were doing and utilize his experience and international expertise."

How much did Beckham himself try to take over the direction of the Galaxy through Byrne? It was impossible to believe that Beckham wouldn't have shared his opinions with his best friend and personal manager. And Beckham certainly had opinions. When Beckham had been injured in 2007, he often sat next to teammate Chris Albright in the players' box during games. What did they talk about? "What he sees, what I see, what changes we think should be made," said Albright. "Everybody jumps into the role of the coach." In that case, was Byrne's role a way for Beckham to influence the Galaxy without leaving any fingerprints? Or was it just another example of Beckham's handlers insisting on as much control as possible without Beckham's knowledge?

Many of Beckham's teammates wanted to give him the benefit of the doubt. "I don't think David's the type of guy who would want to control the new coach," said Chris Klein. "Maybe I'm being naïve, but I don't think he's like that. I hope the people around him are not like that either. I hope it doesn't become about his handlers trying to control our team."

It became a common question inside the Galaxy: Was Beckham pulling the strings? Or was he living in a bubble of blissful ignorance while his handlers used their Beckham connection to take control of the team? From Lalas's perspective, neither scenario made Beckham look good. "If David knew what was going on and condoned it, then shame on him, okay?" Lalas would say. "If David didn't know, then it confirms many people's suspicions that he's completely naïve and that there's a machine working behind him. Either way, it's kind of shitty. Because these are people that work for David. They make their living off of David, and ultimately he has the ability to hire and fire them."

Then again, you could legitimately make the realpolitik argument: If Beckham was the franchise, why *shouldn't* he and 19 have had a big influence over the direction of the team? That was Leiweke's contention many months later, when he was trying to deflect the blame for what had happened. And indeed, as the CEO of the Galaxy's ownership group, Leiweke could hand over control of the team to whomever he (and Phil Anschutz) wished. The problem, however, was the aura of secrecy, the unwillingness of anyone to be honest with the team's players (or its fans) about what was going on. The Galaxy never made Byrne's role public. As for Beckham, he went out of his way to insist that he had no influence over any of the choices made by the Galaxy front office. "Obviously, decisions in the club are not down to me," Beckham said. "As far as that goes, it's none of my business. I'm here to play soccer. I'm not here to make decisions on who goes, who stays."

At best, Beckham was being willfully ignorant and had his head in the sand. At worst, he was flat-out lying.

Leaving aside 19's shadow takeover, the fate of the Galaxy's 2008 season would rest largely on the answer to one question: Was the decision to hire Ruud Gullit as the team's coach a good one? Gullit's accomplishments as a player were beyond reproach. A two-time World Player of the Year, the Dutchman known for his iconic dreadlocks led AC Milan to three Italian championships and two European Cups, teaming up with two countrymen (Frank Rijkaard and Marco van Basten) who also played alongside him on the Netherlands' 1988 European Championship winners. Gullit was rightly considered one of the greatest midfielders of his generation, even if many of the Galaxy players had to go to YouTube to learn about their new coach's playing career.

But Gullit's record as a coach was decidedly more mixed. He had won the English FA Cup in 1996 as the player-coach at Chelsea, but he was fired the following season, despite Chelsea's second-place position in the Premier League, owing to conflicts over potential player acquisitions with the club's directors. Gullit lasted barely more than a year in his next job, at Newcastle United, where he clashed with club hero Alan Shearer, reached the 1999 FA Cup final (losing to Manchester United), and resigned just five games into his second season. He went on to become a popular television commentator in England, coining the term "sexy football" to describe his favored entertaining style, but Gullit had coached in only one season since 1999—a forgettable fourth-place finish at Holland's Feyenoord in 2004–05 before he resigned there as well.

The positives of hiring Gullit were self-evident: He was a world-renowned name with a big personality who would have a commanding presence in the Galaxy locker room. If Frank Yallop's weakness had been that he was too much in awe of Beckham, too hesitant to tell him he couldn't play on consecutive days in London and Los Angeles, that shouldn't have been a problem with Gullit. The hope also was that Gullit would light a fire under Landon Donovan and turn the Galaxy into a team that combined the tactical nous that Gullit had learned in Italy, the balls-out effort of his days in the English Premier League, and the sexy football associated with the Dutch attacking style.

But there were far more reasons that Gullit was a risky hire, reasons that were clear the moment he was chosen to take over the Galaxy. For one thing, big-name foreign coaches had always failed in MLS. There were no exceptions. The list was a convincing one: Carlos Alberto Parreira, Carlos Queiroz, Bora Milutinović, Walter Zenga, Hans Westerhof. The few foreign-born coaches who had succeeded in MLS—Steve Nicol, Peter Nowak, Thomas Rongen, Juan Carlos Osorio—had already spent years in American soccer at levels below that of MLS head coach before they made the jump. Just because you were steeped in the culture of European or South American soccer didn't mean you would have a clue when it came to the unique (and often frustrating) rules that governed the world of MLS. "We've had some phenomenally well-known coaches," said Sunil Gulati, the U.S. Soccer president. "But MLS is a much bigger challenge than being a national-team coach for a foreigner. It's not even close."

During his days coaching in the Premier League, Gullit could walk into his chairman's office, ask for 20 million pounds to spend in the transfer market, and purchase players to improve his team. In MLS, he would have to make do with a $2.1-million-per-team salary cap and learn a minefield of MLS-specific terms and rules, including: roster limits, the draft, senior internationals, youth internationals, allocations, developmental rosters, discovery signings, waivers, and so on. For a coach who had a history of quitting jobs in frustration, it would be a monumental task. You might as well have been asking Gullit to learn Chinese in three months. "Coaching in the States is such a unique process, and a foreign coach could never survive it," said Sigi Schmid, a two-time MLS champion coach. "Foreign coaches think, 'Okay, I have an eighteen-player roster, so now my right back gets injured, so he's out for the season, so let me go sign another right back at X amount of dollars.' You're told, 'No, you can't because of your salary cap, and you can only have eighteen. So [if you do sign someone] who are you going to let go?' There are no roster limits in Europe, no cap. To understand that makes it really difficult." One of the keys to success in MLS was the ability to find $30,000 players who could help the team, but that required hard work scouting U.S. college games. "A guy like Gullit, he's not going to do that work," said Schmid.

Perhaps most damning, U.S. Soccer Federation officials had interviewed Gullit for the U.S. head-coaching job on two separate occasions, in 1998 and again in 2006 (at the request of Gullit's agent). On neither occasion was he given serious consideration.

Ultimately, Gullit was the kind of choice you would have expected 19 Entertainment, Terry Byrne, and David Beckham to come up with for the Galaxy. And perhaps you couldn't really blame them. What did they know about what it took to be a winning coach in the strange, rules-constricted world of MLS? After all, Beckham had been in the league for only four months. The better question was: Knowing that, and knowing the spectacularly poor history of big-name foreign coaches in MLS, why had Tim Leiweke given 19 the power to go down that road? And why on earth had Leiweke created a structure atop the Galaxy in which friction between Europe and America, between one camp (Ruud Gullit and 19) and another (Alexi Lalas), was inevitable?

On a gorgeous afternoon in Southern California, Ruud Gullit sat down for an interview at the outdoor café on the sprawling concourse of the Home Depot Center. His trademark dreadlocks were long gone, replaced by a shorter, heavily moussed haircut that went well with the tailored Italian suits he wore on British and Dutch television programs. Gullit was a handsome man, with piercing brown eyes and a charming smile, the son of a white mother from Amsterdam and a black father who had immigrated to the Netherlands from Suriname. When Gullit spoke, he did so in formal-sounding paragraphs; he often used the word "therefore" before finishing his comments, as though what followed was a kind of scientific conclusion.

As he took his seat, Gullit flagged down Galaxy press officer Justin Pearson. "Justin, could you get me an espresso, please?" When Pearson returned from the café counter, he had bad news: They didn't serve espresso.

Gullit frowned. He wasn't in Europe anymore. He was in America, a fact highlighted by what *was* available at the café, the Special of the Day advertised on a nearby sign: CHILI-CHEESE DOG. If there was a defining metaphor for Year Two of the Beckham Experiment, this was it. Could Europe and America coexist on the Los Angeles Galaxy, especially after Tim Leiweke had dropped millions of dollars on high-priced Europeans (David Beckham, Ruud Gullit, Terry Byrne) whose arrivals had turned the worlds of the team's ruling Americans (Landon Donovan, Alexi Lalas) upside down?

Yet Gullit vowed he was going to adjust. Not to chili-cheese dogs, mind you, but to the peculiarities of MLS. "I have to adapt myself to the American way," he said. "I'm not going to put myself in a position that I know better than the rest. I can't. I don't want to be a wise guy and tell them I want to change this and this. I have to accept it." Already, however, the transition had been difficult—and the source of the predictable worlds-colliding unintentional comedy. Just days after Gullit had taken over, Lalas tried to explain to him the rules of the MLS expansion draft, which called for each team to submit a list of twelve protected players. The first-year San Jose Earthquakes could select one player from each team who wasn't protected. (The Galaxy ended up losing Gavin Glinton.)

"Ruud, you can protect twelve players," Lalas told him.

"No, I want to protect them all," Gullit replied. "I don't want to lose any of them."

"Okay, Ruud, I understand what you're saying, but the rules are you have to protect twelve."

"Why would I not protect them all?"

"Well, you can't."

"Then the player should just refuse the transfer!"

"Number one, it's not a transfer. Number two, this is MLS, and you can't refuse that. There's very few players with no-trade clauses."

Gullit threw up his hands in disgust. He felt the same way about the MLS salary cap and roster limits. As preseason training neared, Gullit wanted to bring in new players, but it wasn't nearly as easy as it had been in the Premier League. "This trading thing, it's so complicated," he said. "It's like a stock market. If you want a player, then you have to get rid of another player to get under the salary cap."

Early on, at least, Gullit always combined his frustrations with MLS with promises to adapt—a reflection of the complex (and often opposing) feelings he had about his new job in a new country. On the one hand, he was excited about the chance to work with Beckham and make soccer more popular to 300 million Americans. Gullit had a feeling that soccer in America was on the verge of changing, that Beckham's mere presence might combine with the millions of youth players to awake a sleeping giant. When Terry Byrne called him about the Galaxy job,

Gullit's first thought was that it could be an adventure. On the other hand, Gullit wondered if Uncle Sam patriotism, of all things, would halt soccer's progress. Gullit's idea of American patriotism was very different from the one Beckham exalted. "Do the Americans really want soccer to become popular?" Gullit asked. "Because they are very patriotic. They want to protect their own sports." It was a strange theory that bordered on paranoia. American sports fans might ignore soccer, but it was hard to believe that they would actively work against it out of a fear that its rise would harm, say, baseball. Yet Gullit would come back to the theme often during his tenure.

Gullit had other concerns that weren't quite so half-baked. On the one hand, he believed that American players would be easy to work with, would do what he asked them to do, would play with the hustle and heart that most Europeans associate with U.S. athletes. On the other hand, after watching U.S. football and soccer players, Gullit wasn't sure if Americans were wired to do much more than that. "When I see the American sports, because it's stop-and-go, it's more like people following an assignment," he said. "The only one who has some diversion is the quarterback. The rest just play the scheme, almost like soldiers. So I was afraid of having people who would only follow orders. I don't want that. I want to be creative on the pitch. Because of the mentality of sports in America, this is going to be the most difficult issue, to get players to be creative."

In many ways, the arrival of Gullit produced the same kind of tension with Lalas that Beckham's arrival had created with Donovan. Leiweke hoped they would be positive tensions, synergistic relationships in which the Americans were motivated to work alongside their European colleagues and vice versa. But that was a lot to ask when Lalas and Donovan, two proud U.S. soccer products, endured so many slights as the result of Leiweke's decisions. In fact, it was hard to know which friction point might be the most toxic source of tension between Gullit and Lalas. Would it be Lalas's resentment over being left out of Gullit's hiring process and Gullit's assumption of powers that used to be his? Would it be both men's underlying awareness that Gullit had achieved more as a player than Lalas had? (Lalas liked to joke with Gullit that their first Italian game against each other had resulted in Padova's 2–0 upset of AC Milan, with Lalas scoring one of the goals: "my brief, shining moment against Milan," Lalas cracked.)

Or would it be simply the clash of Europe and America? "You had Ruud and the way that he thought about life in a very European mentality," Leiweke would say, "and you had Alexi and the way he thought about life in a non-European mentality, almost *anti*-European mentality, quite frankly." Lalas made no apologies about his belief that there was soccer, and then there was *American* soccer. If he had gone to Italy with the humility that he needed to learn about Serie A before telling anyone how they should do things, Lalas felt it was only right for foreigners to bring the same humility to MLS, which was nothing like the European leagues. Too often, Lalas believed, clueless American soccer executives (in MLS, in youth clubs, in television) treated foreign accents alone as expertise. "There's this incredible arrogance that exists when it comes to expats and people coming from other countries," Lalas said, "that just because it's *not* American it has some authenticity or credibility. And that's just not the case."

The funny thing was that, just as Donovan and Beckham had plenty in common when it came to their backgrounds and personalities, so too did Lalas and Gullit. Both men were highly personable, larger-than-life characters who were among the world's most provocative and compelling soccer broadcasters whenever they appeared on television. Both men were born entertainers who became known for their iconic hairstyles—Lalas's beard, Gullit's dreadlocks—before they made major life decisions to shear their locks. For Lalas, the Samson act came during his year-long first retirement. For Gullit, it came the day before he married his third wife, Estelle, the niece of Dutch soccer legend Johan Cruyff, in 2000. "That gave me a new launch in my life," Gullit said. "I'm proud of the things I have done, and I like the attention. But you want to be left alone sometimes. In L.A., people don't know me. I can just relax."

Indeed, both Gullit and Lalas had occasionally grown jaded with their fame, just as both men had pursued interests that ventured far beyond the soccer field. While Lalas had his music, Gullit had campaigned against South Africa's apartheid regime during his playing career. When he won the 1987 European Footballer of the Year Award, Gullit dedicated it to Nelson Mandela, who was still imprisoned on Robben Island at the time. After Mandela was released and became South Africa's president a few years later, he awarded Gullit a medal on behalf of his country. "Ruud, now that I am out of prison I have a lot of friends," Mandela told him, "but you were one of the warriors that stood up for me when I was in prison." Mandela had also returned the favor by appearing on the Dutch talk show that Gullit hosted.

Initially, Gullit and Lalas tried to make their relationship work. On the Galaxy's exhibition tour of Australia and New Zealand in November, the two men joined Cobi Jones and Paul Bravo for long dinners and shared stories from their playing careers. It was Lalas's job to teach Gullit Chinese, in effect, instructing him on the labyrinthine rules of MLS: the salary cap, the college draft, roster limits, and all the other things that made Gullit's head spin. Unlike the previous season, in which Lalas was clearly Yallop's boss, Lalas now had to accede to Gullit's wishes. When Gullit said he wanted a goal scorer, Lalas signed Carlos Ruiz, the talented but mercurial Guatemalan striker who had scored twenty-four goals for the Galaxy's MLS Cup–winning team in 2002. The acquisition carried huge risks. Ruiz earned $460,000, which meant the Galaxy would have dangerously little money left over for the rest of the team under the salary cap. As a result, L.A. was also forced to make several moves to get under the cap, trading Joe Cannon and Chris Albright and waiving Kelly Gray and Kyle Martino.

Gullit and Lalas found themselves agreeing on a few things, including the notion that Landon Donovan was not yet maximizing his vast talents on the soccer field for the Galaxy. "My early impressions are that he's a very good player, he has a lot of talent," Gullit said after the tour of the Antipodes. "And when I saw him play, I thought to myself, 'You take it a little bit the easy way. You try to sometimes create excuses.' Some of the excuses were true. But for someone who has so much talent, I will not accept that." After all, Gullit's unwillingness to accept some aspects of MLS might not be such a bad thing. Take the league's paltry player salaries. "Sometimes you feel guilty about it, you know?" he said. "If I say to players in Europe that they earn $20,000 here, they look at me and say, 'What?' It's very odd. It's almost like, why should I play soccer, then? For what reason?"

Sure enough, a few days later, just weeks before the start of training camp, twenty-three-year-old Galaxy defender Ty Harden walked into Lalas's office. "Hey, can I talk to you?" Harden asked. In 2007, Harden had been the Galaxy's top rookie, a rugged centerback who started twenty-four of the team's thirty games, bottled up some of MLS's best forwards (to say nothing of Chelsea's Didier Drogba), and earned every cent of his $30,000 salary. Lalas shut his office door and listened.

"I don't think I can continue doing this," Harden said.

Lalas thought Harden was joking at first. But it soon became clear that one of the Galaxy's best returning players was retiring from professional soccer to start a career in community service. "I wasn't going to change his mind," Lalas would say months later. "And nobody's heard from him since."

It was unlikely that one of David Beckham's teammates—especially one who played regularly—had ever retired from soccer in his early twenties to pursue another career. When Gullit learned the news, all he could do was shake his head.

Only in MLS.

CHAPTER 10

BECKHAM 2.0

ven though "putting the bulge in the auld onion bag" was Tommy Smyth's trademark goal-scoring call on ESPN's soccer broadcasts, it was probably wise that Emporio Armani opted against that as a slogan when it released its new underwear campaign featuring David Beckham in December 2007. In truth, the first publicly released image spoke for itself. Wearing little more than a pair of tight white briefs and his wedding ring, Beckham was sprawled suggestively on his back, hands behind his head, his six-pack abs flexed in their full glory. The black-and-white film gave the pose a timeless feel, like an art-house photograph. It wasn't the first time that soccer players had done underwear ads, of course. Swedish star Freddie Ljungberg had appeared in his skivvies on a Calvin Klein billboard in New York City's Times Square, drawing raves from admirers who had no idea he played for England's Arsenal. And members of the Italian World Cup–winning team in 2006 had starred in Dolce & Gabbana underwear ads all over Europe.

But the Armani campaign did mark the first time that Beckham had stripped into the nearly altogether for public viewing, and in typical fashion he and 19 Entertainment did it up *big*—in every way. Gigantic billboards sprang up in cities around America: in Manhattan's SoHo, where Becks watched over the trendy neighborhood like a ruling metrosexual colossus, and in San Francisco's Union Square, where Beckham would later make an appearance before hundreds of screaming fans and sign autographs for anyone who spent at least $200 on Armani underwear. When Jay Leno asked Beckham about the shoot on *The Tonight Show,* Beckham confessed that he wasn't as comfortable as he looked. "I was so nervous about doing that campaign because, obviously, I've done photo shoots before, but I've never actually done photo shoots in my underwear," he said. "I was quite nervous because, obviously, I knew that my wife and friends were going to see it, but my mum is going to see it."

Not everyone was focusing on Beckham's Blue Steel gaze, however. In fact, considering the size of the billboards and the layout of the photograph, it was impossible to miss—how best to put this?—the bulge in the auld onion bag. Getting people talking was precisely the point. If you did a Google search for *Beckham* and *underwear*, any number of message-board threads popped up, including this discussion from the gay-themed website Towelroad.com:

> **That's a HOT ad! (the wedding ring makes it even hotter)**
> POSTED BY: JORDAN

> **Now, that's airbrushing done right.**
> POSTED BY: STEVEN

> **It looks like he's wearing a cup.**
> POSTED BY: MICHAEL

> **Looks like Becks decided it was going to be a two-sock night. Damn sensual, until he opens his mouth (to talk, anyway), but he's wearing more padding than a $25.00 hustler.**
> POSTED BY: RUDY

> **Breathtakingly gorgeous. Who cares if he's dumb? I'm never going to get a chance to talk with him, but there will be plenty of opportunities to look. And sigh.**
> POSTED BY: SEATTLE

> **I can't explain it, but I do love Becks. And photos like this one keep me a fan. Woof!**
> POSTED BY: JONATHON

> **Uh smokin' hot. This dude reeks of sex. Unfortunately those who are less blessed tend to be the most vocal.**
> POSTED BY: GEEWIZZ

Judging by the crowds Beckham would draw in San Francisco, women—teenage girls, especially—were just as enthralled. As for the "two-sock night" discussion topic, Victoria Beckham went out of her way to address the issue in a conversation with David (captured in a January 2008 *Elle* magazine cover story) that wasn't likely to be a talking point in the Galaxy locker room:

> I relay to David what Victoria said about sleeping naked, and he smiles, blushes. His wife pokes his arm: "Would you like me to add that you have a large penis?" "No," he says, blushing deeper. Any comment, Mr. Beckham? "Yeah!" Victoria prods. "What do you have to say for yourself?" "No comment," he says, smiling. "I agree with everything my wife says."

Not surprisingly, Emporio Armani reported a 150 percent increase in underwear sales after the debut of the Beckham ads, and Victoria herself would join David in a smoldering follow-up campaign that came out in early 2009. While the underwear billboards were the most-talked-about aspect of David's first off-season in America, it was Victoria who generated the lion's share of the family's attention. David certainly kept busy on his own: He attended the Ricky Hatton–Floyd Mayweather title fight in Las Vegas; appeared on Snoop Dogg's reality show (giving Snoop's kids a soccer lesson); had an hour-long meeting with British prime minister Gordon Brown (who later visited Beckham's soccer academy); accepted a Tribute Award for his career achievements from the Football Writers Association in London; flew to Sierra Leone with UNICEF as a goodwill ambassador; popped over to Brazil to announce a new training center bearing his name; and trained with Arsenal to stay fit for potential national-team selection. (He also won a dubious award from the Carbon Trust, an environmental organization, for producing perhaps the largest carbon footprint in human history: an estimated 163 tons per year, more than twenty times that of the typical American, due to his constant air travel and fleet of gas-guzzler cars.)

But the Beckhams' main event of the winter was the Spice Girls reunion tour. David joined Victoria and their three children for the first show in Vancouver on December 2 and also attended the pop group's concerts in Los Angeles, San Jose, Las Vegas (where they were joined by Tom Cruise and Katie Holmes), London, and Madrid. Often, David would end up in the front row taking pictures for the family album with his own camera. The concerts themselves were high camp: Highlights included Victoria's *Zoolander*-style runway walk, a backup dancer doing the Macarena, and the Spice Girls walking their male dancers on rhinestone-studded dog leashes. The tour sold out several AEG-owned venues—including two shows at L.A.'s Staples Center and all seventeen shows at London's O2 Arena—and made plenty of money for the Beckhams, for 19 Entertainment, and for AEG: a gross of $23.3 million, according to *Pollstar* magazine, nearly the same as the reunion tour of The Police. When *Forbes* magazine released its list of Hollywood's Top-Earning Couples from June 1, 2007, to June 1, 2008, the Beckhams were No. 3 with combined earnings of $58 million, behind No. 1 Jay-Z and Beyoncé Knowles ($162 million) and No. 2 Will and Jada Pinkett Smith ($85 million) but ahead of Tim McGraw and Faith Hill ($35 million), Brad Pitt and Angelina Jolie ($34 million), and Keith Urban and Nicole Kidman ($25 million). According to the survey, David had earned $50 million (including $35 million in endorsements) while Victoria had brought in $8 million (from the Spice Girls tour and her namesake product lines).

The celebrity media is a list-obsessed lot, of course, and the Beckhams' constant inclusion (for good and ill) was evidence that Simon Fuller's choreographed media rollout in July 2007 had worked wonders in the American celebrity realm. Victoria earned a badge of honor of sorts by topping Mr. Blackwell's Worst Dressed of 2007 list. ("Forget the fashion spice, wearing a skirt would suffice! In one skinny-mini monstrosity after another, pouty Posh can really wreck 'em.") Yet not all of Victoria's press was negative. The designer Marc Jacobs became a close friend, giving Victoria the imprimatur of taste by association, and by late 2008 Victoria's new clothing line (said to be heavily influenced, and perhaps more, by 19-managed designer Roland Mouret) was receiving positive reviews in the fashion media. As for David, *In Touch* magazine named him No. 1 on its Top 10 Hottest Abs in Hollywood list, while *Vanity Fair* included him on its 2008 Best-Dressed List. ("Style icon: Steve McQueen.")

Beckham's injury-shortened season may have been a nightmare, but from a business perspective, at least, the Beckham Experiment was a bonanza for the Galaxy and MLS in 2007. The Beckham Galaxy shirt was the top-selling player jersey in the world with in excess of 300,000 sold, more than three times the number for NBA superstars Kobe Bryant and LeBron James (who were in the 75,000–80,000 range). Not only did the Galaxy's sponsorships double, but for the first time ever the team was profitable even after the end-of-season cash call by MLS to fund the single-entity league. "And not profitable in just a little bit of profit," said Alexi Lalas. "We are in the positive in a major way. Mr. Anschutz's asset in the Galaxy as a professional sports team has increased exponentially, too. If the Galaxy were to be sold today as opposed to a year ago, it's a very different type of proposition." A few months later, Tim Leiweke would reveal that he was offered—and turned down—$125 million for the team.

When Beckham's Galaxy went on off-season tours to Australia, New Zealand, South Korea, China, and Hong Kong, it made more than $1 million every time it stepped on the field. "Right now we are on par with your SuperClubs around the world in terms of our appearance fees," said Lalas, who considered the Galaxy's preseason tour of Asia to be beneficial on multiple levels: for revenue (to pay for Beckham's contract), for competition, for team bonding, and for the branding of the Los Angeles Galaxy as a flesh-and-blood team, not just, as Lalas put it, "some mythic thing that exists over in the United States." The risk, however, was that once those Asian fans actually saw the Galaxy brand, they knew it wasn't a SuperClub. One MLS executive said his friend in Hong Kong took some high-rolling business executives to the Galaxy's 2–2 exhibition tie against Hong Kong Union. The Galaxy was "an embarrassment," he said. "My friend goes, 'They're thinking American soccer is crap. Because they view this as your best team, your Manchester United.' And I tell him the Galaxy didn't make the playoffs last year. 'But this is your team with Beckham, and they're crap.' They thought it was a bunch of boys. That's not a good thing."

Yet the money kept rolling in. What's more, MLS as a whole was profiting from Beckham, and not just from its increased exposure around the world. An MLS-hosted philanthropic event with Beckham and Pelé in March 2008 raised more than $1 million for FC Harlem. "That event was a coming-out party for soccer in America," said commissioner Don Garber. "We called up Simon Fuller and said we want to build a field in Harlem, we're having this fund-raiser, and the one guy we need to help us show the New York City philanthropy community it's a special event is David Beckham. And David was the first guy to commit." Beckham ended up presenting Pelé with a Lifetime Achievement Award for his contributions to American soccer. "For me to be here to present this to the greatest sportsman of all time, I feel particularly honored," Beckham said. "This absolutely is a highlight moment for me." And judging by the look on his face, you could believe it.

Still, Lalas was fully aware that Beckham needed a "reintroduction" (his word) to the U.S. and Los Angeles in 2008, especially as a soccer player. The Galaxy's season-ticket base had fallen from 11,000 in 2007 to around 8,000 in 2008, not least because so many new season-ticket holders had seen Beckham play in only two MLS games during his first season. If the Beckham Experiment was going to work, the 2008 season needed to be about the soccer. *Winning* soccer. David Carter, the executive director of the USC Sports Business Institute, argued that Beckham's injury-filled 2007 would put enormous pressure on the Galaxy and MLS to present a Beckham 2.0 that provided what the consumer wanted. "If Beckham doesn't come back and play to their level of expectation, people are going to be wondering what's next, who's next, and most importantly, why should we spend our hard-earned money and our precious time on MLS and the Galaxy?" Carter said. "It's the old saying: Fool me once, shame on you. Fool me twice, shame on me."

The historic media buzz from the summer of 2007 was a distant memory—I couldn't convince my editors at *Sports Illustrated* to approve a Beckham 2.0 story—but Beckham still appeared on several television shows to promote the 2008 season, including *60 Minutes, Ellen, The Tonight Show,* and Barbara Walters's "10 Most Fascinating People of 2007" special alongside Victoria.

Some promotional efforts were cut entirely, however, including the 19 Entertainment–produced show *David Beckham's Soccer USA,* which had drawn poor ratings on the Fox Soccer Channel in 2007. The premise of the hour-long show was to attach Beckham's name (and exclusive access to Beckham and the Galaxy) to a recap of MLS highlights from the week. It was a little like the old *This Week in Baseball* show with Mel

Allen, except the host was a British pop tart named Natalie Pinkham, who mispronounced the Mexican champion's name as Pa-choo-CHA. From the start, ESPN had no desire to broadcast the show, another case in which Simon Fuller overestimated Beckham's soccer appeal in the United States. "We didn't think it was worth the money," an ESPN insider said. Instead, *Soccer USA* ran on the lower-profile Fox Soccer Channel, where it became a weekly reminder that Beckham was still injured. As for the show's regular exclusive Beckham interview, "he hated doing it," said one Beckham associate. *David Beckham's Soccer USA* died at the tender age of three months. Frankly, nobody missed it.

As the Galaxy's preseason training started in early February, there was one regular event that kept Beckham in the local spotlight as a citizen of Los Angeles. Making like Jack Nicholson, Dyan Cannon, and Penny Marshall, Beckham became a regular front-row spectator at Los Angeles Lakers games. Using (and paying for) AEG's courtside tickets, Beckham would wear Lakers T-shirts while sitting next to a rotating roster of companions, including his sons, Victoria, the actor David Arquette, and the musician Marc Anthony (the husband of Jennifer Lopez). Sometimes Beckham even sat alone, mesmerized by the action (and perhaps thrilled to be associated with a winning team again). "I love basketball," he said. "I'm hooked by it, and I love the Lakers."

Why basketball? Beckham had always been fascinated by American hip-hop culture, and no sport reflected that influence more than basketball. Beckham's first autobiography included photographs of him playing hoops by himself at a gym in England, and even if his shooting form needed some work, it was refreshing to see Beckham show so much curiosity about another sport—one that was joining soccer in its global reach. Beckham chose to wear the number 23 when he joined Real Madrid as an homage to Michael Jordan. "I don't consider myself the Michael Jordan of soccer," said Beckham, who had once sought out His Airness to introduce himself at a London restaurant, "but I'm honored to have the same number as him." After Beckham attended ESPN's annual sports awards show a few months later, he said the athletes he was most excited to have met were two-time NBA MVP Steve Nash and

Boston Celtics stars Kevin Garnett, Ray Allen, and Paul Pierce. And when Beckham was asked if he was watching any games from the Euro 2008 soccer tournament—for which England had failed to qualify—he said he was too devastated to watch, though he might check out a match at some point "when I'm not playing basketball with the kids."

If anything, Beckham's Lakers fandom helped make things more relaxed with his teammates inside the Galaxy locker room at the start of 2008. Good locker rooms in any sport are filled with back-and-forth banter about common interests, and the fortunes of the Lakers gave even the lowest-paid Galaxy players the chance to treat Beckham as one of the guys, to bust his chops about, say, an upset loss to the Denver Nuggets. "He's talking basketball with the guys," said Chris Klein. "He feels a lot more comfortable sharing with the guys and being part of this team." Peter Vagenas even gave Beckham a helpful suggestion before his first game in the courtside seats.

"What happens if the ball bounces to me?" Beckham asked. "What if I don't catch it or throw it back properly?"

"Just pick it up and kick it," Vagenas replied, "and everybody will get a good laugh out of it."

Vagenas already had a solid comedy routine going with Abel Xavier, his road roommate, and now he was doing the same with Beckham. One day before practice, Beckham walked into the locker room as red as a tomato.

"Man, what happened?" Vagenas asked. "Did you go to the beach?"

"No," Beckham said, "I was playing in the garden with the kids."

"Dude, you were in the *garden*?" Vagenas said, imagining Beckham and his sons tending roses or vegetables. "What were you doing there?"

After several minutes, it turned out that Beckham meant the backyard. "Now he'll catch himself and say *backyard* instead," Vagenas said.

After so many fits and starts in 2007, Beckham knew how important it was to become a normal presence in the Galaxy locker room. "You feel as if you need to fit in as quickly as possible," he said. "Because obviously, everything that surrounds me as well, people read things and hear things, and it's not until I'm in the team and around the guys that they know me as a person and a player, and how I am as a guy as well."

Yet Beckham's healthy presence on the practice field did more than anything to accelerate his integration into the team. Due to his injuries and England call-ups, Beckham had only two full practices with the Galaxy during the 2007 season. It took time for any new teammates to develop an understanding of one another, to learn how a player liked to work a give-and-go, how he made his runs off the ball, where he sent his passes, and when you needed to cover for him on defense as he advanced upfield. That finally began happening with Beckham and his teammates on the Galaxy training fields in February 2008. Landon Donovan, for one, now started believing the stories he had heard about Beckham being a good teammate in Europe. "I wouldn't have been so quick to say that last year, because I wasn't sure," Donovan said. "But now he's more comfortable, and I think he realizes that as much as we need him to do well, he needs us so that he can succeed."

As the team prepared for its three-week preseason trip to Hawaii and Asia, it was clear that Beckham was developing an especially good connection on the field with three teammates: Donovan (no surprise considering his understanding of the game), Klein (who knew when to overlap Beckham on the right side and when to cover on defense), and Alan Gordon (who was especially adept on the give-and-go). In typical fashion, Gordon also liked having fun with Beckham in practice and in the locker room by initiating all manner of friendly bets. Beckham didn't gamble for money, but he was fiercely competitive, and he enjoyed winning wagers in which the loser had to perform a service for him. Beckham's first bet with Gordon took place on the practice field during a finishing drill. "It was a very, very skeptical win," Gordon joked. "He cheated, but I had to make him coffee after training and bring it to him."

Later on, when the Lakers and San Antonio met during the NBA playoffs, Gordon tried to up the ante. "I'll make a bet with you," Gordon told Beckham in the locker room. "If San Antonio wins, I get to drive one of your cars for a week. And if the Lakers win, you can have *anything* of mine that you want."

"That's not a fair bet," Beckham said.

When you thought about Beckham's reply, it was a brutally honest statement of fact. But Gordon was too easygoing to call him out on it.

"What do you mean? You can have *anything* of mine, and I'd only drive *one* of your cars. Relatively speaking, I think that's a fair bet."

But Beckham would have none of it. They finally settled on the loser having to serve the other one breakfast for a week. Gordon lost again—and found himself bringing Beckham coffee and toast every day in the locker room.

In fact, Gordon recalled one day, he had never beaten Beckham in any of their bets. Not one. The Englishman didn't like to lose.

Sometimes Alan Gordon resembled those participants on *Survivor* who found a way to keep sticking around, even though they rarely stood out, even though most people couldn't believe they were still there when so many others had been voted off the island. On the Galaxy message board at Bigsoccer.com, where the anonymous fans could be merciless (sample thread title: *Alan Gordon: It's Just Not Funny Anymore*), one poster summed up the feelings of a section of the supporters: "I respect his efforts, but I doubt he'll ever produce consistently for the club. I like the dude. When I have criticized him, I have done so with endearment. In 2005, I remarked that he was akin to 'a 3-legged dog' who keeps coming back, and I have also said that 'he couldn't hit a cow in the ass with a banjo.' I don't mean these things in a BAD way. I just question whether we will ever see him strike fear in the hearts of opponents, no matter how lovable he is."

Granted, Gordon was often injured, lacked a clean first touch, regularly scudded shots into the stands, and was so slow that he had earned the nicknames Snowshoes and Flash from fans. But there was a reason that Ruud Gullit had become the third Galaxy coach in four years who liked Gordon enough not just to keep him on the roster *but to put him on the field*. Several reasons, actually. For starters, Gordon did produce on occasion: Despite missing the first three months of 2007 to injury, Gordon finished the season with six goals in nineteen games in all competitions. He also gave maximum effort at all times, knew what he could and couldn't do, served as a positive team-first presence in the locker room, had a ridiculously cheap salary for somebody who actually played (no small attribute in MLS), and brought the height of a raw but powerful 6'3" target man to the field. (A 6'3" target man was a rare thing indeed in MLS, kind of like a left-handed relief pitcher in baseball.)

When Beckham trained alongside Gordon or exchanged friendly barbs with him in the locker room, he could not have possibly imagined what the life of a low- to mid-level MLS player was like away from the Home Depot Center. By September 2007, Gordon had known it was a make-or-break moment for him as a professional soccer player. He was earning $30,870 a year with the Galaxy, coaching a girls' youth team on the side to make extra money, thinking of firing his agent (who almost never called him), and taking risky cortisone injections in his left foot to stay on the field during the last year of his contract. He was also living in a filthy, dorm-room-style apartment in Redondo Beach with teammates Gavin Glinton and Kyle Veris, who often blasted his music until 3:30 A.M., even though Gordon's girlfriend, Sandi Epperson, had to wake up at 5 A.M. every day for her nursing school classes.

So Gordon hatched a plan. One night over beers, teammate Chris Albright mentioned that he and his wife were about to move out of their two-bedroom apartment near the beach in Redondo now that they had a baby. "Hey, Alan," Sandi joked, "you should move into Chris's place!" But Gordon wasn't joking. He and his roommates were locked into their apartment lease for nine more months, but Gordon wanted to move out, knew that Veris would almost certainly be waived (thanks to his howler against Chivas), and suspected that Glinton might be leaving the Galaxy as well. And so, knowing that he would have to take over Albright's lease by October 1, Gordon lied to his landlord, saying that he was being traded by the Galaxy. It was a stroke of genius: The landlord was too clueless to notice Gordon's continued Galaxy participation in the newspapers. Gordon found a new roommate for Glinton and Veris on Craigslist and moved into Albright's apartment, but not before he had to borrow $1,800 from Sandi for his first payment. "Everything's tight with money," Gordon said. "I wouldn't have been able to get in the place if it wasn't for her."

But Gordon wasn't done yet. Sandi wasn't ready to move in permanently, so he logged on to Craigslist again to find someone who could live in the second bedroom. "Let me tell you," Gordon would say, "that is the *worst* idea." His new roommate, a pharmacologist named Matt, managed to achieve a remarkable feat: He didn't get along with Alan Gordon. "He'd sit there and tell me things about his emotions, and by Week Three I was tuning him out," said Gordon. "His girlfriend broke up with him, and he told me he needed to go to the museum. He needed some art stimulation or something. What am I going to say to that?" Shut out by Gordon, Craigslist Matt turned his attentions to Sandi, chatting her up in the kitchen for as long as an hour and a half while she cooked dinner. "It got a little weird," she confessed, "when he said he could smell me from the car." Craigslist Matt never went to the beach (even though it was only two blocks away) and rarely left the apartment, which explained why Gordon couldn't stop laughing when he heard his explanation for moving out after six months.

"I think I need to be closer to the Scene," Craigslist Matt told him.

"But you haven't partied here once, bro," Gordon replied. "Really?"

Not that Gordon was complaining. In early January 2008, Gordon got a call from his new agent, Richard Motzkin (who also represented Landon Donovan). Gordon's four years of earning $30,870 were over. His new contract with the Galaxy would pay him a base of $72,504 with additional incentives if he reached certain statistical thresholds. Gordon breathed a sigh of relief. The pressures, the cortisone injections, the coaching job on the side: They had all been worth it. It wasn't a superstar's salary by any means, nor was it even guaranteed, but it was more than he was earning before. "I was at least happy to be making enough to where I'm not living paycheck to paycheck and worried about rent and gas," he said. "Obviously, I think we should all be making more money, but that's not the situation." Gordon celebrated that night by taking Sandi out to dinner. A few days later, he paid her $1,800 loan back.

Sandi soon moved in, and when Craigslist Matt shipped out, Gordon no longer needed a tenant for the apartment's second bedroom to cover the rent. Yet those weren't the only changes in Gordon's life as the result of his new contract. After four years of coaching his girls' youth team, he sat down with the players and their parents, thanked them for the opportunity, and told them that even though he wouldn't be with their team any longer, he would still look forward to seeing them at Galaxy games. As for his increased income, Gordon began contributing

15 percent of his salary to a 401(k) for the first time and started an individual retirement account. "Seventy-two thousand dollars isn't a ton of money, especially today, and some days I feel like it's still tight," he said, "but at least we're able to do some things without completely stressing." It helped that his friend Chris Klein had set up those accounts and volunteered to become Gordon's financial adviser for no charge. ("I got him a bottle of wine for it, and he didn't even want that," Gordon said.) Klein started teaching Gordon how the stock market works, showing him how to read the *Wall Street Journal* stock tables. Word spread around the locker room, and within weeks Klein became the financial adviser for a half-dozen of his teammates.

If Gordon appeared to some fans like the unexpected winner of *Survivor: Los Angeles Galaxy*, then that was fine with him. He still kept in touch with his departed apartment mates from the previous year. Gavin Glinton had been selected by Frank Yallop's San Jose Earthquakes in the expansion draft after scoring four goals during the Galaxy's ill-fated push for a playoff spot. Meanwhile, Kyle Veris was playing with the Norwegian club IL Hødd. In an embarrassing amateur-hour display, the Galaxy front office (Alexi Lalas and director of soccer Paul Bravo) had neglected to inform Veris that he'd been waived while he was on the team's trip to Australia and New Zealand in November. Gordon, Veris's road roommate, saw the news in an Internet article and asked Klein what he should do. "You should tell him," Klein said.

Gordon returned to the room and sat down with his friend. "Dude, I don't know how to tell you this," he said, "but you got waived." Veris was stunned—not so much that he'd been released, but that *the Galaxy's fans* had known before he found out.

If you were a low- to mid-level MLS player, you lived an entirely different existence from David Beckham. Sometimes Gordon liked joking with Beckham about it in the locker room. "Hey, you should come over to the apartment tonight," he'd say. "We've got a roast cooking!"

Neither man took the offer seriously. Sandi had met Victoria Beckham, but while Posh had been polite, she almost never interacted with any of the Galaxy's wives and girlfriends, not even at the games. The notion of having the Beckhams over for dinner—or attending one at their house in Beverly Hills—caused Sandi to laugh. "I don't think Victoria's at home cooking a chicken," she said.

For any number of reasons, the fans of professional sports teams like to think that their heroes are best friends away from the field, that all the players' families spend their Sundays together in backyard barbecues by the swimming pool. Those things do happen, of course, but the reality is that most teams are just like any other workplace: There are cliques of friends, pockets of tension, and the tacit acceptance that most locker rooms fall somewhere between the extremes of the late-1990s Oakland Athletics (all BFFs) and the 1978 Boston Red Sox (twenty-five players, twenty-five taxicabs). Yet nearly everyone associated with the Beckham Experiment—David and Victoria Beckham, Alexi Lalas, Landon Donovan, and others—had been vocal in mid-2007 about their desire that the Beckhams would in fact spend time with the families of David's Galaxy teammates away from the field. David went so far as to say that he hoped there would be Sunday barbecues in L.A. like the ones he used to enjoy during his days at Manchester United.

It was a feel-good statement for public consumption, an indication that Beckham felt as though he really could be just one of the guys despite their mammoth differences in wealth and fame. But it was also a fairy tale. Beckham unwittingly made that clear one day in early 2008 when a reporter asked if any of the friends Beckham talked to back home in England wanted to come play in MLS. "The majority of my friends," Beckham replied, "are not soccer players." That was especially true in Los Angeles. Beckham may have been *friendly* with a few Galaxy teammates—including Alan Gordon, Peter Vagenas, Chris Klein, and the newly acquired Greg Vanney—but to say they were close friends was a stretch. By the end of the 2008 season, fifteen months after Beckham's arrival in L.A., not one of those players had ever set foot in Beckham's house (or vice versa). It was a revealing fact, considering that the Beckhams opened up their house to handpicked members of the media (as long as they signed a statement swearing not to reveal details of the house's contents).

That didn't mean Beckham avoided his teammates on road trips. "When we're on the road, he loves hanging out," said Gordon, recounting stories of Beckham joining his teammates for dinners, postgame drinks, and games of pool. Beckham himself viewed the Galaxy's three-week preseason tour as a chance to build team camaraderie, at least when he wasn't making promotional appearances for his many sponsors. "When you're away for three weeks with the guys and away from your family, it bonds you as a team and as individuals as well," Beckham said. "We've had that this season. We had it a little bit last season. Because it's a good bunch of guys in the squad . . . You have to have that togetherness, because then you want to win for each other."

Still, there were never any Sunday barbecues with teammates in Los Angeles, at least not after the meet-the-team event that the Galaxy had hosted at the HDC in July 2007. David and Victoria did attend a retirement party for Cobi Jones in December 2007, stopping by after one of the Spice Girls' L.A. concerts, but that was the exception to the rule. The lack of social interaction was due to a few reasons. For one thing, many of the Galaxy players lived extreme distances from one another in traffic-choked Southern California. Peter Vagenas's house in Pasadena, for example, was fifty-eight miles north of Chris Klein's house in Newport Beach. Most of the players lived in the Southland near the HDC, whereas the Beckhams' house was an hour to the north in Beverly Hills. Lalas, too, stopped organizing events for the players and their families, in large part because he was no longer the man in charge.

But the main reason for Beckham's isolation from his teammates in L.A. was simple: His family led a life that was nothing like those of his teammates. "I don't know how much anybody has in common with them," said Landon Donovan. "They're such a different breed, and they just live in a different world." After their initial get-to-know-you dinner with the Beckhams and Yallops at Mastro's in Beverly Hills the previous July, Donovan and his wife, Bianca Kajlich, had not gone out with the Beckhams again. Although Bianca had visited Victoria at the Beckhams' house once, their interactions were now reduced to the occasional text message. Victoria Beckham had clearly decided not to create a Galaxy WAG outpost. "They don't hang out," Donovan said of his wife and Victoria. "But I think that felt forced a little bit for probably both of them last year, and this year I think it's been easier just to be us and for them to be them and not worry about that."

Although David and Victoria's schedules were busy, they did have plenty of time to socialize, albeit with a completely different crowd: Tom Cruise and Katie Holmes; Tony and Eva Longoria Parker; the British actress Kate Beckinsale and her husband, Len Wiseman; and the model Heidi Klum and her husband, the singer Seal. When David wanted to surprise Victoria on her birthday that April, he flew her to Napa Valley wine country, where all those friends (minus the Parkers) joined them for a surprise party. "We have really nice friends, with nice kids," Victoria told *Harper's Bazaar*.

The Beckhams certainly enjoyed their stay. A few weeks later came the news that they were buying their own Napa Valley vineyard.

Celestine Babayaro couldn't believe it. There must have been a mistake. As the Galaxy's new high-profile signing boarded the plane for the team's flight to Hawaii and the preseason Pan-Pacific Championship, he saw David Beckham take a left turn into first class. Then he saw Ruud Gullit do the same thing, followed by Cobi Jones and the other assistant coaches. Babayaro double-checked his boarding pass. It said he was sitting in *coach*. This wasn't what his agent had told him about the Galaxy. He'd said L.A. was the Real Madrid of Major League Soccer, the kind of SuperClub where Babayaro would fit in perfectly, the kind of SuperClub that had given Beckham a $250 million contract.

As recently as a few months earlier, Babayaro had played with New-castle United of the English Premier League. Before that, the dynamic left back and midfielder had spent seven years at Chelsea as a fan favorite known for his celebratory backflips after he scored a goal. Babayaro, twenty-nine, had played on Nigeria's 1998 and 2002 World Cup teams after winning a gold medal with the Super Eagles at the 1996 Olympics. In January 2008, Terry Byrne and Ruud Gullit called on one of their old Chelsea connections, and the Galaxy made Babayaro its primary European-bred acquisition of the Gullit-Byrne Era, signing him to a three-year contract. In the media, the Galaxy hailed Babayaro as a long-term answer to its left-sided attacking problems, a counterweight to the right-sided strength of Beckham and Chris Klein. "Terry said this guy is available, and his agent will call you," Lalas would say. "I was told by Tim [Leiweke] from the start: Give Ruud whatever he wants. And he wanted Celestine Babayaro."

After he took his seat in coach, Babayaro couldn't hide his anger. A comically overweight American passenger was bulging over the armrest into his personal space. From his seat across the aisle, Landon Donovan looked over and noticed Babayaro's exaggerated agitation.

"Baba, what's going on, man?" Donovan asked.

"This is fucking bullshit, man," Babayaro said, loudly enough for other passengers to hear. "Fucking bullshit!"

"What is it, dude?"

"What the fuck is this, man? I'm a fucking *professional*. They should have just told me we were sitting back here, and I would have bought my own fucking seat up there!"

Donovan couldn't help laughing. If it had been the previous season, when Frank Yallop was in charge, he and Babayaro would have been munching on their warm mixed nuts in first class. But the seating arrangement was Gullit's call, and under the new regime only the coaches and Beckham sat up front. Donovan didn't really care—he had sat in steerage for years before Beckham arrived—but Babayaro was apopleptic. "I think that was the beginning of the end for him," Donovan said. "He's made so much money and done everything, and he just said, 'I'm not dealing with this.'" Having to share a hotel room was another insult to Babayaro. As the days went by, his attitude only got worse. Teammates could hear Babayaro muttering on the practice field. *Why am I doing this? . . . Why am I here? . . . This is ridiculous.*

Babayaro's lack of effort was so obvious in his uninspired play that Gullit finally spoke with him. "You have to give more than you are doing at the moment," Gullit told him. "This is not the Baba I know." But it made no difference. On March 5, five days after Babayaro's brutal forty-five-minute showing in South Korea against FC Seoul (in which he was whistled for a yellow card and a penalty on separate plays), the Galaxy waived the Nigerian star. Lalas had insisted on signing Babayaro to a contract that allowed the team to cut him outright without taking a hit on the salary cap. Yet the fallout from the Babayaro fiasco would be extensive: The Galaxy would go six months without an adequate left-sided midfield option. (At times Gullit would just throw up his hands and leave an open space on the left side of the field.) In their first stab at MLS player procurement, Gullit and Byrne had failed miserably.

Not that Lalas's major signing was faring much better. Unbeknownst to the Galaxy, Carlos Ruiz was carrying a right knee injury when L.A. acquired him from Dallas, an injury requiring surgery that kept him out of training for most of February. (Lalas later took the blame for relying on the assurances of the FC Dallas medical staff and not arranging a physical for Ruiz before signing off on the trade, a major lack of oversight.) Even if Ruiz had been healthy, he represented a gamble due to his unpredictable behavior: He had once skipped the MLS All-Star Game, only to be photographed at the opening of a Hooters restaurant in Guatemala City. Ruiz's salary ($460,000) also meant the Galaxy's roster was so top-heavy with three expensive players (Beckham, Donovan, Ruiz) that there was almost no room left under the salary cap for the rest of the team. Signing a third cap-eating player like Ruiz flew in the face of every roster-building success story in the history of MLS. The Galaxy already had its piano players (Beckham and Donovan), as the French liked to call their brightest talents. What it needed were more piano carriers. "It's a risky strategy," said Klein. "Very, very risky. If it works, it works. If not, then I don't know. I don't know how many teams can pull this off. The model is what Houston and New England have done, sticking with your core group of American players and building around them with high-quality guys." If L.A. endured multiple injuries (as in 2007) or if several rookies failed to perform at a high level, then the Galaxy would be in serious trouble, judging by its painfully thin roster (see table on p. 180).

Part of the problem was that so many people were influencing the Galaxy's personnel moves that the team never had a coherent plan. It seemed as though every member of the front office had "a guy." Babayaro had been Gullit and Byrne's guy, while Ruiz was Lalas's guy. The Galaxy made three other significant additions in 2008. Alvaro Pires (Paul Bravo's guy) was a twenty-three-year-old defensive midfielder

THE 2008 LOS ANGELES GALAXY

POSITION	NAME	COUNTRY	SALARY
M	David Beckham	England	$6,500,000
F	Landon Donovan	United States	$900,000
F	Carlos Ruiz	Guatemala	$460,000*
D	Chris Klein	United States	$197,250
F	Edson Buddle	United States	$157,000
D	Abel Xavier	Portugal	$156,000
M	Peter Vagenas	United States	$138,437
D	Ante Jazic	Canada	$120,250
M	Alvaro Pires	Brazil	$110,775*
D	Greg Vanney	United States	$91,800*
GK	Steve Cronin	United States	$75,000
F	Alan Gordon	United States	$72,504
F	Israel Sesay	United States	$57,083
D	Sean Franklin	United States	$48,500*
GK	Josh Wicks	United States	$38,000*
D	Mike Randolph	United States	$33,000
D	Troy Roberts	United States	$33,000
M	Josh Tudela	United States	$17,700
M	Brandon McDonald	United States	$17,700*
D	Michael Gavin	United States	$17,700*
F	Ely Allen	United States	$12,900*
F	Bryan Jordan	United States	$12,900*
D	Julian Valentin	United States	$12,900*
GK	Charles Alamo	United States	$12,900*

*New acquisition in 2008

from Brazil who impressed Gullit enough on trial during the Asian tour to earn a contract offer. Greg Vanney (Cobi Jones's guy) was a whip-smart thirty-three-year-old defender whose lack of athleticism was mitigated by his experience: Vanney had played on some of the Galaxy's best teams from 1996 to 2001. And Sean Franklin (another Bravo guy) was a freakishly fast twenty-three-year-old outside back—the Galaxy's first pick in the 2008 draft—who would slide over to centerback after the bizarre retirement of Ty Harden.

Several other youngsters would be thrown into the deep end under Gullit. The Galaxy was relying on the unproven twenty-four-year-old goalkeeper Steve Cronin to step in full-time after the trade of Joe Cannon. And in the season opener at Colorado, Gullit would play three rookies who were earning less than $20,000 a year: defender Michael Gavin and midfielders Ely Allen and Brandon McDonald.

Yet for all the questions facing the Galaxy at the start of the new season, there was one gigantic positive. David Beckham was healthy, he was rested, and he would be with the team for the entire season. England's failure to qualify for Euro 2008 may have been devastating for Beckham, but for the Galaxy it was a godsend, an unexpected chance to have Beckham for a month during the middle of the season. The more Beckham was on the field, the more likely it was that the Galaxy would start winning some games—and that was the whole idea, right? "For me it's all about winning," said Chris Klein. "Tom Brady is Tom Brady because they win. Michael Jordan was who he was because he won. And David Beckham is going to make his mark on American soccer not because of his looks and all that, but because he's on a winning team. You either become a sideshow or you become a legitimate team, and this team can't be a sideshow. I don't think the public will put up with it for too long if this team is a sideshow."

Indeed, the stakes were high for everyone on the Galaxy in 2008, not least for Alexi Lalas, who knew his future depended on the success of a coach he had never wanted to hire. After all, Lalas was in the last year of his contract. "For me personally, it's my job," he said. "If it doesn't go well, that's it." Sometimes Lalas caught himself wondering what it might be like for the Galaxy to have an easy season with no injuries, an epidemic of wins, and none of the drama that had surrounded the club ever since he'd arrived. But then he caught himself. When would that ever happen? "That would be anticlimactic almost," he said. "And God forbid that we ever become boring."

CHAPTER 11

A RUUD AWAKENING

The Agony of Alexi Lalas might sound like a perfect title for his next solo CD, but it was also a fair assessment of the L.A. Galaxy president's mental state in the parking lot of Dick's Sporting Goods Park just before midnight on March 29, 2008. If you had seen his shadowy, pacing figure from a distance, you would have thought he was a Colorado Rapids fan who'd had too many tequila shots at the postgame tailgate while celebrating the home team's 4–0 season-opening victory. Rarely a calming presence even in the best of times, Lalas was so angry after the Galaxy's miserable performance that he refused to board the bus carrying the team back to the hotel—and made his front-office lieutenants, Paul Bravo and Tom Payne, stand with him for more than half an hour in the cold Rocky Mountain air as they waited for a taxi.

Pacing so frantically that he was wearing a groove in the asphalt, Lalas replayed the lowlight reel of awful moments in his mind and wondered: Did anyone get it? Did Ruud Gullit understand that MLS wouldn't be a cakewalk? Was the Dutch coach as high as an Amsterdam hash fiend when he decided to put the Galaxy's most dangerous connecting tandem (Beckham and Landon Donovan) on opposite wings where they couldn't pass to each other? Did Gullit realize that playing three rookies making under $20,000 might be a bad idea? That their preseason performance against FC Seoul and Hong Kong Union might not have been the best predictor of how they'd play in a real, live MLS game? And what was up with those postgame excuses, Gullit blaming the altitude and Beckham criticizing the referee? Sure, the ref was terrible—how can you call a penalty when the fouled player doesn't even fall to the ground?—but you can't explain away *four-freaking-nil*!

Nothing had gone right, Lalas concluded. From the opening whistle, it was clear that Gullit's 4-3-3 formation wouldn't work. Central midfielder Peter Vagenas couldn't distribute the ball to Beckham and Donovan with any regularity, so Gullit replaced Vagenas at halftime with Brandon McDonald, a rookie who managed no better. Colorado dominated possession, and Beckham and Donovan looked frustrated and tired, not least because both had played three days earlier for their national teams. (Beckham had won his historic 100th cap for England in a 1–0 friendly loss to France in Paris.) After Terry Cooke's goal gave the Rapids a 1–0 halftime lead, the Galaxy's wheels fell off early in the second half. In the fifty-eighth minute, referee Abbey Okulaja whistled a dubious penalty on Abel Xavier—Colorado's Omar Cummings hadn't even fallen down in the penalty box—and the Rapids converted the penalty to go up 2–0. Eight minutes later, Colorado's Cummings made it 3–0, and Colin Clark skinned Xavier in the seventy-ninth minute to put the Rapids up 4–0.

Lalas punched the air in frustration as the gaffes and indignities kept rushing back. To lose 4–0 with Beckham, Donovan, and Carlos Ruiz on the field was embarrassing enough, but the game descended into a new circle of hell in the final minutes. Xavier, who had a tendency to let his frustration morph into five-alarm rage, got sent off by Okulaja in the eighty-ninth minute for dissent and went forehead-to-forehead with the referee before teammates could pull him away. ("The ref is a fucking disgrace," Xavier said to reporters afterward.) But the worst blow came in injury time, when Colorado's Ciaran O'Brien took out Ruiz from behind, drawing another red card from Okulaja. Perhaps due to Ruiz's reputation as the worst diver in the league, nobody realized he was genuinely injured until he remained on the ground for several minutes. For Lalas, it was a worst-case scenario: The player he had signed at such a high risk, the player who consumed so much of the Galaxy's salary budget, would miss the next six weeks with a torn meniscus in his right knee.

The first game of a season is often a bellwether of things to come, and several alarming trends were already starting to emerge. For one thing, the Galaxy played no defense, leaking goals left and right. Xavier, in particular, was a nightmare: As other MLS teams had realized the previous season (when they passed on the chance to sign him), the thirty-five-year-old couldn't keep up with younger, faster attackers one-on-one anymore, and his powder-keg temper was a red card waiting to happen. Even worse, Lalas had given Xavier a two-year guaranteed contract in 2007, which meant Xavier's $156,000 salary would count against the cap for the entire season even if the Galaxy cut him. Not that the rookies were faring well, either. Of the four first-year players who saw time in Colorado, only Sean Franklin looked like he was ready to be a positive force at the MLS level. As for Beckham, his frustrations over not seeing enough of the ball would only continue, as would his complaints about MLS referees. "Certain decisions change games, and I think that's happened tonight," Beckham said of Xavier's penalty, adding that he didn't think the Rapids' red card was deserved either. That, too, would become a common (and tiresome) Beckham refrain: that MLS officials were so bad, they screwed up the decisions on both sides.

From a mainstream media perspective, the Galaxy's 4–0 loss was a disaster, the worst thing that could have happened to kick off Year Two of the Beckham Experiment. The *Los Angeles Times*, which like all newspapers was suffering economically, wouldn't bother to send its soccer writer to another Galaxy road game for the rest of the season. Meanwhile, the city's second-largest paper, the *Orange County Register*, would soon stop covering the Galaxy entirely. In most ways, the excitement over Beckham's arrival in 2007 had been a top-down, media-driven phenomenon, but now even the media was starting to shrug. The Galaxy knew that it would never again credential 700 journalists for an event, as it had for Beckham's introductory press conference, but it certainly didn't imagine that Beckham would speak to as few as three or four journalists at some press gatherings after Galaxy training sessions in 2008.

Inside the Galaxy locker room, the players were shell-shocked. "You always get the sense that you're maybe farther along than you really are," Donovan said. "It opened everyone's eyes—Ruud's eyes, David's eyes, my eyes, the team's eyes—that we're not nearly as good as we think we are." Then again, Gullit argued, how could he have known? The Galaxy had played against only one MLS team during the entire preseason, which kept Gullit from realizing how much work really needed to be done. Now he had learned the hard way. But if Lalas was angry enough that he was barking at the moon in an empty stadium parking lot near midnight, he couldn't have known how upset he would become once he understood exactly how much work Gullit had been neglecting already.

A few minutes after the final whistle, Peter Vagenas sat in the visitors' locker room, eyes down, shaking his head. He was angry about the embarrassing 4–0 defeat, angry about being yanked for a rookie at halftime. But there was one thing about Gullit's preparation for the game—for the entire season, in fact—that he still couldn't fathom. "You know," Vagenas announced to a nearly silent room, "maybe we should go over set pieces before the next game." Call me crazy, Vagenas thought, but if your team has David Beckham, the world's premier dead-ball specialist, then perhaps you should do everything in your power to maximize that advantage. Amazing but true: Several players said the Galaxy had not practiced set pieces during the entire two-month-long preseason. Not in L.A., not in Hawaii, not in Asia. Not once. It was like an NFL team with Walter Payton that just decided, for one reason or another, not to practice running plays.

The thirty-year-old Vagenas had seen a lot in his nine years with the Galaxy: four coaches, two MLS championships (one in 2005 when he was the captain), and enough wins and losses not to get too wide-eyed about anything or anybody. With Cobi Jones's retirement, he was now the Galaxy's longest-serving player, the only holdover from the 2002 title team, and his institutional memory was a major reason Lalas had held on to him in the wake of trading Galaxy veterans like Chris Albright, Kevin Hartman, and Tyrone Marshall. Another reason was Lalas's personal relationship with Vagenas, a close friend, former teammate, and fellow Greek-American. "Had I not been president of the Galaxy, I think Peter Vagenas would not be with the Galaxy," Lalas would admit. "But we had traded a lot of players who'd been around the Galaxy for a while and knew about the culture of the Galaxy."

Along with Alan Gordon, Vagenas was the team's funniest player, the owner of a dry wit who could always make Beckham laugh in the adjoining locker. "I have him sign things on a daily basis," Vagenas joked of his most famous teammate. "In the afternoon it's on eBay, and I make a hundred bucks every day!" But unlike Gordon, who was almost always in "hey bro" mode, Vagenas also had a brooding edge that could appear during tough times. He was bitter that Bruce Arena and Bob Bradley had never included him in their U.S. national-team camps, for Vagenas considered himself "the best player in my position in the *league*, not just on the team." All professional athletes need confidence to perform, but Vagenas (who'd struggled in Colorado) seemed delusional in that regard. What's more, Vagenas had a habit of bellyaching in the locker room that didn't always sit well with his teammates. "Pete's a moaner by nature," said Donovan, who sometimes wished that Vagenas would pipe down and "get on with it."

But Vagenas was not overreacting about Gullit. Failing to practice set pieces was no trivial matter. In fact, it was shocking, the ultimate irony on a team whose best-known player had a movie named after (you guessed it) his set pieces. Once the news got back to Lalas—either through Vagenas or, as Vagenas claimed, another player—Lalas approached Gullit looking for an explanation. "I say this all the time: Water is to life what set plays are to soccer," Lalas would say. "It's one thing you can actually control. If you ever wanted a[n American] football comparison in soccer, here you go: I'm going to draw it up, run here, and there you go. This is stuff that any coach in the world would be doing, and when a coach isn't doing that, then you know there's a problem." After Lalas's meeting with Gullit, the Galaxy worked on set plays before its next game. But that wasn't the only fallout: According to Vagenas, Gullit assumed that Vagenas had leaked the information to Lalas and gave him an express ticket to the Gullit doghouse. Not only did Vagenas not start another MLS game for two months, but he *played* only thirteen minutes over the next ten league games in April and May.

Vagenas was crushed. "It was hurtful in a way because there was an accusation," he would explain, but Vagenas was also well aware of Gullit's history in other clubs with veteran players. Soon after Gullit joined Newcastle United, he reportedly stripped midfielder Rob Lee's captaincy, took away his number, and forced him to train alone—all for what Lee described as representing the players' concerns as their captain (which included occasionally telling the coach things he didn't want to hear). Banishing players was the kind of thing you could do as a coach in Europe, where the lack of salary caps and roster limits allowed you to bring in new players easily. But in MLS, on a team that had precious few veterans, exiling Vagenas and his experience was dangerous. Several Galaxy players thought that Gullit was doing it specifically to spite Lalas. "One reason I think Ruud wanted to release Pete was because of the closeness of his relationship with Alexi," Greg Vanney would say. But for now, at least, Vagenas was simply left in purgatory on the Galaxy bench.

While Lalas's frustrations with Gullit were increasing, so were Gullit's about MLS. Every week the league contested reserve games—European-style junior varsity matches—that allowed the coaches to observe rookies and second-team players in live-action games against other teams. But MLS had strict rules limiting how many minutes players could be on the field on consecutive days, which (combined with teams' small rosters) meant Gullit could field only ten players in the reserve game at Colorado and had to call on two members of the Galaxy's sales department staff to play in the following week's reserve game. "I can't deal with that," Gullit explained one day, his face tightening with anger. "It's unbelievable. The league has to do something." The way Gullit saw things, there was a huge difference in MLS between the very good players and the average players, largely due to poor coaching in U.S. colleges. He concluded that he could have had his biggest impact polishing "the rough diamonds" on the reserve team, but only if he could watch them in serious games. (MLS's solution at season's end was straightforward enough: It abolished the reserve league.)

Still, Gullit vowed to push ahead. "I wanted to come here," he admitted. "It was my choice. I have to adapt." Gullit certainly showed a willingness to adjust tactics and lineups. Needing to rebound from the Colorado debacle in the Galaxy's second game—ESPN2's Game of the Week against Frank Yallop's San Jose Earthquakes—Gullit junked the 4-3-3 formation for a more traditional 4-4-2 and moved Donovan to forward, where he could connect more readily with Beckham. The results were magical. In the ninth minute, Donovan intercepted a San Jose back-pass, instantly saw Beckham running to goal, and fed him a perfect ball for the one-time finish through the legs of former Galaxy goalkeeper Joe Cannon. It was Beckham's first goal in an MLS game, and he returned the favor just before halftime, sending a pass over the top to Donovan, who lobbed Cannon for a 2–0 lead. Up in the Beckham box, Victoria stood and cheered next to Los Angeles Lakers star Kobe Bryant and his family, while Beckham jumped atop Donovan's shoulders and bathed in the adoration of a roaring home crowd. Granted, San Jose played like an expansion team, but the sheer domination of Beckham and Donovan in the 2–0 victory was as plain as day. These men saw a different game, thought a different game, played a different game.

Indeed, scoring goals wasn't the problem for Gullit's Galaxy; the intractable challenge was preventing them at the other end. For every step forward the Galaxy took during the first half of the season (usually by fashioning majestic, highlight-reel strikes), the team lurched another step backward, either through off-the-field turmoil or on-the-field incompetence (read: shambolic defending). The Galaxy's back line was undeniably poor—somehow too old and too young at the same time—but it wasn't solely to blame for the defensive problems. Far too often the forwards and midfielders (including Beckham) failed to put pressure on opposing teams, allowing them to make unchallenged passes into the Galaxy box, and Gullit never prioritized defensive discipline. It made for thoroughly entertaining soccer with video-game score lines (3–2, 3–3, 5–2, 4–1, etc.), but the Galaxy found itself just as often on the wrong end as on the right one.

If there ever seemed like a sure three points in MLS, it was when Toronto FC came to town. The red-clad Canadian outfit arrived in Los Angeles the following week with an 0–2 record, whereupon the Galaxy defense promptly made its attackers look like the second coming of Brazil's 1970 World Cup winners. Three times Toronto took advantage of mistakes by Greg Vanney, and the visitors never trailed, prevailing 3–2 on an eighty-eighth-minute goal in which Vanney fell down while trying to keep up with the faster Jeff Cunningham. Donovan scored both Galaxy goals (one on a penalty), but he also inexplicably failed to finish two first-half breakaways (courtesy of Beckham passes) that would have given the Galaxy the lead. "It's about creating chances and having the confidence to finish them off," Beckham acknowledged afterward in a not-so-subtle dig at Donovan. "It's about putting the goals away. Hopefully, that will start soon."

Whatever aggravations Beckham had with not seeing enough of the ball on the right side or (when it did come) sometimes receiving terrible passes, he rarely showed much visible anger with his teammates aside from occasionally pointing to his head (*think!*) or raising both hands in the air when he was open. Chris Klein, for one, knew that Beckham had to be frustrated—he was going from playing with Zinédine Zidane, Raúl, and Roberto Carlos to teammates lacking refined soccer skills— but he admired Beckham for encouraging the Galaxy rookies, for treating them like human beings, even if Beckham sometimes felt like he was in charge of a remedial soccer class. "It's a long-term project with the MLS for many years to come, so it's also about teaching the young lads the game," Beckham said. "The biggest thing is keeping the ball and learning how to pass that sort of final ball, when it's right to pass. But at the moment it's just about teaching the lads movement and where to pass it and when to pass it." You could have called it "Soccer for Dummies with David Beckham."

Beckham urged the fans and media not to panic after the Galaxy's 1–2 start, but the mere fact that he felt the need to do so was a refreshing change in a league where there usually *wasn't enough* urgency during the regular season. Unlike the European leagues Beckham had always played in, MLS's forgiving playoff structure meant that individual regular-season games mattered little in the grand scheme, and the relative lack of significant pressures (media attention, fan support, player salaries, and competition for playing time) conspired to dial down the heat. What's more, every team lost games. MLS did as much as possible to create parity across the board, and no team dominated the way the three or four wealthiest clubs ruled over the leagues in England, Spain, and Italy. In a thirty-game season, Klein noted, "even the best teams in our league have eight to ten losses." You could have a spirited debate over which system was better. MLS was clearly a more competitive league top to bottom, but fans also want to see excellence, not a muddle of mediocrity. There were so many curbs on excellence in MLS that sustained achievement was next to impossible. "That's one of the things I've realized," Beckham said. "It's going to be one of those seasons where we play really well in one game and win, and then we play really bad and lose like we did in the first game. It's been like that already even three games into the season."

Such wild swings in quality would even take place within the same game. The Galaxy was so poor in the first half against defending champion Houston on April 19 that the home fans booed as the team left the field at halftime down 1–0. In the second half, the Beckham-Donovan combination ignited again as Beckham's lasered crosses found Donovan for two equalizing headers, one in the sixty-seventh minute and the other in the eighty-fourth. It was thrilling stuff, the combination of world-class passing and finishing, and Donovan got such a charge after one of the goals that he stood over his fallen defender, Patrick Ianni, and barked like Muhammad Ali looming over a beaten Sonny Liston. If the Galaxy had only defended with as much energy, it might have won the game instead of settling for a 2–2 tie.

Despite the Galaxy's firepower, two troubling trends emerged in the first four games: Donovan and Beckham had scored all the team's goals, and L.A. had given up the opening goal in every game but its lone victory. Both changed the following week in the Galaxy's intracity rivalry showdown at a sold-out HDC against Chivas USA. With Tom Cruise and Katie Holmes watching from the Beckham box alongside Victoria, Donovan struck first with a scorching left-footed blast from twenty yards in the eighteenth minute and added another goal early in the second half. But Chivas equalized after both strikes, victimizing the painfully slow-footed Abel Xavier twice. Just when it appeared the Galaxy was headed for another multigoal game without securing the victory, an unlikely change agent came on as a sub in the seventy-first minute and triggered a transformation.

Alan Gordon.

Gordon had played so badly in the first four games that he wasn't even earning his five-figure salary. When an ESPN.com columnist wrote a live blog of the Galaxy's 2–0 victory over San Jose, he devoted much of it to taking potshots at the man the fans called Snowshoes: "71 mins: [Ely] Allen plays a tremendous ball which sends Gordon free yet again into the Quakes box. He's wide open, ahead of the Quakes defenders with the San Jose goal at his mercy, but trips over the ball, falls down and loses it with only Cannon to beat. Seriously . . . I'm not making this up." In Gordon's defense, Gullit had played him out of position in the central midfield during the next game against Houston, but an out-of-his-depth forty-five-minute performance meant that Gordon could hear a smattering of boos and whistles from the home fans when he entered the 2–2 game against Chivas. "It got to my confidence a little bit," Gordon admitted. "This team is under the microscope, and I got caught listening to the media."

All of which made the next quarter hour so remarkable. In the seventy-sixth minute, Chivas defender Lawson Vaughn headed an innocuous-looking high ball back toward his goalkeeper Brad Guzan, a U.S. international who was about to move to Aston Villa of the English Premier League. For some reason, Gordon decided to try to beat Guzan's hands to the ball using his head. The 6'3" forward launched himself skyward, catching Guzan by surprise, and barely reached the target first, nodding the ball improbably into the net: 3–2 Galaxy. It was classic Gordon—an aesthetically deficient goal based entirely on hustle—and his teammates mobbed him on the field. But there was more to come. One minute later, Gordon assisted Donovan on his third goal of the night, another left-footed screamer from outside the box: 4–2 Galaxy. Amazingly, Gordon found the net again in the eighty-fourth minute, finishing after a gorgeous passing sequence between Donovan and Beckham. On the night he won back the fans, the only shame was that Gordon hadn't come up with a Snowshoes goal celebration to poke fun at the nickname given by his fiercest detractors.

For all of Gordon's late heroics, though, the Man of the Match was Mr. Hat Trick. Five games into the season, Landon Donovan had scored eight goals—only four fewer than his highest output for an entire MLS season. When Donovan returned to a raucous locker room after the 5–2 victory, the Galaxy's best player did something symbolic. He ignored Tom Cruise and made a beeline instead for another well-wisher who knew a thing or two about hat tricks: Wayne Gretzky.

Landon Donovan lived in a two-floor Mediterranean-style house in Manhattan Beach with mahogany furniture, wide-paneled oak floors, and a sprawling, sunlit open space that included a high-ceilinged living room and a well-appointed kitchen. It was the kind of place that the head writer of a successful network sitcom might have called home: by no means ostentatious, but exceedingly tasteful, welcoming, and (given the tony location not far from the beach) no doubt seven-figure expensive. On a Friday afternoon in early May, Donovan was home alone eating a lunch of crab cakes and an artichoke. An ultrathin MacBook Air laptop computer sat open on the marble-topped island in the kitchen.

Donovan and his wife, Bianca, were dog people. As he took a seat with his plate on the living-room sofa, Donovan was surrounded by the couple's four pooches: Thor, a five-year-old shepherd/Labrador retriever mix; Loki, a four-year-old ridgeback/black Lab mix; Luna, a three-year-old purebred Boston terrier; and Santi ("like Santiago"), a four-month-old pit bull/Lab mix. "I grew up with dogs in my house, and so did Bianca," said Donovan, who played peek-a-boo with the puppy. "*You're so cute! Santi!* You can push him off the couch. *Good boy*."

The scene communicated many things, most of all that this was not the house of a young, immature twentysomething. There were no Bob Marley posters, no lava lamps, no half-eaten containers of takeout on the kitchen counter. The furniture, the modern design, even the food: They were the signs of a forty-year-old, not a twenty-six-year-old. To hear Donovan, none of it was a coincidence, for he had undergone a "personal transformation" in the two years since his disastrous 2006 World Cup. "Leading into 2006, I kind of got complacent, got to a point where I could just show up and play and it wasn't a big deal and whatever happens happens," he said. "And that's not fair. I've realized I only have one career, and I need to make the most of it." That meant lifting weights with abandon. That meant taking practice seriously. That meant eating right every day: Donovan was about to read *The Omnivore's Dilemma*, Michael Pollan's book on the sources of America's food supply, and he preached against the evils of McDonald's to his younger teammates after finishing the book *Fast Food Nation*.

Yet Donovan's biggest change, he believed, was mental. Instead of waiting until Friday to visualize that weekend's game, he would start preparing on the previous Sunday, keying up so much that by the opening whistle he was a mass of tightly coiled energy ready to pounce on opposing defenders. (That explained his uncharacteristic Muhammad Ali pose above Houston's Patrick Ianni, he said, even though the taunt was kind of bush-league.) Now that Donovan was no longer the captain, he never met one-on-one with the head coach, and though he missed speaking on behalf of the players, he took the opportunity to focus entirely on his own performance. He wanted to claim his fourth MLS championship, of course, but he also set a goal of leading the league in scoring and winning the Most Valuable Player Award—neither of which he had done before, owing to MLS's bizarre practice of scheduling games on FIFA international dates. "How does a league have its best player never be in the MVP race?" asked Chris Klein. "Landon misses ten games a year playing for the national team, but a rested Landon is by far the best player in our league. If he played a full season with the Galaxy, thirty goals wouldn't be out of the question for him."

Donovan knew he wouldn't keep up his nearly two-goals-per-game pace, but he acknowledged that his confidence was at an all-time high. What's more, as a voracious consumer of sports media, he was fully aware that continued scoring would quiet the legion of critics (aka the Landycakes Brigade) who acted as if he had a personal character deficiency for not plying his trade in Europe. "I understand the criticism from the World Cup for sure," Donovan said. "I understand any criticism from not playing well in certain games, but what I don't like is when things are said that are personal. That pisses me off. As far as soccer goes, I know I haven't always played the same way I've played these five games. But if I do play the same way all year, there's nothing anybody can say."

After months of reflection, Donovan felt that he had worried too much about Beckham's arrival, wasted too much time and energy complicating matters by wondering if they and their wives would have a close relationship away from the field. It was too much like the bad parts of high school, Donovan decided, and it didn't have to be that way. In fact, life was a lot easier now that he realized where he and Beckham *did* connect: on the soccer field, where their shared passion, competitiveness, and talent had a sort of elemental purity, a simplicity that Donovan craved. "We're both soccer players," Donovan said, "and we have a common goal: We want to win. It's not much more complicated than that, as complicated as it can seem at times. I don't have to go hang out with David on weekends. There's no pressure to do that. So by having that mentality we've gotten along really well this year off the field as well. I think there's more mutual respect than there was last year. Not that it was bad, but there was never any real connection."

Of course, forging that soccer bond was impossible in 2007 because Beckham rarely ever played. For all the publicity that Beckham generated outside of sports, Donovan now understood how skilled Beckham really was as a soccer player, marveling at his passing precision and efficiency, the way he hit the ball cleanly every single time. Any kind of ball: a dead ball, a ball moving in one direction or the other. And any kind of strike: from a driven cross to a long diagonal pass, whether he was using his instep, his outstep, or even the top of his foot. Donovan had reached the point, unheard of in MLS, that he expected Beckham's passes to go exactly where they were supposed to without fail—and 95 percent of the time they did. When you combined Beckham's technical ability with his full-field vision for the game, Donovan was in soccer nirvana. "It's just fun," he said. "When he gets the ball my eyes light up, because I know every time there's the potential that we're going to score a goal. And that's an awesome feeling."

From the start, Donovan's primary concern with Beckham had been the same as it was with any other big-name player from overseas: What is he really here for? The money? A vacation? Would he care about beating Real Salt Lake when he'd played for Real Madrid? So far, at least, Donovan was impressed with Beckham in 2008. The team's 2–2–1 start had been frustrating at times, but Beckham showed real emotion when the Galaxy scored, when one of his crosses found Donovan for yet another goal. Producing on the field, Donovan felt, had brought Beckham and his Galaxy teammates closer together—not as friends, necessarily, but as soccer players. "It's kind of like it's validated why he's here," Donovan said. He didn't need to be best friends with Beckham as long as there was respect, for Donovan had made his own friends, both inside and outside the team. Nearly every week on their off day, he joined Alan Gordon, Chris Klein, and Steve Cronin for a round of golf. ("Landon and Klein always make us go to the most expensive courses for some reason," Gordon joked. "I'm paying a hundred bucks every course, so I'm like, 'Come on, guys.'")

At the same time, Donovan's personal transformation had caused him to change his outlook toward the future. After two failed attempts at European club soccer, he was convinced that only now, at twenty-six, was he truly ready to make the jump, mature enough as a person and a player to thrive at the game's highest level. Donovan had already discussed the possibility with his wife: If the right opportunity in Europe came along, he would certainly consider it. "That doesn't mean I have to go back to feel any redemption or feel satisfied," he said, "but now I realize I can be successful there." In one way, at least, Donovan had already gone European. His new charcoal-gray Maserati Quattroporte had arrived from Italy, which meant that he now qualified under the Lalas $100,000 Rule to park his car next to Beckham's and Xavier's downstairs at the HDC near the locker room.

Like the player who almost seemed sheepish to be in first class the year before, Donovan told Gordon that he wasn't sure he wanted to big-time the Galaxy's other American players by parking downstairs.

"I don't want to be *that guy*," Donovan told him.

"Dude, you *are* that guy," Gordon replied. "Just go!"

And so Donovan did what he had been doing all season. He went for it.

CHAPTER 12

EUROPE VS. AMERICA

In the first half of 2008, Ruud Gullit's Los Angeles Galaxy was the ultimate Newton's Law team: For every action there was an equal and opposite reaction. After the adrenaline rush of smacking down Chivas 5–2, the Galaxy promptly gave up two goals in the first eighteen minutes at Real Salt Lake on May 3. The second was due specifically to lazy defending by Beckham, who allowed Javier Morales to send a pressure-free cross to Kenny Deuchar for a 2–0 lead. But Beckham made up for his mistake with a four-minute *tour de force* just before halftime that gave the crowd of 25,571 their money's worth and more. Wonderstrike No. 1 came in the thirty-sixth minute, when Beckham maneuvered into open space twenty-five yards from the RSL goal and bent an angry parabola into the upper left corner for a 2–1 deficit. And Wonderstrike No. 2 was something you had to see to believe: a dauntingly long thirty-three-yard free kick that swerved over the wall like a Fourth of July bottle rocket, reaching the same destination with such speed and precision that you half expected it to produce a sonic boom as it buckled the net. It appeared that Beckham had figured out artificial turf.

But if the 2–2 final score was still disappointing—four minutes of Beckham brilliance surrounded by eighty-six minutes of dreck—the Galaxy's 2–1 loss at home to New York the following week was cause for real alarm. Steve Cronin had developed a maddening habit of giving up rebounds that turned into goals for opposing teams, and it happened again midway through the first half as the Red Bulls took the lead. Alan Gordon tied the score with his third goal of the season in the seventy-seventh minute, using his size to gather the ball and turn before firing past New York goalkeeper Jon Conway, but the positive vibe lasted less than a minute. Galaxy rookie Brandon McDonald, the replacement for the doghouse-dwelling Peter Vagenas, got skinned by Dane Richards on a thirty-yard run before Juan Pablo Ángel scored the game-winner. The Galaxy was now 2–3–2, even though five of its seven games had been at home.

Beckham played poorly, having little impact on the match, and Gullit criticized his captain publicly for the first time, both implicitly (blaming the game-deciding defensive breakdown on "a lack of leadership") and explicitly (arguing that Beckham had played too far up on the right side). Gullit refused to specify which players should be showing more leadership, but there was only one captain, and it wasn't Donovan. As for his positioning, Beckham was frustrated (not for the first time) by his teammates' inability to pass him the ball, and he noted that he had ventured backward in the first half to pursue it before moving forward in the second half to try making "that killer pass," as he put it, that the Galaxy needed. "Sometimes if you don't get the ball you have to go look for it, so that does take you out of position at certain points," said Beckham, whose eyebrows furrowed when he learned of Gullit's criticism. "Sometimes that works for the team, and sometimes it doesn't."

Beckham's forays around the field would become an all-too-common theme of the season, as would Gullit's custom of blaming the players when things went wrong and taking the credit for his halftime changes when things went right—a pattern that drove the players nuts. "Listen to some of the things he says," one said. "It's all about him." On this night, though, Gullit argued that the loss was *nothing* about him, issuing a strange pedantic soliloquy explaining how soccer was different from American sports since a coach couldn't call any time-outs. "You scream whatever you can scream, but you can't reach them," Gullit concluded, effectively throwing up his hands and pleading that he was powerless.

Alexi Lalas clearly felt otherwise. Lalas watched the games, observed Gullit's practices, and spoke to some of the players, paying even closer attention to the coach's methods after he discovered that Gullit hadn't bothered to work on set pieces before the season opener. Granted, Lalas wasn't likely to give Gullit the benefit of the doubt, having been undermined by the coach's hiring, but what Lalas learned was nevertheless troubling. In training sessions, Gullit would almost never spend time on individual technical skills, instead conducting game after game of eleven-on-eleven, like a roll-out-the-balls basketball coach. Gullit simply switched players around every ten minutes until he found a combination he liked, and that would usually be the starting lineup for the next game. "Maybe in his own mind Ruud had an idea of what we were working on in training," Greg Vanney would say, "but the rest of us had no idea." Gullit's mood swings on players were schizophrenic. "I've never seen anybody that would love you one minute and hate you the next, almost like the next day," Alan Gordon would say. For his part, Vanney viewed Gullit's extreme swings and routine benchings of everyone except Beckham, Donovan, and Klein as a lack of respect for the players. "How do you make sense of that," the thirteen-year veteran wondered, "and step on the field with confidence, ready to go to battle for your coach?"

Likewise, several players thought that Gullit's work ethic was bordering on nonexistent despite his $2 million annual salary. In MLS, winning coaches thrived by putting in long hours studying game tapes and providing detailed scouting reports to their players, the better to maximize every tiny advantage with such evenly matched teams. "To be successful in MLS, you have to be 100 percent committed," Lalas said. "Whether you're a president or a coach, you have to be a junkie. I watch every single game. I know all the players." Did Gullit? "Nope," Lalas said. "Not yet." Nor did it seem as though Gullit was showing much desire to learn. On the occasions when he did show scouting videos, players would say, it was painfully clear that he had spent little time poring over the tapes. "We'd watch the first twenty-five minutes of Salt Lake–Kansas City, and he wouldn't say anything," Gordon would say. "We'd just watch it and go out to training saying, 'What is going on? That didn't help us at all.'" Even worse, Donovan observed, Gullit rolled into the HDC at 9 A.M. and left by 12:30 P.M. on many days. (Practice was from 10 A.M. to noon.) "Coaches should be the first one there and the last one to leave, and it just wasn't the case," Donovan would say. "You almost get used to it, but it's not right."

It struck Donovan that Gullit was treating his U.S. adventure as a chance to live in the Hollywood Hills and hang out in Santa Monica. The coach barely communicated with his players—many said they didn't understand their roles on the field, one of the coach's main duties to explain—and when Gullit did talk to them they thought it often made no sense. Once, when the Galaxy was waiting in an airport, Gullit called over Gordon to watch a television showing a Manchester United game. He told Gordon that he wanted him to play like United midfielder Paul Scholes, who had nothing in common with the 6'3" Gordon's target-man skill set. It became a long-running unintentional gag. One week Gullit wanted Gordon to be like Spanish forward Fernando Torres. The next week it was English beanpole Peter Crouch. "He called me like eight different names," Gordon would say. "Scholes, Torres, Crouch, and some old midfielder I couldn't even name." Teammates started asking Gordon: *Who are you this week?* Finally, Gullit's well ran dry. "I wish I could show you videos of myself," he told Gordon one day before practice. "I was a horse!"

In time, even Beckham, whose own advisers had installed Gullit as the head coach, would grow impatient. "What are we doing?" Vanney said more than once to Beckham, who could only shake his head over Gullit's perplexing lineup decisions and practice plans. Of course, none of Gullit's problems with the Galaxy was surprising to anyone who knew the history of big-name foreign coaches in MLS. If you were going to hire a coach from overseas, Vanney reasoned, "that person has to be open to the nuances of the MLS game and the rules, and he has to be a hard worker. Those are the qualities that Ruud probably *didn't* have as a coach. He didn't want to listen to anybody else. He knew everything there was to know."

The humility that Lalas believed was crucial to succeeding in any soccer league as a foreigner, especially MLS, was not something that Gullit had the desire to summon. Lalas didn't know which was more damning, his impressions of Gullit's daily work habits or the coach's tactical decisions in games, which included not choosing to use a left midfielder at times and throwing as many as five forwards onto the field when the Galaxy needed a late goal. Or maybe the issue was what Lalas viewed as Gullit's unwillingness to adapt, no matter how many times he promised to do so. "I've tried from the start to let him go through this learning curve," Lalas said. "But when I'm held accountable for it at the end of the year, I also have to do what I feel is appropriate, because I swear to God, I'm not going down without swinging. And I will do whatever I feel is appropriate to get this team to win, because at the end of the day my ass is on the line."

There was a peculiar irony in Lalas's reduced power with the Galaxy: Although it was Tim Leiweke's decision that kneecapped Lalas in the first place, Leiweke was one of the few people in the management structure, such as it was, who still cared about what Lalas had to say. (Gullit, Terry Byrne, and 19 Entertainment certainly didn't.) Leiweke called Lalas regularly to ask about the team, and he did so again not long after the loss to New York.

"How are things going?" Leiweke asked.

"Do you really want an honest opinion?" Lalas replied.

"Yeah."

"They're not going well, and I don't know if I see them getting any better."

Leiweke had been talking to Byrne, Gullit, and Simon Fuller as well, and the AEG chief knew there were growing tensions between Lalas and Gullit—no surprise considering 19 Entertainment had wanted Lalas to be fired as soon as it had installed Gullit as the Galaxy coach. What's more, Gullit wasn't happy about the team's focus on dollars and cents, which included its refusal to indulge Gullit's wishes for more European-style soccer amenities at the HDC and its scheduling of exhibition games during the MLS season. Gullit was incensed that the Galaxy had to travel to Edmonton, Canada, for a meaningless friendly on May 13 just to punch the Galaxy cash register. For his part, Lalas (whose main role now was on the business side) reiterated that the exhibition games were crucial to covering the team's bottom line. Leiweke knew he had a problem on his hands, and he wasn't the type to let it fester. He set up a summit meeting with Lalas and Gullit at AEG headquarters in downtown L.A. for May 21.

Three days before the showdown meeting at AEG, naturally, the Galaxy played its best game of the season. Beckham had earned the gratitude of his teammates by asking AEG for a private charter that could fly the Galaxy back from their midweek friendly in Edmonton directly after the game. The selling point was an extra day of training before that week's game at FC Dallas, where the Galaxy's explosion for four goals in the first half was all the more shocking considering Donovan and Beckham scored none of them. Chris Klein put L.A. up 1–0, cutting into the box to score after a long overlapping run, and Edson Buddle did him one better, slaloming through four Dallas defenders for his first goal of the season. An own-goal two minutes later gave the Galaxy a 3–0 lead, and then Buddle struck again, heading in a Beckham corner kick for a 4–0 halftime advantage.

Not even the Galaxy's defense could screw up this one, and it didn't, allowing only one Dallas goal in the second half. (Xavier got smoked one-on-one again.) But ugly things can happen at the ends of blowouts, and in the seventy-fifth minute the home team's Adrian Serioux committed a low-grade assault on Beckham, scissoring out his legs from behind with clear and violent intent. It was an obvious red card, and an incensed Beckham had to be restrained by teammates from going after Serioux in the ensuing melee. What followed was first-rate theater, pro wrestling–style, for Beckham's antics showed that he could play the villain on the road with aplomb. Beckham theatrically waved good-bye to Serioux as he left the field, and the sellout crowd started booing the Englishman every time he touched the ball. Ten minutes later, Beckham responded like a classically trained heel, sending a glorious cross to Buddle to seal the 5–1 victory before turning and shushing the 22,331 Dallas fans, who booed more lustily still. If Beckham had only rushed to the locker rooms and slammed Serioux over the head with a folding chair, the scene would have been a perfect slice of Vince McMahon/Jerry Springer Americana. Now this was *entertainment*!

Of course, the five goals were impressive, too, most of all Buddle's out-of-nowhere hat trick. If the Galaxy had one breakout player who thrived under Gullit's influence, it was Buddle, a twenty-seven-year-old son of Jamaican immigrants who grew up in New York's Westchester County with a poster of the dreadlocked Gullit on his bedroom wall. "To have him here in person, it's like my poster came alive," said Buddle, a shy, strapping forward who had excellent dribbling skills if he felt confident enough to use them. Buddle's father, Winston, played professional soccer in Greece and Cyprus, and he was such a fan of the

Brazilian national team that he named his son after Pelé (full name: Edson Arantes do Nascimento). Like his teammate Alan Gordon, Buddle had overcome his own demons of substance abuse. Though he'd scored forty-four goals in his first five MLS seasons with the Columbus Crew, Buddle's career was heading south when he was arrested for driving under the influence over the MLS All-Star Game weekend in 2005. (He refused to take a Breathalyzer test.) Concerned by Buddle's erratic behavior, MLS mandated that he attend a two-week treatment program at the Canyon Ranch in Malibu, California, where he acknowledged that he was an alcoholic. "The first step is admitting it," said Buddle. "You think of your family and what people think of you. I put myself in that position, so it was disappointing when you have an opportunity in front of you to mess up that way." Buddle said he no longer drank a sip of alcohol, and after short spells with New York and Toronto he was finally starting to look like a dangerous striker again with the Galaxy.

Unlike Gordon and Peter Vagenas, Buddle was hopelessly starstruck by Beckham; he even admitted as much. His main goal, he said, was not to mess up any of Beckham's gift-wrapped passes. When it came to Beckham's life away from the field, well, he might as well have lived on a different planet. Although Buddle was making relatively good money— $157,000, the team's fifth-highest salary—he still shared a house with teammate Troy Roberts and Chivas USA's Shavar Thomas. What could Buddle and Beckham even talk about? "He and his wife bought a *vineyard* for her birthday," Buddle said, trying to wrap his mind around the idea. "That's not normal."

Then again, when was anything ever *normal* in the three-ring circus of the Beckham Experiment? After the season's most electrifying win, the team president who most players thought was in charge (Lalas) was about to have a Five Families–style meeting with the coach he hadn't hired (Gullit), the AEG boss who had emasculated him (Tim Leiweke), and an adversarial audience that included David Beckham's best friend and personal manager (Terry Byrne), Beckham's agent (CAA's Jeff Frasco), and another member of Beckham's support staff (19 Entertainment's Rebecca Mostow).

Welcome to the 2008 Los Angeles Galaxy, aka Dysfunction Junction.

The moment Alexi Lalas stepped into the conference room at AEG headquarters on the afternoon of May 21, he knew nothing good would come of the meeting. Not for him, anyway. If he had much juice left at all, there would have been three participants: himself, Tim Leiweke, and Ruud Gullit. Instead, nine people sat at the large round conference table with a tenth on speakerphone. Gullit and Cobi Jones represented the Galaxy coaching staff. Lalas and assistant general manager Tom Payne represented the Galaxy front office. Leiweke, AEG Sports president Andrew Messick, and chief operating officer Dan Beckerman represented AEG. And Jeff Frasco, Rebecca Mostow, and Terry Byrne (who was on speakerphone from the Champions League final in Moscow) represented David Beckham.

Why Beckham needed to have *anyone* here, much less three of his advisers, was baffling to Lalas. But the battle lines had been drawn. 19 Entertainment had installed Gullit; therefore, Lalas's tension with Gullit was tension with Team Beckham. "It was a perfect example of how fucked up the situation got," Lalas would say. "Here I am meeting about the Galaxy, our soccer team, and I have agents, I have managers, I have consultants on the phone. And I'm the goddamn president of the Galaxy. If I want to call my coach out, then that's what I'll do. I don't need to answer to them."

Leiweke, for his part, had intended for the meeting to be a let's-get-along session, a reminder to Gullit and Lalas that the Galaxy's success required them to be on the same page. Leiweke's message, he felt, was simple: Everyone needs to stop shooting at one another. If it doesn't work for one of you, it's not going to work for the other. But as soon as Lalas opened his mouth, the tensions in the room were laid bare.

"I know this has been an adjustment with David," Lalas said, "trying to figure out things, trying to work within all the restrictions. And I know this is a work in progress."

As soon as Lalas said the magic word (*David*), Team Beckham kicked into high gear. Over the speakerphone, Byrne interjected immediately, ominously. "We didn't know this was a meeting about David," he said.

Lalas was notorious for losing his cool in such settings, for letting his anger take over when he felt the whistle-blower's impulse to cut through the corporate nonsense and speak the truth, or at least his version of it. Now the blood was rushing to Lalas's brain like the lava of an erupting volcano. "Guys, don't be naïve," he said. "Do you think we'd be doing this if David Beckham wasn't here? *Everything* is about David." But Lalas wasn't done yet. He mentioned his concerns about Gullit's game preparations, and when the subject turned to the Galaxy's in-season friendlies—games that Lalas felt were necessary to pay for Beckham and hit his numbers for the season—things quickly got heated between Lalas (who wanted to continue the exhibitions) and Gullit (who thought they were a distraction from the MLS season).

"Is this about the business or the team?" Gullit said, his voice rising. "Do we want to win or do we just want to hit the numbers?"

"This is the reality of the Galaxy," Lalas barked across the conference table. "It's part of our business plan. We're not Milan. That's just the way it is."

The two alpha males went back and forth, the intensity of their venom surprising the others who sat at the table. In the end, Gullit got his way. The Galaxy would play no more lucrative exhibitions during the season. "Fine," Lalas said. "But I'm in charge of the business, and the business is going to suffer."

By the end of the meeting, Lalas felt liberated in a sense, even if his honesty was probably to his detriment in the long run. "It was the beginning of the end," Lalas would say. "For the first time to their faces, 19 and CAA knew that I was not happy. They knew after that meeting that the relationship between Ruud and me had deteriorated to the point of no return. They had basically put him in charge, and they had so much invested in it going well that when I say the emperor has no clothes, they're saying, 'Well, you're just against it.' Fine, whatever."

You couldn't argue with Lalas on one thing: The Galaxy was never boring. In fact, even as tensions behind the scenes continued to build, L.A. was about to climb into first place for the first time in three years.

Newton's Law was in full effect again three nights later as the Galaxy players gathered in the locker room at halftime after one of the team's worst halves of the season. The Kansas City Wizards led 1–0 on a goal by the Argentine forward Claudio López, and the Galaxy attack looked anemic, especially in the central midfield. Ruud Gullit stormed into the locker room. He was a large man who knew the force of his personality could induce fear. Even before Gullit spoke, the players noticed he was breathing heavily, as though he had just run directly from the playing field.

"Landon, do you want to win?" Gullit thundered at the Galaxy star in front of the team.

"Excuse me?" Donovan replied.

"Do you want to win?"

"Yeah, of course I want to win."

"Well, then *you* need to start doing what I'm telling you to do and drop back into the midfield!"

"No, I think you're wrong. That's not fair to me. That's what we have midfielders for."

"No! You need to do it!"

Donovan stood up. No coach had ever baited him like this before, embarrassed him in front of his teammates. Donovan's acute sense for disrespect was throbbing like a five-alarm fire siren. He could feel his adrenaline rising. "No, that's not fair! That's putting too much work on my shoulders when other people need to be doing it."

"If you don't want to do it, then I'll put someone in the game who will! Okay? Do you understand?"

Donovan fell silent, considering his options. For an instant, he thought about walking to the showers and calling Gullit's bluff. *Who are you going to put in that's better? Let's see you figure this one out if I'm not around.* Donovan stared at his coach, then finally decided it wasn't worth the trouble and sat down. Gullit launched into his halftime speech; the charged moment subsided.

The Galaxy proceeded to score three times in the second half to win 3–1. Donovan drew a penalty, scoring his first goal in four games by converting the go-ahead spot kick, and Gullit took the credit in the postgame press conference for motivating Donovan at halftime (without mentioning any specifics of their exchange). But the game's lasting image was a bizarre play that took place in injury time with the Galaxy leading 2–1. After Kansas City had won a corner kick, Wizards goal-keeper Kevin Hartman ran downfield to join the attack, leaving his goalmouth open. L.A. cleared the corner kick, however, and the ball came to the foot of David Beckham, who found open space outside his own penalty box and sent a *seventy-yard* rainbow dead solid perfect into the middle of the Kansas City goal. Beckham opened his arms wide and bathed in the roar of the home crowd. It wasn't as lightning-strike impressive as Beckham's legendary goal from the halfway line for Manchester United in 1996—there was a goalkeeper to beat on that one, after all—but the sequence was mesmerizing nonetheless. "The consistency of the way he strikes the ball is mind-boggling, how accurately he hits it over long distance," marveled Chris Klein. "A lot of guys could have hit that shot, but with a guy chasing him I think he could do it again and again and again. That's where the greatness comes in." In a repeat of Beckham's first Galaxy goal in 2007, the seventy-yard strike was viewed 240,741 times on YouTube in the next two days, making it the most popular clip in the world.

Yet the impact of the game on the Galaxy's other star was even greater. Gullit never mentioned the halftime incident to Donovan again, but for Donovan the shouting match told him all he needed to know about the Dutchman. Perhaps it was a reflection of the female influences in his life, perhaps a sign that his immaturity had not yet been fully consigned to his past, but Donovan internalized the exchange with Gullit, took it as an unforgivable act of disrespect. "People in my family will tell you that once you cross me that way, there's no coming back," Donovan said. There were other examples: Donovan's nearly three years (and counting) without any contact with his father; and his refusal to speak to Grahame Jones, the longtime soccer reporter for the *Los Angeles Times*, for weeks after Jones wrote that Donovan had "cheated" to earn the penalty against Kansas City by diving in the box. From now on, Donovan decided, he would simply tune Gullit out. "I'm just not here to play for him," Donovan said. "I'm here to play for myself and my teammates. He's lucky that I have other motivations."

Gullit's "hair-dryer" treatment of Donovan was one example of the difference between European and American soccer coaches, and it was grist for a good debate. Had Gullit crossed the line? Had he blatantly disrespected the star American in a way that he wouldn't have treated, say, Beckham? Or was Donovan being too thin-skinned? Was there any chance that Gullit's tough love was just the thing that Donovan needed to play with more intensity in the second half? The Galaxy players were split. Chris Klein, one of Donovan's closest friends, didn't think Gullit had crossed the line, arguing that the manager could do and say what he wanted. Greg Vanney maintained that every player should be challenged but added that Gullit should have picked a better setting to do so with Donovan. Meanwhile, Alan Gordon agreed with Donovan that Gullit's outburst was uncalled for. For Donovan, it all came down to mutual respect, the kind of professional courtesy that he felt existed with U.S. national team coach Bob Bradley. "I've had many conversations with Bob where we don't see eye to eye, but he always treats me respectfully," Donovan said. "Ruud doesn't do that. There's always an *I know what I'm talking about and you don't* in his voice."

Though Donovan may not have sounded like a league-leading scorer on a first-place team, the Galaxy's victory had pushed L.A. to 4–3–2 and the top spot in MLS's weak Western Conference. The question, now that Donovan and Beckham were departing for national-team duty, was whether the Galaxy could stay there. England was about to meet the United States in a friendly at Wembley Stadium.

England and the U.S. didn't face each other very often on the soccer field—the game at Wembley was only their fourth meeting since 1985—but that hardly meant there was no history between the two sides. In what is still regarded as one of the greatest upsets in World Cup history, the U.S. rode a first-half goal by Haitian immigrant Joe Gaetjens to a 1–0 victory over England at the 1950 World Cup in Brazil. England had dominated their matches since then, though Alexi Lalas was quick to remind anyone that his goal had helped give the Yanks a 2–0 friendly win against England in 1993. Any chance to play in Wembley Stadium against England was something to treasure, which is why Donovan was so disappointed when he was ruled out with a groin injury.

In the end, the game was a disaster for the United States, which played like a collection of amateurs in a 2–0 loss that didn't fully capture the embarrassing disparity in performance. Afterward, one England player would tell associates that the American players' hands were trembling during the pregame handshakes. It didn't matter that Donovan was out or that the U.S. would play much better over the next two weeks in a hard-fought 1–0 loss at Spain (the eventual European champion) and in an electric scoreless draw against a nearly full-strength Argentina at Giants Stadium. For what it was worth, England fans saw an outclassed U.S. team and presumably confirmed their suspicions that David Beckham was wasting his time in a third-rate American league.

MLS executives were always defensive when anyone accused their league of being a Mickey Mouse operation, but while MLS's level of play was better than most Europeans gave it credit for, the decision to continue staging games on FIFA international dates was a blight on the league. MLS honchos talked big about preventing "competitive advantages" by limiting such perks as charter flights, but they had no problem with a system that clearly harmed teams that signed marquee internationals like Beckham and Donovan. They were bound to miss several MLS games each season, while other stars whose national-team careers had ended (e.g., New York's Juan Pablo Ángel and Columbus's Guillermo Barros Schelotto) were available for all their teams' games. "I do wish that would change," Beckham said of the MLS policy. "I think it needs to be looked at, because I think it's tough for teams around the league to lose players at important times, and every other league in the world caters to that."

Not surprisingly, the Galaxy struggled without its two best players, losing to Colorado 1–0 to be eliminated from the U.S. Open Cup (a knockout tournament like England's FA Cup) and falling 2–0 at Toronto in MLS play. Lalas was furious with Gullit after the coach left two strikers on the bench for the entire game in Toronto: Carlos Ruiz, who was now recovered from his knee injury, and Donovan, who despite his groin strain had flown in just before game time and was available to play. It was a bad week all around for Lalas, who had a private lunch with Leiweke on June 3 at the Palm, the same restaurant where Leiweke had offered him his first executive job five years earlier. This time Leiweke was far less enthusiastic.

"My contract is up at the end of the year," Lalas said at one point to his boss, "and I don't really know where I stand here at this point."

Leiweke's response was a short one. "I know your contract is up at the end of the year," he replied, leaving it at that.

Meanwhile, the Galaxy made the most of Beckham's unexpected availability for MLS games during the European Championship. In yet another profoundly strange game, on June 7, the Galaxy went up 1–0 against Colorado in the fourth minute, Alvaro Pires putting the Galaxy ahead after a scramble following a Beckham free kick. Two more Galaxy goals followed on either side of halftime: one by the suddenly surging Buddle and another by Ely Allen off a penetrating through-ball from Peter Vagenas, who was celebrating his exit from a two-month-long stay in Gullit's doghouse. (Not long before, Vagenas had finally asked for a meeting with Gullit, in which he vowed that he wasn't ratting the coach out to Lalas.) The Galaxy's inept defense nearly squandered the 3–0 lead, though, giving up two goals in nine minutes and releasing the HDC's boo-birds yet again. L.A. barely held on for a 3–2 win, but not before the home fans witnessed another scene from the theater of the absurd.

In the eighty-sixth minute, a male spectator in a black T-shirt jumped onto the field and began running toward Beckham. It wasn't the first time Beckham had been the target of a field invasion in his career, but the advancing figure gave him pause nonetheless. "He didn't have a smile on his face, and he didn't have a Galaxy shirt on," Beckham said, "so I didn't know if he was going to come and give me a hug or something else." With no security guards in sight, the fan gave Beckham a high five and made a motion as if he was going to wrap his arms around Beckham in a hug. That was when Chris Klein—devout Christian, mild-mannered family man—turned into the Ultimate Warrior. With scenes of Monica Seles's on-court stabbing going through his mind, Klein charged the man with his arms out and his right knee up in the air, knocking him to the ground before stadium security frog-marched him off the field.

When the gossip website TMZ.com posted a photo of Klein in full enforcer mode taking out the spectator, Alan Gordon couldn't stop making fun of his friend in the locker room. "Here's Klein, the nicest guy ever, and he's on TMZ with fire coming out of his ears charging this poor kid who wants to hug David," Gordon said, laughing. "You see the picture and Klein just looks *evil*. It was classic."

Though everyone had a good laugh about the incident after the game, the Galaxy's near-collapse in the second half wasn't so funny. Gullit took the occasion to remind reporters of the outcome ("We *won*, by the way"), while Beckham had to pause when asked if the 5–4–2 Galaxy felt like a first-place team. "I think we've worked hard together, and we need to stay there," Beckham said. "We need to improve a lot. There's some good aspects. We've definitely moved forward with the team, with the players, with the confidence, but we have to get that consistency. That's when we're going to realize we're a first-place team, a championship team." In other words, no, it didn't feel like a first-place team.

But it did a week later. Before a crowd of 39,872 in Oakland—more fans than the same stadium drew for the New York Yankees, Boston Red Sox, and the 2006 baseball playoffs—the Galaxy demolished the San Jose Earthquakes 3–0 on June 14. Beckham had a quiet game, but with Landon Donovan still on international duty Edson Buddle erupted for his second hat trick in less than a month. His second goal, in particular, was a thing of beauty, the culmination of a Galaxy passing sequence highlighted by a pinpoint *left*-sided cross from the converted defender Ante Jazic. Beckham was so ecstatic after the goal that he wrapped both hands around Buddle's face like a proud grandmother. "I think it's the best we've played, actually," Beckham said afterward. "The goals we scored tonight were great goals, great finishes, but great movement as well from each player." It was, dare it be said, Sexy Football. If the Galaxy could play this way all the time, especially on defense, there was no reason it couldn't win an MLS championship.

Then again, it was one thing to beat a lowly expansion team or, in the case of the Galaxy's other five victories, opponents that all had losing records. It would be quite another to win the following week at home against the Columbus Crew, the owner of the league's best record.

The Galaxy's relentless attack didn't disappoint, staking L.A. to a 2–0 lead over the Crew on goals by Donovan and Buddle. But just when it appeared the Galaxy was cruising to a statement-making victory, the defense imploded again with the fragility of a third-world apartment building. Columbus pulled one goal back on a fluky play in the sixty-seventh minute, when Sean Franklin's header deflected off the face of Alvaro Pires to the Crew's Brad Evans, who made it 2–1. Then, four minutes later, Abel Xavier got worked again one-on-one, losing the fleet-footed Robbie Rogers before a lunging Klein took out Rogers in the box for a penalty, which Barros Schelotto converted for a 2–2 score. The Galaxy thought it had sealed the game in the eighty-second minute when Beckham drew his own penalty and Donovan drilled the spot kick for 3–2, but Xavier gave Columbus a dangerous free kick five minutes later after taking out Rogers just outside the penalty box. *Set pieces again*, thought Lalas in his luxury box, shaking his head. And sure enough, Steve Cronin allowed a rebound on the ensuing sequence, leaving it for the Crew's Steven Lenhart to bang home the equalizer: 3–3.

But the game's defining play took place in the ninetieth minute. As L.A. barreled forward on the attack, Beckham received a pass in the box at full speed, took one touch past a Columbus defender, and found himself in on the goalkeeper with three points on his legendary right foot. All he had to do was finish the easy chance for a 4–3 victory. From his vantage point behind Beckham, Klein knew it was going in, was already celebrating the goal inside his head. "With the way that he strikes the ball," Klein said, "if he gets that shot five times he buries it every time." The Galaxy was going to beat Columbus, staking its own claim as the league's top team, the team that everyone else would fear most heading into the rest of the season. Beckham's game-winning goal and exultant celebration with his teammates would be one of the top stories that night on *SportsCenter*, proof positive that the Beckham Experiment was succeeding where it mattered the most: on the playing field.

And then, with a swift lash of his right foot, Beckham blasted his shot high over the crossbar.

The proud Englishman fell to his knees in agony. It would be the turning point of the Galaxy's season. L.A. had blown 2–0 and 3–2 leads at home, had scored three goals without securing the win, and Beckham himself had choked on a ninetieth-minute sitter with the game on the line. Rarely had a 3–3 tie ever seemed like such a sucker punch. "At the moment," Beckham said afterward, his grim face creased with frustration, "it feels like a loss." Back in the locker room, Beckham apologized to his teammates and asked anyone who had seen the replay what happened.

"Did my foot slip?" he wondered. "Did my plant foot come out from under me? Did the ball hit a bump?" In fact, replays showed that it did appear to have taken a slight hop, but Beckham still didn't stay down on the ball long enough. There was no excuse for not finishing.

On Monday morning, Beckham was still down when he arrived at practice. "I couldn't sleep all weekend," he told Klein. "My wife said, 'What's wrong with you?' But I couldn't get it out of my mind."

The mood inside the Galaxy locker room was funereal all week, par for the course on the league's most schizophrenic team. At 6–4–3, L.A. was in first place atop the Western Conference. It had MLS's top two goal-scorers in Donovan (eleven goals in ten games) and Buddle (eight in ten), to say nothing of Beckham, whose four goals and six assists made him a shoo-in choice for the All-Star Game. If anyone was wondering whether Beckham could excel without ten world-class players surrounding him, the answer was now clear: *yes*. Fans were still turning out in great numbers at home and on the road, and the Galaxy's offense was producing some of the most entertaining soccer in league history.

Yet it seemed as if a thundercloud was hanging over the team. Donovan, still bothered by his dustup with Gullit, was also aware of the front-office turmoil with Lalas, Gullit, and Byrne. Like the rest of the players, he had no idea who was in charge. "All these things don't make for a good environment to play in," Donovan said in Washington, D.C., the night before the Galaxy's next game. "Because, one, you don't know who has the power. Now, if we assume that Ruud has the power, giving the wrong people power is a disaster. Or is Terry pulling the strings? What does David know or not know? How much is he involved? Who knows?"

As for the team itself, Donovan was just as worried, even though the Galaxy had gone 4–1–1 in its six previous league games. "Having David and me and even Edson now providing a few moments of brilliance on the field keeps you in games or can win you games, but all that overshadows what the real issues are in the team," Donovan said. "On the field, we have all kinds of defensive issues that never get addressed, and off the field you have the way Ruud treats people. So there's all this shit, but then you look at the standings and everyone goes, 'Oh, they must be great!' And the reality is a lot of times we're just hanging by a thread where something's gonna happen and someone's gonna snap."

CHAPTER 13

GOOD TEAMMATE, BAD CAPTAIN

I f you took your eyes off David Beckham for a single second, you would have missed it. But the act was unmistakable, a breathtaking loss of decorum that caused anyone who witnessed it to turn to the person next to him and say: *Did you just see what I just saw?* On June 29, 2008, during a game at D.C. United before 35,979 fans and a national audience on ABC network television, the world's most famous athlete directed a universally recognized obscene gesture at referee Jair Marrufo.

And nobody—not the game officials, not the league, not ABC—acknowledged it or did anything about it.

On a day so hot and humid that Beckham's trademark long-sleeved jersey looked more like a torture device, Beckham's anger toward the referee had been building almost from the opening whistle. In the fourth minute, Marrufo called a penalty (correctly, though not in Beckham's view) on the Galaxy's Ante Jazic, leading to a 1–0 United advantage. Eleven minutes later, D.C.'s Jaime Moreno scythed down Beckham from behind, a harsh challenge that, when it was deemed only a foul instead of a yellow-card offense, caused Beckham to spike the ball on the turf in disgust. Beckham was upset again six minutes after that when Landon Donovan's equalizing goal was disallowed, the linesman ruling he was offside even though replays suggested otherwise. Though Edson Buddle did score to tie the game at 1–1, Luciano Emilio's thirty-seventh-minute header put United ahead 2–1, rendering Beckham's mood especially foul when he dropped to the ground after contact with D.C.'s Gonzalo Martínez two minutes later.

Sprawled on the RFK Stadium grass, Beckham stared at Marrufo, expecting him to blow his whistle, but instead the referee gave Beckham the two-handed upward motion that says: *You weren't fouled, get up!* Beckham was livid. As United triggered the counterattack, taking the ABC cameras with it, Beckham balled his fists, brought his left hand across to his right biceps, and theatrically thrust his right fist upward at the referee. Beckham's middle finger was not extended, but there was no confusion about the *up yours* gesture or its intended target. If Fox Sports broadcaster Joe Buck had famously called Randy Moss's pantomime of mooning Green Bay Packers fans "a vile and disgusting act," one could only wonder how he would have described Beckham's obscene taunt of a *referee*, a signal that would have sparked a brawl on the streets of cities around the world.

Beckham never received any punishment for the incident, nor was it even mentioned in the media. The message, in turn, was clear. "The golden goose gets a pretty long leash," said Alexi Lalas. "Look, he has a temper on him, and he reacts in a typical English manner where it's not necessarily disrespectful to call somebody a cocksucker or something. And I know how that sounds, but it's just a different way of how words play out, where they don't have the same effect as they do in a Latin type of culture. I think the referees give him the benefit of the doubt, and you know, sometimes you think you're untouchable."

Many forces were in play when it came to Beckham's antagonistic behavior toward game officials. For one thing, he knew full well that he'd have to break an opponent's leg or wrap his hands around a referee's neck to be ejected from an MLS game and miss the next week's match, where his appearance was the Main Event. Yet Beckham's habit of showing up the refs hadn't started in the United States. In Spain, too, Beckham would often gesticulate wildly after what he felt were bad calls, but in La Liga the referees had no trouble striking back, ejecting him from five games in four seasons as Beckham developed a reputation for picking up unnecessary cards. And in February 2009, Beckham extended his record for the number of yellow cards picked up by an England international (seventeen) when he got booked for dissent in a friendly against Spain. If you wanted to play armchair psychologist, you could argue that Beckham felt his anger showed the fans his competitive fire and commitment, and besides, didn't the fans hate the referees too? You could also argue that venting at the zebras in MLS was a more acceptable way of redirecting the frustrations Beckham felt toward his lower-skilled teammates, toward the quality of the league, and toward losing more frequently than he had ever lost in his career at Manchester United and Real Madrid.

Granted, the officiating in MLS *was* often bad—and far below the standards of European soccer. "The problem with our refs isn't that they try to do things maliciously, they just don't understand the game, and for David that's frustrating," Donovan said. "I would assume at some point he's going to lose it. You can see it in almost every game." Donovan was incensed with Marrufo as well in Washington, most of all because the referee didn't eject United's Marcelo Gallardo just before halftime for what Donovan felt was an intentional elbow to his face, unleashing a gusher of a bloody nose. The half ended with both Donovan and Beckham, MLS's two biggest stars, berating Marrufo as they were allowed to walk next to him for nearly the entire length of the field. It was hardly a good advertisement for MLS in one of its two broadcasts of the season on network television. Donovan was still so angry about the Gallardo incident a few weeks later that when the league asked him to speak at the All-Star Game's referee symposium, his first thought was to reply with a six-word e-mail (TELL THEM THEY CAN FUCK OFF) until he reconsidered. For years he had been encouraging at such discussions, saying the standard was improving over time, but this time he passed, knowing he would simply come off as bitter over the Gallardo exchange.

MLS officiating certainly had its problems, but Beckham's constant rants against it—both on the field and in postgame news conferences—would grow tiresome as the season progressed, making it seem as if he felt the Galaxy's manifold problems were somehow the result of a refereeing conspiracy. L.A. got blitzed 4–1 by D.C. United that day not because of Jair Marrufo's calls, but rather because the Galaxy players weren't in good enough condition for the heat and because their typically lax defending allowed for unpressured crosses and easy finishes. "We were god-awful," Lalas said, "at least in the second half. When we're subbing people in the middle of the game because they're dehydrated and exhausted, that's unacceptable to me."

It seemed like every week of the Beckham Experiment brought a new soap opera, and the trip to Washington was no different. When the players gathered at LAX for their outbound flight, Carlos Ruiz was nowhere to be found. "Where's Fish?" several players asked one another, using Ruiz's nickname, wondering if he'd overslept (or might perhaps be spotted at the Guatemala City Hooters). It turned out that Gullit had not included Ruiz on the travel roster even though he was healthy, even though his $460,000 salary was the third highest on the team and had handcuffed the Galaxy from keeping (and signing) more veterans like Chris Albright in the low-six-figure range. "It's sort of strange and disappointing," Chris Klein said. "Carlos is one of the best pure goal-scorers in the league, so to have this situation is really odd." The prevailing opinion among the players was that Gullit wanted to waive or trade both Ruiz and Peter Vagenas, not least because he viewed them as Lalas guys. "Ruud and Alexi are both big personalities, big egos, and they both think they're right all the time," one player said. "And now that Alexi has just been squashed, Ruud has the power to do whatever. My guess is that with both Pete and Fish he knows those are Alexi's guys. I think he's just saying, 'Fuck you, I'll get rid of them.' He's the type of guy who does that, whether it's good or bad or indifferent for the team. Those sort of things shouldn't be happening, and if I'm concerned about my team I'm going, 'What the fuck are we doing?'"

If the Galaxy needed further evidence that holding first place in the West meant nothing against teams from the Eastern Conference, it came on the night of July 4 at the HDC against the New England Revolution. Abel Xavier had been awful defending faster attackers one-on-one all season, but now he was losing mediocre forwards on set pieces, too, as Adam Cristman scored both New England goals off corner kicks in the first half. If set pieces were to soccer what water was to life, as Lalas so often said, the Galaxy was dying of thirst while its opponents went swimming. Amazing but true: Despite having the world's most renowned dead-ball specialist, the Galaxy would fail to score on a free-kick set piece in the last twenty-four games of 2008 after Beckham's goal at Real Salt Lake in the *sixth* game of the season. Part of that was due to Beckham's lack of useful targets, but Beckham himself simply stopped putting dangerous free kicks on goal.

As for Xavier, he continued to be an enigma. His teammates liked him and said they respected his professionalism, but how could Xavier's refusal to play on artificial turf be considered professional behavior? Nor did the Galaxy have any incentive to waive Xavier despite his horrible defending, since his guaranteed contract meant he would count against the salary cap all season. By now, even Lalas (who had signed Xavier in the first place) was calling his artificial-turf phobia "a joke" and proclaiming that help was on the way. After months of scouting by director of soccer Paul Bravo, the Galaxy was about to sign Eduardo Domínguez, a twenty-nine-year-old central defender from the Argentine club Huracán. "Paul has seen this guy play a bunch of times," Lalas said, "and he thinks he's going to be a good player in MLS."

Domínguez couldn't arrive soon enough. The two goals scored by Xavier's man gave New England a 2–1 victory, Beckham's fifth strike of the season (on a deflected second-half volley) notwithstanding. From a financial perspective, though, the game was a holiday business bonanza. MLS had a tradition of drawing big crowds for its Fourth of July games and postmatch fireworks displays, and the Galaxy's gate receipts totaled nearly a million dollars, the most ever for a stand-alone MLS game at the HDC (and far more than the typical gates in some league cities, which could be as low as five figures).

The loss was the Galaxy's third straight game without a win, bringing its record to an even .500 (6–6–3) at the midpoint of the regular season. Eight of the team's next twelve games would be on the road, where a visit from David Beckham's team was always the biggest event of the season. That meant one thing: If the Galaxy ever needed veteran leadership in the locker room, now was the time.

A few days after the Fourth of July loss, Chris Klein arrived in the Galaxy locker room before practice and found an invitation to an event involving David Beckham. Only, this invitation was nothing like the gold-script-on-red-velvet envelopes that the players received for the

Tom Cruise–hosted party welcoming the Beckhams in July 2007. It was simply a request from Beckham (along with printed MapQuest directions) to attend a players-only dinner at Fogo de Chão, a popular Brazilian rodizio steak house in Beverly Hills. In what hardly seemed like a coincidence, Victoria was in Europe with the Beckhams' two youngest sons, and so the Galaxy captain was organizing his first team get-together in Los Angeles. "I'm bringing Brooklyn," Beckham told Klein. "Why don't you bring Carson along?"

You could look at Beckham's idea for the dinner in two ways. On the one hand, it was about time. For the first time in *eleven months* as the Galaxy captain, Beckham was initiating a team gathering in Los Angeles, the kind of players-only bonding ritual that had taken place on a regular basis when he was at Real Madrid. (Granted, those meals had been paid for by the club, but it wasn't as if Beckham was strapped for cash.) On the other hand, Beckham's teammates realized, maybe this was a sign that he was starting to become a real captain, to make a genuine investment—of time, emotions, and maybe even some money—in the software of team chemistry. For the rookies making $12,900, it was also a rare chance for a nice restaurant meal, even though some of them had heard of Beckham's alligator-arms reputation and arrived wondering if he would pick up the check.

On a professional soccer team, the captaincy is not a ceremonial position. Beckham certainly didn't view it that way. He considered his five years as England captain to be his greatest achievement, a status that precious few players had attained, a status that attached itself to wearing the armband on any team, especially in England. That was why Terry Byrne had pushed so hard for Beckham to become the Galaxy captain before his arrival. That was why the British soccer magazine *FourFourTwo* hailed a Beckham cover story in October 2008 with the headline CAPTAIN GALAXY. When Beckham took over the Galaxy armband in August 2007, it seemed like a no-brainer. The guy had captained England for five years, right?

By July 2008, though, the L.A. players had seen enough to realize: Captain Galaxy was a good teammate, but he wasn't much of a captain. There was a clear difference. A good teammate worked hard in practices and games, arrived on time for team events, and interacted with the players in the locker room. Beckham did all those things. "He's a great teammate," said Alan Gordon. "He jokes around when it's time to joke around, but when it's time to get serious he's a competitive person. On the field, I look to him when it's time to get going, and I would hope that by me working hard and throwing my body around that I'm at least giving somebody motivation." When Beckham's presence was required, he was not aloof from his teammates in the way of, say, Terrell Owens. In late May, Gullit had arranged for a team-bonding day at a local go-kart track. The players competed against one another in teams of three, and while Beckham begged off driving—he said he'd hurt his back the last time he had done so—he and Gordon had fun messing with the teams of Galaxy rookies.

"How can I screw them up?" Gordon asked him, holding a big chalkboard while they stood next to the track. "What should I write?"

"Write 'pit now,'" Beckham replied.

The rookies made their pit stops too soon, and sure enough, the team of Gordon, Klein, and Landon Donovan won the race, earning a cold Gatorade shower afterward as Beckham and the rest of the team hooted with laughter. Although those types of events were all too rare during the season, Beckham was there when they happened. A week before the dinner at Fogo de Chão, Cobi Jones had scored the team passes to an early screening of the Batman movie *The Dark Knight*, featuring the final performance of the late actor Heath Ledger. David and Victoria Beckham attended with two of their children, participating just like the other players and their guests.

Yet it was one thing to take part in team events, the Galaxy players felt, but it was another thing to *lead*, to act like a captain, to rally the players during tough times and represent the greater good of the team—with the coach, with the front office—even when it might not have been in the personal interest of the captain himself. In that department, several Galaxy players found Beckham to be surprisingly lacking. Now that Donovan was no longer captain, he noticed several things in particular. For one, on the few times that Gullit gave the players an optional practice day, Beckham would never show up. ("Sometimes you expect that as the captain you should at least come in and show your face," Donovan said.) What's more, with all the secrecy and rumors about Terry Byrne's role, Donovan thought Beckham should address the team about it and clear up any confusion. "But he hasn't had anything to say to anybody," Donovan said, shaking his head. Most of all, Donovan was upset that Beckham had not supported him in front of the team when Gullit had confronted him at halftime of the Kansas City game. "If I'm the captain and he goes after our best player that way, I would have said, 'Hold on a second, that's not right, this guy is doing everything he can,'" Donovan said. But Beckham had sat stone-cold silent.

The questions about Beckham's lack of leadership didn't come just from Donovan, but from other players who liked Beckham personally and shared dinners with him on road trips. Despite Greg Vanney's struggles in Gullit's system—the thirty-four-year-old defender was a bad match for a run-and-gun playing style—Vanney always had probing insights on team dynamics, the kind of thoughtful opinions that made it clear: *This guy gets the American game.* A ten-year MLS veteran who had never failed to reach the playoffs, Vanney had also played four seasons for Bastia in the French first division, and he missed the U.S.'s quarterfinal run in World Cup 2002 only because he was injured in the next-to-last friendly before the tournament. Like Klein, Vanney was always cranking away at his laptop computer on road trips, and he had his post-playing-career plans figured out. He was already leading a prominent youth soccer club in Phoenix, with the hope that he could eventually be a coach in MLS.

Vanney was an original thinker who didn't buy the conventional wisdom that the quality of play in MLS had improved since the league's inception in 1996 (when he was a rookie with the Galaxy). "We as a league have made the decision to forgo experience for potential," Vanney argued. "Because of the salary cap, experienced players who've been in the league six or seven years are less important than young players who can play for less money. The middle-of-the-road guys who understand the league and make quality decisions over ninety minutes are no longer part of it." Vanney reckoned that, on his Galaxy teams from 1998 to 2000, nine of the eleven starters had played for their national teams. "Now it's three, maybe four or five," he said. "We're a league of a couple superstars and potential." To Vanney, MLS had become like a country with the social structure of Brazil or India or South Africa: an upper class and a lower class with next to no middle class. The 2008 Galaxy was the clearest example, and the soccer suffered as a result.

Vanney liked Beckham, enjoyed playing alongside him and spending time with him off the field. But he noticed that as a captain Beckham didn't rally the players during rough stretches and never called team meetings during losing streaks. In fact, nobody else did, either, prompting Vanney to wonder if *he* should fill the leadership void by doing so. Moreover, Vanney wondered if Beckham just didn't understand the concerns of the common Galaxy player who was making a five-figure salary and being whipsawed in and out of the lineup by Gullit each week with no explanation. It was like the famous moment from the 1992 U.S. presidential debates when George H. W. Bush was clueless about the cost of a gallon of milk. Beckham lived in a bubble, a bubble made of Evian.

In a Wal-Mart league like MLS, a lack of empathy didn't work if you were a captain like Beckham. "I think he's a great guy, a great father, and a very good soccer player who's special in the qualities he brings to the field," Vanney said, "but the difficulty for him is that he doesn't live in the same world that we live in. That's not his fault, but it's very difficult for him to relate to and understand the majority of the players on the team, how we're treated by the coach. He's very much a professional, but it's a difficult jump to ask him to relate to everybody else on this team that he's supposed to be leading, to understand when he needs to step up and say, 'It can't be this way, the players need this.' In his position as captain, maybe it's not in his best personal interests to take a stance, but it's a stance he *should* take because he's the leader of our group." Beckham was indeed more vocal representing the players in private meetings with Gullit, Beckham's side argued, but Vanney thought the players needed to be aware of that, since he saw no evidence of any changed behavior by the coach.

Truth be told, Beckham had never been a captain at the club level before. Roy Keane always wore the armband during his days at Manchester United, whereas Raúl had at Real Madrid. Even when Beckham had been the captain for England, there was always debate over whether he was a natural leader, whether his fame detracted from his abilities to direct the team. Yet Sven-Göran Eriksson had stuck with him anyway. If you asked Beckham to describe his leadership style, the phrase he always used was "leading by example," which was fine if you wanted to be a good teammate but wasn't enough to be a successful captain. "I think there's different ways of obviously captaining teams and captaining players," argued Beckham, who considered Keane to be the best captain he had ever played under. "Roy Keane was obviously a shouter. He was a player that was more verbal than me. I'm a bit more quiet, although Roy Keane led by example on the field. That's what I try and do, but in a slightly different way." Perhaps, but as his teammates noticed, the only times when Beckham ever got vocal came when he was berating the referees.

If Beckham wasn't going to provide much leadership in the locker room, then Lalas at least wanted someone to do so. In Lalas's experience, successful teams didn't rely on the coach for leadership; the players took ownership themselves, and there was always at least one figure (not necessarily the captain) who could hold a slacking teammate accountable by pinning him up against the locker-room wall. On the Galaxy's 2002 championship team, that figure had not been Cobi Jones, the captain, but rather Lalas himself. "Somebody needs to take responsibility and take everybody not by the hand, but by the *throat*, and lead them," Lalas said of the 2008 Galaxy. "It has nothing to do with your name or how much you make or if you wear the captain's armband." But nobody filled that role. Donovan had already been forced out of the captaincy. Klein was too nice. Vagenas and Ruiz didn't play enough. Xavier wasn't good enough anymore. And Vanney felt like the team was set up for Beckham and Donovan to assume the leadership roles.

Alan Gordon had his own theory about the problems inside the Galaxy locker room, and it had to do with the makeup of the roster. "We don't have the dickhead veterans," he said. "When I came in: dickheads everywhere. Like, don't even try to get in the front of the line at the airports. Carry the bags. They made sure we knew what to do. You don't talk back. If someone screams at you on the field, you just work harder. That's the way it was, and through all these changes we've lost it." There were just too many rookies and too few experienced players on the Galaxy—almost no middle class. Maybe Gordon could become a dickhead veteran eventually, but not until he was a regular starter.

At least the Beckham-organized dinner at Fogo de Chão was a step in the right direction, his teammates thought. For two and a half hours, the players sat in a private VIP room wolfing down unholy amounts of sirloin and prime rib and lamb. The veterans got to know the younger players a little better, and even Brooklyn Beckham and Carson Klein had a great time. But the most intriguing development of all came when the check arrived at the table. A group including Donovan, Vagenas, and Klein offered to pay, but Captain Galaxy waved them off. "No, I've got it!" Beckham announced.

The veterans smiled. The rookies breathed a sigh of relief. Maybe Beckham was finally starting to pick things up—and not just the dinner checks.

On the morning of July 10, the day of the Galaxy's second showdown of the year with archrival Chivas USA, Alexi Lalas had breakfast with John Harkes, his old friend and U.S. teammate who would be broadcasting the game that night for ESPN2. Lalas never imagined that he'd be cast in the role of the grouchy soccer purist—he was Mr. Entertainment, after all—but he felt that the Galaxy's lack of tactical discipline under Gullit had swung the pendulum too far toward entertainment at the expense of the defensive organization necessary to win games, not to mention championships. Sometimes Gullit's Galaxy would throw as many as six attackers forward, refusing even to pay lip service to defense. No wonder the team's league-leading thirty-three goals on the season was offset by thirty goals allowed, by far the most in MLS. "Watch what happens tonight," Lalas told Harkes. "It'll be entertaining, but from a soccer purist's perspective it will be difficult to watch, and it will be mind-blowing."

And it was, not so much because of the number of goals on the night (two) but because a professional soccer game degenerated into what Lalas derisively (and accurately) called "streetball." Chaos was the theme. Both teams sent waves of attackers forward, but the play was sloppy and amateurish. At one point, Harkes got so frustrated on the ESPN2 broadcast that he called out Gullit for the Galaxy's complete lack of organization—a criticism that no doubt pleased his pal Lalas, even if so little in the rest of the game did.

For the first time all season, Gullit started Beckham in the central midfield instead of on the right. The idea was to pair him with Peter Vagenas, another player with good ball skills, and starve Chivas of possession. Beckham, too, had grown increasingly frustrated over not seeing enough of the ball on the right side, so much so that he had been drifting all over the field again in recent games. As Lalas put it, "there are times when I scratch my head saying we're paying millions of dollars for a centerback." On the one hand, it meant Beckham wasn't hiding—he wanted to do *something*—but the net effect was a negative for the team. Landon Donovan lost count of how many times Beckham had commandeered the ball deep in the Galaxy's own end, giving his teammates time to run downfield, and sent a long Hollywood pass a yard or two short, only for the opponent to start a counterattack against a Galaxy defense that now had five players out of position. By mid-July, Donovan felt like he needed to say something to Beckham about it, but it was a sign of their distant relationship that he did so by *text message*. I know you're frustrated and I know you're trying, Donovan told Beckham, but we need you farther up the field where you're more dangerous. You're the best player out there and you need the ball, but it doesn't help us achieve anything if you're doing other people's jobs.

Beckham's reply was short (it *was* a text message, after all): We just need guys to be better on the field and do a better job. Donovan tried to follow up with Beckham in the locker room the next day—"You understand what I'm saying?"—but Beckham clearly didn't want to talk about it. "It's difficult to know how to approach him with things, to be critical of him," Donovan said, "because he doesn't take it well."

Gullit's Beckham-in-the-center experiment lasted all of one half against Chivas, as the Galaxy midfield kept giving the ball away, one of the turnovers combining with poor defending by Abel Xavier on Ante Razov's fifteenth-minute goal to give Chivas a 1–0 lead. Beckham moved back to the right side in the second half—nominally, at least, since the Galaxy formation had little shape—and L.A. managed a 1–1 tie through Edson Buddle's seventy-second-minute equalizer, courtesy of a marvelous through-ball from Vagenas.

The sudden resurrection of Vagenas (and even Carlos Ruiz, who played thirty-two minutes) stunned some of the Galaxy players, who had seen his exile to the bench and assumed Gullit would trade or waive him from the team. "Pete went from almost never playing to playing every minute and being the guy the coach really relies on now," said Greg Vanney. "Ruud went from not talking to him to being, 'You're my guy.' How does Pete make sense of that huge swing in his head?"

What had happened was simple: Gullit had finally realized he couldn't act like a typical European coach in MLS, couldn't just write off players and bring in waves of new ones, because the league rules didn't allow it. By the time the Galaxy arrived in New York City the following week dragging its four-game winless streak like a ball and chain, Gullit was at his wits' end. "I must say that it has been an enormous challenge," he said. "Because you just can't buy players. You can't do it. All of these rules are so difficult, because you see where you need improvement but you can't do anything about it. You have to deal with what you have." In the ultimate *Moneyball* league, the European way of doing things didn't work. Gullit now understood that achieving success as a coach in MLS was even harder than it was in Europe, if only because of the handcuffs everyone had to wear. "It's much tougher here," he said. "You're not a miracle man. You can't do miracles."

Yet for all of Gullit's issues with American soccer, his most significant conflict was with one of the Galaxy's two *European* players. Gullit and Xavier had been butting heads behind closed doors for weeks, the coach disgusted by Xavier's dreadful play and the player angry that Gullit, he felt, had amassed too much power over the direction of the Galaxy. On July 18, Gullit stunned the team by waiving Xavier, even though his guaranteed $156,000 contract would still count against the salary cap. The conflict had clearly gotten personal, for Gullit's action showed that he felt the team was better off just paying Xavier to go away. Besides, defensive savior Eduardo Domínguez's work visa had cleared, and the Argentine centerback was making his first road trip for the game against the Red Bulls.

There was only one problem: Domínguez was too sick to play. At the end of the bus ride from Manhattan to Giants Stadium for practice on Friday, Donovan was using the bathroom when defender Troy Roberts opened the door. "Hold on a second," Donovan said. "I'm almost done."

"Hey, man," Roberts replied, "I think Eduardo just threw up."

Domínguez thought he had eaten something bad at Starbucks, and he spent the duration of the practice running back and forth to the bathroom. It was, to put it mildly, an inauspicious start. But he wasn't the only player who was sick. So was Beckham. In fact, Beckham threw up repeatedly the night before the game due to a case of food poisoning. When he showed up at the postgame press conference on Saturday after playing the full ninety minutes, Beckham looked ashen, as though he might vomit right in front of the New York media. The result hadn't made him feel much better. Before a crowd of 46,754—some 20,000 fewer than in 2007, but still the largest to see the Galaxy all season—L.A. had gone up 1–0 on a goal by Ruiz, who was making only his second league start of the year. But the Galaxy defense wet the bed again, giving up two unanswered goals before Donovan's late cross from the left side somehow spun off the artificial turf and into the net for a 2–2 tie.

Despite going five games without a victory, the 6–6–5 Galaxy still didn't appear to be in crisis mode, in part because three of those five matches had been ties. Nobody was concerned about missing the MLS playoffs, since even teams with losing records made the postseason. Likewise, none of the behind-the-scenes turmoil had gone public: not the takeover by 19 Entertainment, not Lalas's tensions with Gullit or Donovan's with Beckham, and certainly not the players' dissatisfaction with Gullit over his poor communication, his roll-out-the-balls practices, and his revolving-door doghouse.

That changed in a hurry once the team returned to Los Angeles. Xavier was so angry over being released that he asked to schedule a news conference at the Home Depot Center, only to learn that teams don't usually organize media events so that former players can rip the current coach. So Xavier did the next-best thing. He unloaded a verbal fusillade against Gullit to reporters from the *Los Angeles Daily News*, the *Washington Post*, and Goal.com. Xavier told the *Post* that Gullit "doesn't respect the players, he doesn't communicate with the players. He never wants to listen to the players. It's a bad environment. He doesn't like the players with personality. The players are afraid to speak out because, for most of them, their jobs are not guaranteed. They are afraid of losing their jobs. Look at Carlos Ruiz: One week Ruud Gullit wants to trade him, and the next week he wants to be his best friend. . . . With all the friction between the coach and the players, how can you have a healthy environment?"

Gullit fired right back in the *Daily News*. "It's bad for a player to point the finger at somebody else," he said. "[Xavier] doesn't stay long with many teams. I asked him an interesting question: Can you do what I ask you to do? He couldn't answer that. It's nothing personal, but he is a bad apple."

Xavier obviously had an axe to grind, to say nothing of a temper that could be frightening, and his performance on the field had been miserable. But privately, several Galaxy players rejoiced that someone finally had the *cojones* to call out Gullit in the media, even if Xavier occasionally sounded like a man possessed. Sometimes, though, Xavier revealed a level of insight that Gullit himself could have learned from. "MLS is different from Europe," Xavier told Goal.com. "You need to integrate with the team. You need to be part of the players and listen to what they say. You need to create a group relationship, especially amongst the experienced players, and he doesn't do that." It was hard to know what was more fascinating: that Xavier was talking like an American, not a European, or that he could have issued the exact same complaint about Captain Galaxy, David Beckham.

Nearly everyone inside the Galaxy had a reaction to Xavier's one-man media offensive. Just as Lalas had welcomed (and even encouraged) his friend Harkes's criticism of Gullit on ESPN2, he wasn't complaining about Xavier's outburst either. "I talked to Abel," Lalas said. "I'm never going to tell a player that he shouldn't say what he feels is the truth." Meanwhile, Chris Klein took issue with Xavier's claim that Gullit had too much power in the team. Far too often, Klein asked himself a different question: Who's in charge here? "Who's making the decisions in our club?" Klein wondered. "Is it Tim Leiweke? Is it Alexi Lalas? Is it Paul Bravo? Is it Ruud Gullit? Is it Terry Byrne? If we're fighting amongst ourselves, how is this thing going to be successful? Because we have so much talent here, there's no reason for there to be a power struggle. And it becomes very disappointing when you see that it *is* a power struggle."

Nobody realized that the Galaxy's downward spiral was about to get worse. A lot worse.

Strange things always seemed to happen when the Galaxy traveled to North Texas: the 6–5 Superliga win in 2007; the 5–1 Galaxy victory in May 2008, which cost Dallas coach Steve Morrow his job; and even Adrian Serioux's vicious red-card tackle on Beckham that day, followed by Beckham's uncharacteristic taunting of the crowd. But what took place at Pizza Hut Park on July 27, 2008, was remarkable, a fiasco that unraveled the Beckham Experiment more than any other single game. Three days after Beckham and Donovan had played at the MLS All-Star Game in Toronto, you could tell something wasn't right with the Galaxy from the opening whistle. If anyone had bothered gambling on MLS games, you would have wondered if the Galaxy was on the take. The players couldn't complete simple passes. They didn't make runs away from the ball. The first Galaxy shot on goal didn't come until the sixty-first minute; the first corner kick not until the seventy-second.

Beckham, wearing long sleeves in the 100-degree heat, looked just as bad as his teammates. In the sixth minute, his first free kick, taken from thirty-five yards, sailed over everybody out of bounds. Seven minutes later, Beckham shanked a cross out of play. And then the Dallas goals started pouring in. Kenny Cooper beat Ante Jazic to give Dallas a 1–0 lead in the fifteenth minute, and Cooper struck again two minutes later after Eduardo Domínguez, making his first start, muffed a backpass in the Galaxy's own end. When Dallas forward Dominic Oduro smoked Domínguez in the thirty-sixth minute for a 3–0 lead, you couldn't help but ask what Paul Bravo had seen during his year of scouting the Argentine centerback, whose ineptitude made Abel Xavier look like a defensive stopper. *This* was the help that was on the way?

Then again, the blame for the Galaxy debacle went across the board. Not a single player showed well. By the time Abe Thompson had sealed Dallas's 4–0 victory with a late goal, the only question remaining for MLS watchers was whether the league had ever witnessed a ninety-minute meltdown more complete than the Galaxy's that day. "Probably one of the worst performances in Galaxy history," said Lalas, whose descriptions of *poor* got more inspired each week. "The score is obvious, but more importantly the lack of effort—and not just for parts of the game, but for the *entire* game—was appalling, to say the least. There's an element of everybody had a bad day, but to compound it by what looked like a complete giving-up was difficult to stomach. This is a game where you ask: Who was the least horrible? It was varying degrees of dismal to *we should tear up your contract right now and you should retire.*"

For the second time in 2008, Beckham had endured the ignominy of losing 4–0 in an MLS game. It was baffling: How could a team with two players who would join AC Milan and Bayern Munich on loan after the season (Beckham and Donovan) look so awful against meager MLS opposition? Afterward, Beckham didn't bother with his usual positive spin after a loss. The Galaxy showed "no fight or passion," he said. "We didn't deserve to win," Beckham added. "We didn't play well and didn't start the game well. Our attitude was bad before the game." Perhaps, but Beckham was poor, too, the latest in a run of bad-to-mediocre form that coincided with the Galaxy's six-game winless streak. Unlike the first half of the season, in which Beckham had combined so well with Donovan and Buddle, Beckham's crosses were no longer putting defenders on their heels. He spent more time venturing deep into the Galaxy's own end to find the ball and less time barreling upfield. Even worse, Beckham's fitness appeared suspect: He didn't run with his usual sense of purpose. And his set pieces? Punchless.

"There is no doubt he hasn't played the way he played the first third of the season," Lalas said. "He's had some low games, and that's a problem. We're definitely not getting what we're paying for right now, and it's not just him."

If the Galaxy hadn't been in crisis mode after the tie in New York, it definitely was now. During the reserve game against Dallas, word filtered to the Galaxy players: Tim Leiweke wanted to meet with the team when it returned to Los Angeles, and he wasn't happy. As Leiweke had watched the game on television, his anger rising steadily, he concluded that the players made a conscious decision to quit on Gullit. "You just can't have that," Leiweke said. "Yeah, maybe there's tension or friction, and maybe Ruud was going through a tough transition here, but at the end of the day players get paid to show up no matter who their coach is." After practice that Tuesday, Beckham and the rest of the Galaxy players gathered in an event suite at the HDC. Lalas and Leiweke walked in. "Guys," Lalas said, "you know Tim."

Leiweke did not address the team often, and when he did it was because things were either very good or very bad. In 2005, Leiweke had met with the players after they won the MLS Cup to make good on his promise to give them a luxury suite at the Staples Center for Los Angeles Lakers games if the Galaxy had claimed the championship. This time it was not such a joyous occasion. For the next ten minutes, Leiweke was blunt. He told them that he and Phil Anschutz had never been so embarrassed by a team as by the Galaxy's performance against Dallas. He said it was unacceptable to give up in a game and not to provide 100 percent effort for ninety minutes. It was one thing to lose, Leiweke added, but it seemed like nobody had even cared.

Then Leiweke issued an ultimatum: If the Galaxy didn't turn things around in two weeks, AEG would make major changes to the team. "If you try to make excuses," he said ominously, looking at each player, "then you'll be out the door too."

The players filed out of the room silently. Still, not everyone agreed that their attitudes had been poor (Beckham's opinion) or that they had quit on Gullit (Leiweke's view). Greg Vanney, for one, was adamant that whatever American soccer players may have lacked in the skills department, they never rolled over and gave up. Gullit could ask them to run ten miles, he said, and the players might not be happy but they'd do it. The problem against Dallas, Vanney argued, was that the players experienced the same type of confusion that permeated the Galaxy's front office, only the question for management (Who's in charge?) was replaced by another one for the players (What's my role?). And the blame for that, Vanney believed, lay at the feet of Gullit. "Guys are stepping on the field not 100 percent clear what their role is," Vanney said. "We're like eleven guys all on different pages. If you pulled the eleven starters in separately and asked what the game plan was for today, I'd be shocked if you got eleven of the same answers. I'd be surprised if you got three. When you step on the field, that uncertainty looks terrible."

If Beckham was ever going to earn his captain's armband, the time to hold a team meeting and rally the players was now. But Vanney was floored that Beckham *still* hadn't addressed the locker room, *still* didn't realize that he had an obligation to say something as the captain. Was Beckham checking out on the team? Or was firebrand leadership just not in his nature? "My internal conflict is: Do I say something and bypass David and Landon, or do I pull them into a private discussion and say this needs to be said?" wondered Vanney, who would consider his reluctance to speak up as his biggest regret of the 2008 season. "As players, we need to address each other, get some stuff out there, and get ourselves on the same page." Yet Beckham was frozen, paralyzed by . . . what exactly? Distrust? Anger? Ambivalence? Nobody knew for sure.

The moment that sealed Beckham's "good teammate, bad captain" reputation might have been the moment that Chris Klein started questioning whether Beckham was well-suited for the armband. If you polled MLS teams on the best-liked player in the league, Klein probably would have won the vote. But now he saw Beckham's limitations as a captain firsthand. "I really like David as a person, and I respect him as a man," Klein said, "but it's a different type of leadership that has to go on with all this. Sometimes it's the rah-rah American sports leader that needs to be like, 'All right, guys, come on!' and have a team meeting. It's difficult for a foreign player to do that, especially one in his position, because you don't know what the college kid had to go through, you don't know what it's like to make $12,000 a year. You can't get your mind around that to relate to those guys. It's impossible." Perhaps, but Beckham should have been able to find common ground as a teammate, not least because that was his job as the captain. The more Beckham disengaged from the Galaxy players, the more some of them wondered if his five-year captaincy with England had been as ceremonial as the role of the British royal family.

Then again, maybe some of those American players didn't understand Beckham, didn't understand how important it was to win, didn't understand that losing was not something to be met with a shrug of the shoulders. Was that what happened when you made only $12,900 a year? Was there just not enough incentive to win at all costs? Needing a victory against the lowly San Jose Earthquakes on August 2, the Galaxy fell behind 2–0 in the first half, only to think it had earned a point when Edson Buddle tied the game 2–2 in the seventy-sixth minute. But the Galaxy defense failed again in the ninetieth minute, Steve Cronin allowing yet another rebound that Ryan Cochrane bundled in for a 3–2 San Jose win. It was a brutal goal, a terrible way to lose, and the reeling Galaxy (6–8–5) had now gone seven games and nearly two months without a victory.

Afterward, Beckham was as livid as he had ever been since joining the Galaxy, a mood that didn't carry over to all of his teammates. "He was so angry that I couldn't even speak to him after the game," said one Beckham associate. "He wanted to kill somebody, and other guys on the team are laughing and having a good time. I think that drives him insane." Once again, though, Captain Galaxy chose not to address his teammates, even though the team was in free fall.

By the next day, the news of Leiweke's win-or-else meeting—and his two-week ultimatum—had broken in the papers. Lalas spent the day answering reporters' questions about his job future. The vultures were starting to take flight. "Everyone's kind of circling," Lalas said wearily, the usual energy drained from his voice. "There's a certain sport to the hirings and firings of personnel, and they can smell blood."

CHAPTER 14

"WE'RE THE OWNERS, AND WE'RE GONNA ACT LIKE IT"

August 8, 2008—8/8/08—was supposed to be the luckiest of days, at least in Chinese culture, which revered the number 8 as a symbol of good fortune. The Opening Ceremony of the Beijing Olympics was set to take place on 8/8/08, and the former Olympian Alexi Lalas was planning on watching it at his Manhattan Beach home that night with his wife, Anne, and their two-year-old daughter, Sophie. Any day now, Anne would be giving birth to their first son, who'd be a redhead like his father. They had already picked out a name: Henry.

The call came from Tim Leiweke's office that morning. The boss wanted to meet with Lalas at 4 P.M. at AEG headquarters downtown. As soon as he hung up, Lalas knew exactly what was about to happen. It was a Friday. If there was one cliché that Lalas had learned in the world of business, it was this: You always fired people on a Friday afternoon. "I knew what I was driving into," Lalas said. "I was driving into the gallows." With hours to spare before the 4 P.M. meeting, Lalas got in his teal 1994 Mercedes and started driving. He didn't call anyone, didn't turn on any music. A million thoughts flashed through his mind as he wandered through downtown L.A., Hollywood, and Koreatown on a postcard Southern California afternoon. *Should I go down swinging? Should I tell him what I really think? Should I say I told you so about Gullit?* Lalas could feel his heart racing. He decided that it wasn't worth wasting his breath. He would make a few short points, take it like a man.

Finally, just before 4 P.M., Lalas parked his car in a lot on the south side of downtown. He walked past the AEG-owned Staples Center, past

AEG's $2.5 billion L.A. Live entertainment project, past the Palm restaurant where Leiweke had offered him his first executive's job in 2003. Lalas had fired people before—hell, he'd sacked the man who was now the U.S. national-team coach—and while it was never fun, he knew there were ways to cushion the blow, to show some understanding and compassion for someone who *right then* was experiencing his worst moment as a professional.

Tim Leiweke was not going to cushion the blow.

AEG was a multibillion-dollar empire, a conglomerate that owned sports teams, promoted concerts, and constructed arenas and stadiums in countries around the world. Leiweke was always traveling to London or Dubai or Shanghai, always pushing to build or promote the Next Big Thing, always juggling $100 million projects with the ease of a circus performer. But he didn't have to act like firing the president and general manager of the Los Angeles Galaxy was a trivial matter, decided Lalas, who got the impression from the moment he arrived that Leiweke viewed him as a nuisance in his busy day. Whether you're a first-year intern or a CEO, Lalas thought, what you're told when you're fired will have a lasting impact. And this was what Leiweke told him on 8/8/08 during the Closing Ceremony of Lalas's five-year tenure as an AEG executive:

"This doesn't even rate in the top ten problems I have to deal with right now."

8/8/08 was not a lucky day for a few other people, either. Gullit was out, too, Leiweke told Lalas during their meeting. The Dutchman had decided to resign, although there was no disputing that Leiweke had given him a hard push. When Lalas saw the first draft of the press release announcing his own departure, it avoided saying he was fired and intimated that he was leaving because his contract was set to expire at the end of the season. Lalas called back to demand a change in the wording. "I'm leaving because you *want* me to leave," he said. "I want you to say what the reality is, and that is that I was fired, I was sacked, I was canned, whatever word you want to use for it." Lalas never had any patience for corporate doublespeak, and while he was bitter that the public viewed him as the scapegoat for decisions that he didn't control, there was no shame in being fired, he felt. It happened in sports all the time.

Why Gullit and Lalas were out remained in some dispute, however. At root, the reason was simple: The Galaxy was 6–8–5, had gone seven games and nearly two months without a victory, and appeared to have stopped playing for its coach. But Leiweke refused to admit that hiring Gullit and letting Terry Byrne run the search had been bad decisions. "The mistake we made here was not who we chose or how we chose him," Leiweke said. "The mistake we made here was not being smart enough—and it's my fault—to see inevitably the conflict that was going to come out of this. And it's too bad. Because is Ruud a good coach or not? I think he's a good man. Is Alexi a great president and GM? I think Alexi's a good man, and he's done his country and his team well every-where he's been. They have proven themselves in their ability to under-stand the sport on the pitch. That said, it doesn't mean that everyone's on the same page. And the mistake we made is not getting everybody on the same page."

The players didn't know who was in charge, Leiweke finally realized, and it's a dangerous thing when players start worrying more about the dysfunction of the team than doing their jobs on the field. As for Lalas's firing, Leiweke argued that he wasn't being held accountable for Gullit's failures (since Lalas didn't hire the coach), but rather for his decisions on players over the previous three years, for trading Galaxy veterans like Chris Albright and Kevin Hartman. "Did we make good player-personnel decisions? Obviously not," Leiweke said, ignoring the fact that Frank Yallop (not Lalas) had wanted to trade Hartman to make room for Joe Cannon. "It's been two months since we've won a game. We can sit here and debate it all we want. Those are the facts."

Lalas, however, said Leiweke told him there was another dimension to his firing, one that was far bigger than the Galaxy soccer team: Guil-lotining Lalas would go a long way toward helping Leiweke save the re-lationship between AEG and 19 Entertainment, a partnership that produced tens of millions of dollars each year in the music business. Gullit was 19's handpicked choice, after all, and if Gullit had to go, well, then Lalas—the nemesis of 19 and Gullit, the man Simon Fuller blamed for Gullit's demise—had better go, too. "When the *American Idol* tour goes through the Nokia Theater and all the different venues that AEG owns next fall," Lalas said, pointing to himself, "... *this guy*! Tim knew if he had any chance of salvaging the relationship with 19 he needed to fire me. So it's an eye for an eye. All is fair in love, war, and business!"

In many ways, Lalas's contention rang true: Leiweke admitted that his relationship with 19 was strained over his decision to show Gullit the door. But while the Lalas-for-Gullit, eye-for-an-eye theory made perfect sense—at least to explain the timing of Lalas's firing *on August 8*—there was no reason to believe that Lalas would have kept his job after his contract ran out at the end of the 2008 season. The Galaxy had turned into too much of a debacle during the Beckham Experiment, and whoever replaced Lalas and Gullit needed to have full control over the team's new direction.

That Saturday and Sunday was a rare radio-silent weekend for the Galaxy during the MLS season. There was no game on the schedule, not even a lucrative exhibition match, which was the original plan until Gullit had put a stop to them. Lalas took the occasion to clean out his office at the HDC: the win-loss charts in bars of green, yellow, and red; the containers of Red Vines; and the guitar with the Galaxy logo. The players, meanwhile, remained unaware of the Leiweke-triggered bloodbath. As Chris Klein drove to practice at 8:30 on Monday morning, he argued that another coaching change—the second in nine months—was exactly what the Galaxy *didn't* need. "The organization has to realize that consistency carries the day in this league," Klein said. "If you keep blowing things up, it won't work."

In less than an hour, Klein would find out: The Galaxy was blowing things up again.

As the players arrived in the locker room on Monday morning, they saw a note on the bulletin board announcing a meeting at 9:45 in the lounge. It didn't last long, no more than five minutes. Beckham and the rest of the players took their seats, and Leiweke walked in and announced that Gullit had resigned and Lalas had been fired. He had named Cobi Jones the interim Galaxy coach, and it was now up to Jones and the players to steer the Galaxy to the MLS playoffs, starting with that Thursday's ESPN2 game against Chivas USA. "There are no more excuses," Leiweke told the team, reminding them (not for the first time) that the MLS Cup final was being played at the HDC. "You can't blame the coach or the general manager. This is on *you*."

It would be a stretch to say that the players were surprised. Leiweke had already given them a two-week ultimatum, after all. And while several were hardly sad to see Gullit go (or Lalas, for that matter), they were also embarrassed over their own performance, since coaches aren't usually removed unless a team has serious problems. From a player's perspective, you could view the changes in two ways. On the one hand, the arrival of a new coach brought uncertainty and the need to prove yourself to another boss. On the other hand, it heralded the opportunity to improve what had become a toxic environment under Gullit. Whether that meant solving the leadership issues in the locker room as well was anyone's guess, however.

Donovan, for his part, thought it was about time that Leiweke made a move. In his mind, the Galaxy hadn't been set up to succeed under Gullit and Lalas, and only now was Leiweke taking steps in the right direction. "Alexi's a good guy, but that doesn't mean he's good at his job," Donovan said a day after the Galaxy housecleaning was announced. "This is supposed to be the flagship team in MLS, and he was put in a role where he didn't know what he was doing. Then you had a new coach who didn't know the league or anything about the players. Is that going to help you win?" Then again, given the cloud over the team during the past two months, Donovan didn't see much that made him think the 2008 season was somehow going to turn out well, new coach or not.

What Beckham really thought was a mystery to any of his teammates, who found Captain Galaxy harder to read than ever. Beckham had a future playing poker in Vegas, they thought, for he showed no emotions one way or the other during Leiweke's meeting, and it went without saying that Beckham refrained from calling a team meeting of his own to deal with the biggest news of the season. "I don't think he gives a shit who's the coach or the GM," said one Beckham associate, "but he just can't stand the fact they're not winning." Perhaps, but Beckham's best friend, Terry Byrne, had essentially hired Gullit with Beckham's blessing, and now that move had been deemed a failure after just nine months. Beckham couldn't have been happy about that. "Ruud was [19 Entertainment's] guy," Leiweke told the *Los Angeles Times*, sounding like a man who was pointing fingers, "so Ruud resigning and us accepting that obviously is not a great day for them."

Greg Vanney was curious enough that he stopped Beckham after Leiweke's meeting. "What does Terry think of all this?" Vanney asked.

"They don't really talk to him, either," Beckham replied. Leiweke was treating Byrne the same way he was dealing with Gullit and Lalas.

That was the truth. For the news of the day wasn't just that Gullit and Lalas were leaving the Galaxy, even though they were the only names on the official press release. Although his one-year contract would continue paying him until October, Terry Byrne was being dropped as the Galaxy's paid consultant, too. And while Beckham may not have cared much about Gullit or Lalas, he most certainly did care about his best friend and personal manager. Tim Leiweke wasted little time finding a new head coach, and unlike the decision to name Gullit nine months earlier, 19 Entertainment and Terry Byrne had absolutely nothing to do with the hiring process. Not long before the game against Chivas that Thursday night, Leiweke saw Donovan in the hallway outside the locker room. "I want you to know," Leiweke told him, "we've hired Bruce Arena."

That night Leiweke watched the game at the HDC Stadium Club with Arena, the most accomplished coach in U.S. history, the man who had won five NCAA titles at Virginia, two MLS Cups at D.C. United, and a berth in the 2002 World Cup quarterfinals coaching the United States. Arena couldn't start soon enough. The Galaxy struggled against Chivas, barely salvaging a 2–2 tie on Alan Gordon's injury-time goal. It was L.A.'s eighth straight game without a victory, and only ten matches remained for the 6–8–6 Galaxy to turn things around and capture a berth in the playoffs. To make matters worse, Beckham and Donovan would miss two of the next three games on international duty. Yet Leiweke remained undeterred. "The Galaxy hasn't made the playoffs for a couple years," he said. "Punting on this season is not acceptable."

The man who landed David Beckham for the Los Angeles Galaxy sighed deeply and took a sip from a bottle of Diet Coke. Nineteen months earlier, Tim Leiweke had predicted that "David Beckham will have a greater impact on soccer in America than any athlete has ever had on a sport globally." Leiweke wasn't issuing such bold proclamations anymore. His hands clasped behind his head, Leiweke leaned back on a couch at AEG's headquarters in downtown Los Angeles and put one foot up on the coffee table in front of him. Performing autopsies on a failed coaching hire, to say nothing of the rapidly tanking Beckham Experiment, was not his idea of a fun time.

"It bothers me when we don't do well," Leiweke said, taking another sip of his drink. "It bothers me when we're not living up to potential. It bothers me when we have this kind of dysfunction. The one thing that gives me comfort is for the first time in well over a year I sleep better about the Galaxy. I am 100 percent convinced that if there's a guy that's going to create the right environment for David to succeed here, it's Bruce. That's nothing against Ruud or Frank or anyone else. I just think Bruce is the right guy for the unique situation we have here."

For the second time in a row, Leiweke's coaching hire was an attempt to rectify the failures of the previous regime. In Ruud Gullit, Leiweke had chosen a coach with a world-renowned name and the kind of dominating personality that Frank Yallop had lacked. In Arena, Leiweke had selected a coach who was familiar with all the league's players and knew the complexities of MLS's salary cap, roster limits, and other quirks—all the details, in other words, that Gullit had barely tried to learn. What's more, by naming Arena the head coach *and* general manager, Leiweke had eliminated any confusion over who was in charge of the Galaxy. That meant napalming the entire dysfunctional management structure, including Gullit, Lalas, and, not least, Terry Byrne. "Terry's a good guy, and I value his opinion and like him very much," Leiweke said, "but Bruce is the coach and general manager, and we ended any speculation or any potential conflict that could be created by different opinions. We have *zero* different opinions in the organization today on where this team is headed."

The translation of Leiweke's message to 19 Entertainment was simple enough: *You had your chance, and you screwed it up. Now I'm taking my team back.* The more Leiweke spoke, the more he laid bare not just his defensiveness over having let 19 take over the Galaxy, but also the first signs of his dissatisfaction with David Beckham—a player he had always treated with so much deference that you wondered if Leiweke thought Beckham could walk on water. "I am well aware of the fact there are people that think at the end of the day 19 ran the team because of David," Leiweke said, his voice rising. "David was unaware of the changes that were made with coaching. He was unaware of the new coach. I didn't talk to David. I didn't talk to Terry. I didn't talk to Simon Fuller. This was our decision 100 percent. If they had as much control as people think they did, then why did we do that?"

Leiweke was rolling now, leaning forward in the couch, tap-tap-tapping the table as he spoke. His face was turning red. Not once did he move to loosen the black-and-white striped tie from his starched white collar. The Beckham Experiment was *his* idea, after all, and he did not like to be embarrassed. It didn't matter if Simon Fuller or anyone else at 19 Entertainment was upset or offended by the removal of Ruud Gullit and Terry Byrne. Tim Leiweke needed to act. Their input was no longer needed or desired. "I think what David and his people will tell you is they're probably not a huge fan of mine based on Bruce," Leiweke said. "I didn't ask them. Did they know at the end of the day that we were going to go ahead and Ruud was going to resign and go back to Europe and Alexi was going to be relieved? Yeah. Was that a good day for them? No. Again, are they happy with me? No. Now Simon Fuller and I have a very strong personal relationship. Terry Byrne and I had a friendship. I think we still do, but am I real popular with them as it relates to us owning this team and the decisions we have made [recently]? Absolutely not. But I didn't go back to David and ask his opinion. It's not David's place."

This was an entirely new tone from Leiweke when it came to talking about Beckham, a fascinating reversal of fortune. Long gone were the days of "When David or his people spoke, we obviously listened." In fact, Leiweke was starting to sound like a jilted lover who was now minimizing even the good times in the relationship. When asked how much of the Galaxy's value as a franchise was tied to Beckham, Leiweke's response was surprising: "Some, but not as much as people think. . . .

David has helped, but he's not what drives the value of this team." And when pressed to provide his opinion of Beckham's play for the Galaxy in 2008, Leiweke refused to even say. "Not my job," he argued. "You go ask Bruce that. If I give you an opinion as a fan, people think I'm giving you an opinion as an owner." Needless to say, it was hardly a rousing endorsement.

What made Leiweke's comments so startling was this: Leiweke was fully aware that he was the only person at the Galaxy whose opinions mattered to Beckham. If the relationship between Beckham and Leiweke faltered, there was nothing to keep Beckham with the Galaxy much longer, only a contract that some European club could buy out for the right price should Beckham decide to leave MLS. And there would certainly be suitors. Hadn't Beckham turned down AC Milan to join the Galaxy in the first place? Did Leiweke ever wonder if Beckham might wake up one day and decide the Beckham Experiment was a failure? Did he wonder if Beckham might want to go back to Europe? Leiweke took another sip of his Diet Coke. "Do I worry that ultimately David wakes up and he's not having fun anymore?" he said. "Yeah. A lot."

But Beckham wasn't in charge here, Leiweke wanted to emphasize. *He* was. Too many people thought Leiweke had handed over the keys of the Galaxy to Beckham and his advisers, and it was time to set them straight. "Does the David Beckham Experiment work? I think next year is a really important year for us," Leiweke said. "Really important. Because if we go through a third year like the first two, you know, here's a bigger question: Does David sit around wondering if Tim wakes up one night and says, 'I'm not happy with this anymore'? So we're the owners, and maybe we needed to act like it. We're acting like it now, and if I've made a mistake here, I guess I forgot about that. We haven't forgotten about it. *We're the owners, and we're gonna act like it*."

In the days and weeks after the Massacre of 8/8/08, a vibrant (and entertaining) blame game played out between the parties involved in the Reign of Error over the Beckham Experiment. Naturally, since there were several actors and nobody had ever quite been sure who was in charge, nobody wanted to accept full responsibility for the fiasco, either. It was far easier to point fingers at the other guys, and that was exactly what happened. Still, taking some time to sift through fact and fiction was worth the trouble (and sort of fun). Who won the blame game? Who lost? Was the culprit . . .

Alexi Lalas? As he nursed his battle scars in his Manhattan Beach home and woke up in the middle of the night to attend to his crying infant son, Lalas started gaining some perspective on his two-and-a-half-year tenure as the Galaxy's president and general manager. "I do want people to understand there was much more to the story behind the scenes, but I also don't want to whine and say I got fucked," Lalas said. "I got a great opportunity, and to a certain extent I fucked it up." But only to a certain extent, he thought. In the wake of the 19 takeover and the hiring of Gullit as the coach, Lalas argued that 90 percent of his energy was devoted to the Galaxy's business side. Lalas loved to talk about the Galaxy's financial success, which was indisputable, and his biggest regret (other than not resigning when he got kneecapped in November 2007) was that neither he nor Tim Leiweke had ever publicly defined his diminished role with the Galaxy in 2008. "Because of my background and my name, I am constantly associated with the soccer," Lalas said, "but for the most part I was immersed in the business."

Since the public always thought Lalas had hired Gullit—instead of counseling Leiweke and Terry Byrne against him—Lalas probably did receive too much blame for the 2008 Galaxy debacle. But he *had* been in charge in 2006 and 2007, years in which he gutted the Galaxy roster and was responsible for poor trades, bad signings, and a salary-cap miasma of epic proportions. "An example of mismanagement of a roster and the salary cap would be the New York Knicks in the NBA," Bruce Arena would say, implicitly comparing Lalas to Isiah Thomas. "I'm not saying we're the New York Knicks, but we're sure giving it a shot." Then there were Lalas's tensions with Gullit and 19 Entertainment. It was safe to presume that David Beckham and Simon Fuller would not be sending Lalas Christmas cards in 2008. "19 looks at me as being against Ruud from the start and therefore integral in his downfall," Lalas said, "but the reality is that Ruud, through the Galaxy and ultimately through me, was given every opportunity to succeed. We bent over backwards. We changed our business philosophy for this coach." Maybe, but what Lalas saw as protecting the Galaxy—observing practices, speaking privately to players, reporting concerns to Leiweke—gave the impression that he was working against Gullit, no matter how many shortcuts the Dutchman took.

In the end, it came down to this: Lalas had a three-year contract, and in those three years the Galaxy never once made the playoffs.

Ruud Gullit? On the day after his "resignation" was announced, Gullit briefly addressed the Galaxy players, thanking them and issuing vague complaints about not receiving enough support from management. Gullit never spoke with any media who covered the team after his departure, but he did return to the HDC two months later as part of a promotion for an automobile company. "The rules and all the things that they do here are so different from what we do in Europe," he told Reuters, blaming the structure of MLS for his problems. "Everything that looks logical, they do in a different way." In his nine months with the Galaxy, Gullit proved to be as bad a fit in MLS as any of the previous failures among big-name foreign coaches, only he had a higher salary than all of them. In the eyes of many players, Gullit didn't put in the hours to learn what he needed to know, and by the time he understood the magnitude of the task it was too late. Worse, he lost the support of the players in a way that Frank Yallop never had. Then again, Gullit's issues with the players and the league structure could have been predicted (and *were*, in fact) the moment he took over the team. Could he really be blamed for the Galaxy's half-baked decision to hire him?

Terry Byrne and 19 Entertainment? It was hard to know what David Beckham's best friend and personal manager thought of his experience as a paid consultant for the Galaxy, since Byrne refused all interview requests before and after Leiweke told him his services were no longer needed. But sources on Beckham's side contended that

Leiweke had (1) put an unfair burden on Byrne, asking him to find a coach for a league he didn't know, (2) pulled the plug on Gullit too soon, and (3) blamed 19 Entertainment in the media when Gullit didn't work out. What's more, they added, Gullit had been at the bottom of Byrne's list of recommendations, and the Galaxy would have fared much better had it broken the bank for, say, José Mourinho or Fabio Capello. Ultimately, they argued, it was Leiweke who should be responsible for making the final calls on the Galaxy's important decisions and it was the Galaxy's fault (mainly Lalas's) for not building a better team to support Beckham once he arrived.

In truth, there was no chance that Mourinho or Capello would have accepted the job, and while Lalas deserved plenty of blame, it was hypocritical for 19 to say he screwed up the team when Byrne had taken over the most important move of 2008 (finding the new coach) and botched it completely. Nor was Byrne ever truly held accountable for his paid position at the Galaxy, since neither the team nor 19 ever made it public. It takes a lot of chutzpah to seize control without responsibility, but Simon Fuller's 19 Entertainment had made behind-the-scenes power plays an art form. "That they became such a part of how the Galaxy functions is disgraceful," Lalas argued. "I don't necessarily blame them, because you give an inch, they take a mile. It's their responsibility to get as much control as possible, and we gave that to them. That's disappointing, and I am complicit to a certain extent."

David Beckham? The jury was still out on Beckham, considering the season wasn't over yet, and Captain Galaxy himself didn't point any fingers, at least not publicly. (Besides, he had handlers to do that for him.) But how much of the Galaxy's predicament was Beckham's fault? Certainly the Galaxy was a deeply flawed team before and after Beckham had arrived, but the takeover by 19 Entertainment had been a failure, and the people of 19 and Terry Byrne worked for Beckham. On the field, Beckham had been magnificent during the first 40 percent of the MLS season, but his performance had tailed off dramatically during the Galaxy's free fall. What's more, as had been the case on every one of Beckham's teams—Manchester

United, Real Madrid, England—he was not the best player on the Galaxy, either.

"Let him be the captain, you be the star," Lalas had told Landon Donovan in 2007. Donovan had done both. He was still leading the league in goals, and he had hoped that Beckham would be a good captain. But like the Galaxy's other players, Donovan was perplexed by the way Beckham had disengaged from his leadership role during the Galaxy's winless streak, not once calling a team meeting or explaining Terry Byrne's role with the Galaxy. "It's disappointing, candidly, because you just want to see a heartbeat, a pulse," Donovan said. "Not that he doesn't care, but it's hard when he's not showing it on a daily basis to people." Donovan said he thought all the time about convening the team himself, but that was supposed to be Beckham's role as captain, and he felt that 75 percent of the players—the rookies, the foreigners, and the veterans who didn't want to listen to him—wouldn't digest what he had to tell them anyway.

Donovan was hardly alone in wondering why Captain Galaxy had gone AWOL. The Galaxy players' verdict on Beckham was in: *good teammate, bad captain.* "The players don't see a lot of that leadership he may be able to claim he puts out there," Greg Vanney said. "A lot of us don't see much of what he's doing."

Tim Leiweke? It was safe to say that the *Sports Business Journal*'s Sports Executive of the Year would not be winning back-to-back awards. Depending on when you spoke to him, Leiweke could sound contrite and accept a measure of responsibility for the Galaxy's mess, or he could also sound like the most active finger-pointer of all. "We've made mistakes," he'd say in one breath, "and what gives us some comfort here is we're at least acknowledging we've made some mistakes, so let's fix it." But then, in another breath, Leiweke would blame the Galaxy players ("Unfortunately, you can't fire twenty-two players."), Alexi Lalas ("If you look at our personnel decisions, can you blame AEG for that?"), Ruud Gullit ("With Ruud it was a difficult transition for him and a difficult transition for us."), 19 Entertainment for recommending Gullit in the first place ("Did they have input? Yes, one hundred percent, they had a lot of input."), and MLS's restrictive rules and salary cap ("Are we penalized for going out and taking the risk we took on David? I think we are.").

In some ways, it was hard to criticize Leiweke. He wanted to make MLS one of the best leagues in the world, and more than any other owner he was willing to spend the money to do it. If Leiweke had his way, MLS's salary cap would be a lot higher, the star power would be a lot brighter, and the soccer would be far more exciting across the board. He was a dreamer who did not hesitate to proclaim that the United States was going to win a World Cup. If you were an American soccer fan, these were impulses to admire, not to denigrate. But Leiweke was also too stubborn to admit that you couldn't build a global SuperClub the way MLS was structured, that re-creating top-level European soccer in a heavily salary-capped league just wasn't possible yet. As for the Galaxy's struggles, it was Leiweke who created the dysfunctional management structure that left players and executives wondering who was in charge of the team. And it was Leiweke who, despite knowing the miserable history of big-name foreign coaches in MLS, let Terry Byrne handpick a big-name European coach.

Now it finally appeared that Leiweke had learned at least one lesson. He had landed Bruce Arena. He was buying American, David Beckham's preferences be damned.

CHAPTER 15

THE GALAXY DEATH RATTLE

David Beckham always said he admired the in-your-face honesty of New Yorkers, but whether he'd embrace that quality in a Gotham-born coach was an entirely different proposition. "You can accuse me of a lot of different things," said Bruce Arena, a fifty-six-year-old Long Island–bred wise guy who counted Howard Stern as one of his greatest inspirations, "but I am more honest than anyone I come across." It was an honesty that could amuse, instruct, or outrage, an honesty that had won him friends and enemies, an honesty that (combined with his runaway success) had made Arena the biggest personality in U.S. soccer during the heady days before the 2006 World Cup.

Winning comparisons with legendary American coaches from Vince Lombardi to Bill Parcells to Phil Jackson, Arena entered Germany 2006 as the longest-serving manager in the thirty-two-team field, the mastermind who in nearly eight years on the job had brought the U.S. to the 2002 World Cup quarterfinals and an eyebrow-raising No. 4 ranking in the world. Then it all fell apart. Arena's Yanks managed only a tie and two losses at the 2006 World Cup, and a month later he was out of a job. He took over the New York Red Bulls that summer and lasted barely more than one season before alienating his bosses and leaving the team under mutual agreement. Now Arena was seeking to prove with the Galaxy that he still had the magic touch. "Anyone in sports wants to show you can compete with the best," he said. "I want to prove we can build a good team here."

How Beckham would react to Arena was anyone's guess. On the one hand, Arena's short-but-intense practices and exhaustive game preparation would likely be traits that Beckham would appreciate. But would

Beckham have any lingering resentment over being shut out of Arena's hiring process? Would Beckham respect a U.S. coach who'd have the *co-jones* to tell him things he might not want to hear? Would Beckham respond to Arena's American style of communication, which called for frequent (and often informal) chats with the captain? And perhaps most intriguingly, would Beckham trust Arena, knowing the coach had close ties with Donovan, whose relationship with Beckham had grown even icier during the Galaxy's nosedive?

After barely speaking to Gullit, Donovan was suddenly back on the inside with the Galaxy's head coach, just as he had been with Frank Yallop. Arena had given Donovan his first chance with the national team in 2000, had trusted him enough to make him a starter as a twenty-year-old at the 2002 World Cup. Donovan felt an enormous sense of gratitude toward Arena, as well as pangs of regret over the way Arena lost his job after the U.S.'s first-round exit in Germany four years later. "We had a lot of success together, but I didn't do him any favors in 2006," Donovan said, "so you always feel a little bit guilty if a coach gets let go. But we've always had a great relationship." In fact, during a period when Arena could have been bitter over Donovan's no-show in '06, the coach had written him occasional e-mails offering his congratulations and thanks. It was almost as if Arena suspected that someday they might be working together again.

The ground is constantly shifting in world soccer, however, and on the day after Arena took the Galaxy job, Donovan learned that Arena had received a call from his friend Jürgen Klinsmann, who was now the coach at the German giant Bayern Munich. Klinsmann, a longtime California resident, was interested in acquiring Donovan. When they spoke over the phone a few days later, Klinsmann explained to Donovan that he wanted him to join the team, but the Bayern board of directors preferred arranging a loan instead of an outright purchase, given the perception that Donovan had already failed twice in Germany. While Donovan said he understood, he also knew that a loan during the MLS season was impossible. Klinsmann agreed to table the discussions until after the Galaxy's season, but for Donovan the interest was flattering, even if it meant possibly returning to the site of his career's lowest moments.

"Part of me says, 'Oh God, it's Germany,'" Donovan admitted, "but the reality is that I was too young, I wasn't ready as a player and probably not as a person. And Munich's a great city. Jürgen's there, and you can never overestimate the value of a coach wanting you. Plus it's a direct flight for Bianca. The more I thought of it, *it's Bayern Munich*. It's one of the best clubs in the world. It's Champions League. That's as good as it gets from that standpoint." It was worth asking, though: How much had Beckham's arrival and the Galaxy's dysfunction pushed Donovan toward wanting to leave for Europe? Chris Klein, for one, had no doubt. "A *lot*," he argued. Donovan himself wouldn't go quite that far. "It may have something to do with it," he allowed, adding that the main reason was his personal transformation and his feeling that he wanted to challenge himself while he was nearing the height of his powers.

For Arena, the potential of losing his best player in 2009 was one more variable in what figured to be a monumental turnaround process. The new coach was already putting together a lengthy report for Leiweke outlining what needed to be done, from acquiring allocation money to freeing up cap space to overhauling the Galaxy's youth-development program, the better to provide low-priced talent to offset the team's expensive stars. In the short term, though, Arena transformed the Galaxy's practices and game preparations. Gone were Gullit's endless eleven-on-eleven scrimmages in training, replaced by skills work, improved fitness sessions, and actual instruction for the rookies. Gone were Gullit's vague-to-nonexistent scouting reports, replaced by detailed breakdowns of opposing teams. Gone was the mass confusion over defensive organization and the players' roles, replaced by increased communication with the coaching staff and one another. And gone were Gullit's laissez-faire work habits, replaced by long days from Arena and his assistants, who encouraged players to visit them in their offices.

The change in the team's mood under Arena was palpable, whether you talked to Donovan ("the level of detail is night and day"), Greg Vanney ("the drama in our locker room has died down"), or Alan Gordon ("Bruce is one hundred percent prepared, and I don't think we were five percent prepared with Ruud"). Beckham's own impressions would have to wait, however, since he would miss Arena's first week (and two of his first three Galaxy games) on national-team duty. With only ten matches left and an uphill climb to qualify for the playoffs, the pressure was only increasing on a team that hadn't won a game in more than two months. "At the end of the day, the Beckham Experiment on the field looks like a little bit of a farce if this team doesn't find a way to be successful," Vanney said. "And there is no waiting-till-next-year type of stuff. It's something that has to happen *now*."

For all the improvements inside the locker room, this was still the same Galaxy team, the same group of players whose confidence had been shattered, and the weeks without a victory kept passing by with the numbing regularity of the news on Wall Street, which was enduring its worst crash since the Great Depression. MLS's decision to play on FIFA international dates certainly didn't help. Missing Beckham and Donovan, L.A. lost 1–0 to Chicago on August 21 in Arena's home debut, extending the Galaxy's winless streak to nine. In one bit of good news, though, Arena signed left-sided midfielder Eddie Lewis, a veteran U.S. international who could fill the void that had existed ever since Gullit's fiasco with Celestine Babayaro. The hope was that Lewis, regarded as the best crosser of the ball in America, would provide some long-sought width to the Galaxy's attack and a balance to Beckham's threat on the right side.

Of course, that required Beckham to be physically *present*, an increasingly rare proposition as his focus turned elsewhere during the MLS stretch run. Beckham was gunning for Bobby Moore's all-time caps record for England field players (108), and he hit 103 in a friendly on August 20 against the Czech Republic. But Beckham not only didn't try to play for the Galaxy the next day (as he had in 2007), he didn't even return to Los Angeles immediately, flying instead to Beijing so that he could represent London's 2012 Olympics delegation at the Closing Ceremony. (His task was to kick a ball from the top of a double-decker bus on the stadium floor.) The side trip didn't cause Beckham to miss any additional Galaxy games—he finished his global circumnavigation by landing at LAX on Monday morning and headed straight to practice—but it did spark a *Rashomon*-style debate. On the one hand, the elective trip added thousands of miles to the fatigued Beckham's already punishing travel schedule while the Galaxy was still in free fall. "David flies halfway around the world so he can go out there and drop-kick a ball into the crowd," said Donovan, "but he's our captain and we're going through a shitstorm with a team that hasn't won a game in two months. I'm like, 'Where are your priorities?'"

MLS executives saw Beckham's appearance before a global audience of one billion as valuable publicity for the league, however, and other Galaxy players had no problem with Beckham's trip. "We had the weekend off anyway," Vanney noted.

What Beckham and the Galaxy needed more than anything was a victory. It was hard to measure the psychological effect of so much losing on Beckham, but his frustrations on the field (with his teammates and the referees) were plain to see. "I don't think I've ever gone nine games without a win," Beckham said before L.A.'s game at New England that week, and he was right. Before his U.S. arrival, a Beckham team had never gone more than *five* straight league games without a victory during his thirteen-year career at Manchester United and Real Madrid. In his thirteen months with the Galaxy, Beckham's teams had already posted winless streaks of seven league games in 2007 and nine (and counting) in 2008. "You have to stay confident," Beckham said, sounding for a moment like a captain, "and you have to keep the players up for the fight and up for playing games, because when you do go through a tough time it's all about sticking together as a team."

In that regard, the Galaxy's comeback from a 1–0 deficit against New England on August 30 was a positive step. Though Beckham was largely ineffective, showing signs of growing fatigue, Donovan scored two marvelous goals on either side of halftime off through-balls from Peter Vagenas and Eddie Lewis to give the Galaxy a 2–1 lead. "You'd better start defending me or I'll get three!" Donovan screamed at the Revolution's hulking hardman Shalrie Joseph. If Donovan had been looking for Beckham to show a pulse, he certainly did when he ran fifty yards to bear-hug Donovan after the goal.

The Galaxy outplayed New England on the night, but just when it appeared that L.A. was headed for its first victory in two and a half months, Joseph broke through the defense and scored the equalizer for the 2–2 tie. The winless streak was now ten, though even Beckham sounded a note of encouragement about Arena's new regime. "This last week has been a week of training hard and doing things that we should be doing," Beckham said afterward, "and tonight is the first step of getting us back on the right road. . . . As a team we stuck together, and we haven't had that for a few months."

But two more World Cup qualifiers for Beckham and Donovan led to two more steps backward for the Galaxy. A 2–2 tie at home with Real Salt Lake on September 6 (without either player in attendance) ran the winless streak to eleven, and both stars acted like they were in different time zones during the Galaxy's next match in Kansas City on September 13. Beckham had played six minutes for England in its 4–1 win at Croatia three days earlier, while Donovan had gone ninety minutes in the U.S.'s 3–0 win against Trinidad and Tobago. In an awful game played in the rain on a field scarred with American football lines, Beckham did his best impression of a potted plant on Kansas City's second goal, watching from five yards away as his man, Davy Arnaud, blasted a long-range screamer to seal the Wizards' 2–0 victory.

Three months after the Galaxy's last triumph, the winless streak that started with Beckham's choked ninetieth-minute sitter against Columbus on June 21 had now reached an astonishing twelve games, the longest in team history. Beckham's American adventure had officially turned into a nightmare on the field, the soccer equivalent of *Ishtar* or the Spruce Goose.

At the news conference afterward, Beckham appeared in a drab-blue Galaxy sweatshirt, not the designer attire that he usually wore to such events. "Good evening—or afternoon," he said. "I'm not sure what it is at the moment."

Beckham often led off his press gatherings that way. It was funny at first, the wry lament of the ultimate jet-setter. But as the Galaxy's losses piled up like dead fish after a red tide, it became the tired refrain of a man who hadn't learned his lesson. No matter how many times Beckham argued that his travel itinerary wouldn't keep him from playing (and playing well) for club and country, it was obvious now that he was spreading himself too thin. (The trip to China now appeared especially unnecessary.) Beckham wasn't running at full speed and hadn't for several games. When asked if his legs felt sluggish, Beckham nodded. "Yeah, a little bit, I must admit," he said, even though he'd played a total of only sixteen minutes in the two England games. "After the Croatia game, I flew back to London and from London to Los Angeles. I got back yesterday, I think, or the day before, then traveled early morning on Friday, which obviously is tough because I'm trying to also get myself back into the time zone. I didn't sleep well last night. That didn't add to it, but that didn't help obviously with the game today."

Beckham may have liked to think he was indestructible, but in fact he was a thirty-three-year-old soccer player whose powers of recovery were nowhere near what they had been a decade earlier. His ill-fated attempt to play ninety-minute games on consecutive days in London and Los Angeles in 2007 should have been a sign to tone things down, yet Beckham continued trying to meet the demands of being a global brand. It showed.

At the airport after the Kansas City game, Arena told Beckham to take off the next three days. "Go home," the coach said. "We don't want to see you until Wednesday." Arena felt it was important to get off on the right foot with Beckham, and he made a point of announcing publicly (while sitting next to Beckham at a news conference) that he had made a mistake by playing a fatigued Beckham and Donovan in Kansas City so soon after their national-team games. It was clear that Arena's comments were directed less at the media than at Beckham, the coach showing a willingness to accept blame that he hoped Beckham would appreciate—and perhaps return the favor with his effort in the upcoming must-win games.

Even after his three-day break, Beckham struggled in his first practice back that Wednesday. His play was still off, and the coaching staff thought he looked unnecessarily angry with his teammates. Arena pulled Beckham aside at one point. "Are you doing all right?" he asked.

"Yeah," Beckham replied. "I'm still just a little tired."

The next day's training session went better. Dave Sarachan, Arena's top assistant, walked up alongside Beckham afterward. Sarachan knew the league, having been an MLS head coach himself for four and a half years with Chicago, which he led to the 2003 title game. The adjustment to coaching a global icon had been strange at first—Sarachan's daughter had a poster of Beckham on her bedroom wall—but the new staff had sought to earn Beckham's respect by treating him like any other player. Still, Sarachan had observed Beckham's interactions with his teammates on the field and in the locker room, and he felt Beckham could do more as the team's captain. "You need someone to look up to, someone who's going to address issues," Sarachan said. "Everybody seems to be kind of dancing around a lot of stuff. I think we'd like him to engage more. Maybe he needs to feel really invested in this project and team."

Yet Beckham hadn't completely checked out, Sarachan thought. Not based on their exchange that day on the practice field.

"How're you doin'?" Sarachan asked.

"Good," Beckham said, taking a swig of water.

"We've gotta win this Saturday."

"Yeah, I know. We just need one win to get things going. We can still make the playoffs."

It was true. In any European league, the Galaxy—with a twelve-game winless streak and a league-worst 6–10–8 record—would be fighting for its life in a relegation battle at the bottom of the standings. But in the Alice-in-Wonderland world of MLS, L.A. was still only four points out of a playoff spot with six games remaining. Anything was still possible, even a championship.

Of all the bizarre pregame presentations the Galaxy could have arranged, making David Beckham shake hands with a *Star Wars* storm trooper before the match against D.C. United on September 20 might have been at the top of the list. But any Hollywood mirth was extinguished seventy-one seconds after the opening whistle when the Galaxy gave up its quickest goal of the season on a post-corner-kick scramble in the box to go down 1–0. The boos from the home crowd rained down in torrents, and Landon Donovan turned to see Captain Galaxy directing a look of disgust at his teammates.

Donovan shook his head. Not again. He wondered if Beckham was even going to try for the rest of the game. "David!" he yelled. "Let's go, dude! We've gotta get on with it!" Donovan had grown weary of what he viewed as Beckham's sulking and diminished effort, not least because he was earning so much money and wearing the captain's armband. "I would assume he'd admit he's not been very good for a long stretch now," Donovan said that week. "For people who know soccer, they know the reason he makes the money and he gets the attention is not necessarily based on soccer. He's a good player, but he's not the guy where you're going to say, 'Lead us, take us to the promised land.'"

On this night, at least, that player was Donovan. His first goal came in the twenty-first minute, tying the game 1–1 on a world-class finish at full speed on a pass from Chris Klein. Donovan's second goal was even better: a twenty-two-yard missile from the left side twelve minutes later, in which he created his own space for the shot like a basketball point guard. (As it happened, an NBA point guard, Tony Parker, was watching the game from Beckham's box.) Just before halftime, Alan Gordon made it 3–1 with a classic Gordon strike, a mishit ball that he aimed for the far post but somehow squeezed between the goalkeeper and the near post for his fifth goal of the season. ("You can tell me in ten years whether you were going far post or near post," Arena would joke during that week's video session with the team.) Reserve Galaxy goalkeeper Josh Wicks gifted United a goal early in the second half by misplaying a routine cross, but Donovan had two more blasts of brilliance left. On a Galaxy counterattack in the eighty-first minute, Donovan stopped on a dime in the United box and lifted a delicate lob pass over the defense to Peter Vagenas, who side-volleyed the finish: 4–2. Donovan finally sealed his hat trick and the 5–2 victory in injury time, breaking past the United defense for his third goal of the night and his league-leading nineteenth of the season.

The Galaxy's epic twelve-match winless streak was over, the result of one player taking over the game and releasing the full potential of his talents. Just as striking, Beckham had been a complete nonfactor, playing no role in any of the Galaxy's five goals. His only positive contribution was earning a dubious second-half red card on United's Marc Burch that Beckham himself disputed after Burch's ordinary foul had caused Beckham to fall into the advertising boards. At times, it seemed as if Beckham focused nearly all of his energies on venting at the referee and linesmen, even at the expense of rallying his teammates and playing the game. For his part, Beckham was convinced that he was a better player when he was angry. "I think I am," he argued. "People always say to me, 'Shouldn't that part come out of your game?' And I've always said it's the way I am, the way I play. I'm passionate, and sometimes it's too much, but it's something I can't control . . . I hate losing. So the last few months have been tough, and it's very frustrating. But it's something that is in me, and it will never go now."

Donovan, meanwhile, felt his nineteen goals and nine assists gave him the leeway to question Beckham's lackluster performance, his priorities, and his penchant for showing up the referees. Donovan wished more journalists would press Beckham. "Why would someone not ask David: 'Are you concerned that the only time you seem to care or get emotional is when the referee makes a bad call? What are you doing?'" Donovan said. "In England they'd be *killing* him." The Galaxy had followed the recipe for fostering Donovan's resentment to perfection. Violating one of the cardinal rules of professional sports, the team had brought in a new player (Beckham) on a higher salary than the best player (Donovan), and the new guy hadn't been better himself. Compounding the problem, the Galaxy had lost games with spectacular regularity during the Beckham Era. Nor did it help that Donovan felt the team had forced him to give up the captaincy, only for Beckham to be a feckless leader.

Donovan vowed that he didn't hold a personal animus toward Beckham, that he didn't care what Beckham did on his own time away from the team. But the American was honest about feeling slighted during the Beckham Experiment, not least because Donovan had far and away been the Galaxy's top player in 2008. "I'd be lying if I said that as a proud person, as a proud athlete, that it doesn't hurt when you kind of get overlooked," Donovan said. "What I do want people to appreciate is that I really care and bleed for the team, and I hope some of that rubs off on David, too." From the start, Donovan insisted, he'd had issues with Beckham only when he felt the Englishman wasn't helping the Galaxy. "But there have been numerous times this year when he's hurt us on the field," Donovan said.

By now, the Galaxy's two biggest stars hardly spoke to each other, their distance even greater than the one between their giant banners looming over the southern corners of the HDC. And so Donovan had taken to observing Beckham, looking for details that might explain his mood, his unwillingness to trust, to share, to explain the secrecy that shrouded him and the role of 19 Entertainment with the Galaxy. Donovan knew that Arena's arrival had coincided with the ouster of Terry Byrne, and he wondered if what he viewed as Beckham's sulking and petulance was connected to that departure, or if perhaps it was simply the result of so much losing on the field. Donovan certainly noticed one change. When Gullit was the coach, Beckham had lingered in the locker room after practices, receiving massages and ice baths and even hanging around to eat and chat with his teammates sometimes. "But since Bruce has been here," Donovan said, "David has consistently been the last person to show up almost every day and the absolute first person gone from training every day. . . . By the time I have ice on my knee and talk to reporters and get downstairs, he's dressed and leaving. And I'm like, *Jesus Christ . . .*"

In Beckham's defense, he wasn't skipping practices or arriving late, and not all of his teammates noticed what Donovan was seeing. Greg Vanney didn't think Beckham was disgruntled, but he did believe there were a Beckham camp and a Donovan camp among the players, the result less of any obvious tensions than of a natural competition inside any team that had two focal points. On the other hand, Chris Klein agreed with Donovan that Beckham *had* changed in his demeanor toward the Galaxy players. Klein had picked up on Beckham's last-to-arrive/first-to-leave practice habits, and he couldn't remember a single time that Beckham had stayed after training to work on free-kick set pieces with his teammates, even though the Galaxy hadn't scored on one since early May. "I've definitely seen a shift of him being concerned with 'Is this team winning?' to getting caps with England," Klein said. "Now that he's involved with that, the most important thing to him seems to be to get the caps record, and that just doesn't register for us."

For Klein, Beckham's distance from his teammates owed largely to his difficulty relating with them, due in equal measures to his shy personality, his rarefied tax bracket, and his foreign nationality. When Beckham was following the Lakers, Klein felt, the players could engage him in the banter that was typical in any healthy locker room by talking about NBA basketball. But since the NBA Finals had ended in June,

Beckham had shied away from the other topics that dominated locker-room discussion. The 2008 U.S. presidential election was a constant talking point—Klein, a vociferous Republican, loved instigating locker-room debates—but Beckham had always professed his disdain for politics, refusing even to vote in British elections. Likewise, the Galaxy locker room had not one but two fantasy football leagues once the NFL season started, but Beckham had no interest in American football and never joined in the trash-talking sessions on Mondays.

"As our country's best player, Landon does an amazing job with that," Klein said. "He loves sports and football and college stuff, and it's the best way for him to engage with a developmental player. It makes him real to other guys. I think that's what people crave: a teammate that's real and they can count on, who will have them to your house and do those types of things." Other big-money foreign stars in MLS did that. New York's Juan Pablo Ángel, a Colombian who had played in England and Argentina, invited nearly all of his Red Bulls teammates over to his house for dinner during the 2008 season, maintaining that it helped improve team chemistry if they saw him as an ordinary human being.

The only time Beckham's teammates saw his house that season was when they opened *People* magazine.

No matter how many times it happened, you still couldn't get used to the idea of David Beckham staying in the same charmless hotels as the rest of us mortals. The Chicago Fire's stadium, Toyota Park, was located in Bridgeview, Illinois, a gritty industrial suburb light-years removed from Michigan Avenue and the city's tonier precincts. As a result, the league-mandated road hotel for visiting MLS teams was a nondescript Marriott housed in the Midway Hotel Center, a collection of equally dreary hotels (Fairfield Inn, Hilton Garden Inn, Courtyard by Marriott) a short drive away from Chicago's Midway Airport. It was not the safest part of town. For two nights, Beckham and the Galaxy stayed in a neighborhood composed of dimly lit bodegas, boarded-up car-repair shops, used-car dealerships, and a railway yard.

"I'm not much for team walks," Bruce Arena cracked to his players the day before the game, "but if you guys want to get out and walk around tomorrow, I would probably take a security guard with me." The coach was only half joking, his concern not so much over rabid fans as armed assailants.

As MLS contests go, it was a big game: a nationally televised showdown on ESPN2 in a sold-out stadium featuring the league's two marquee draws—Beckham and Chicago's Cuauhtémoc Blanco, a Mexican national hero—with postseason implications. Remarkably, the Galaxy was only two points out of a playoff spot with five games to play. Three of those would be on the road against some of MLS's top teams: Chicago, Columbus, and Houston. Some of the league's heaviest hitters were on hand, including ESPN honcho John Skipper, the man who'd bet on Americans paying attention to soccer on TV, and MLS commissioner Don Garber.

In nine years on the job, Garber, a former NFL executive, had presided over MLS's slow but steady growth. Since the league's low point in early 2002, when the demise of franchises in Tampa Bay and the Miami area reduced the total number of teams to ten, Garber had guided MLS through a transformation. By 2008, the league had modest national television contracts with four networks, to say nothing of fourteen teams, eight of them playing in soccer-specific stadiums. Continued expansion was projected to add four more teams (and up to six more stadiums) by 2011. Garber certainly deserved the lion's share of the credit, having crafted a promising long-term strategy while uniting the league's disparate owners, attracting new ones, creating a side business to promote lucrative non-MLS games in America (including European club exhibitions and Mexican national-team games), and pitting expansion-candidate cities against one another to increase the demand for joining MLS.

Garber had grown to enjoy the sport he promoted, but he was a marketing man at heart and he did not hesitate to spin the media when it suited his needs. Despite the Galaxy's failures on the field, Garber argued that the Beckham Experiment had been a rousing success from his perspective, if only for the reason that it had made millions of people (in the United States and around the world) aware of MLS's existence. During his family's 2008 vacation in the mountains of western China,

Garber noted, their guide not only knew of Beckham but asked how he was performing for the Los Angeles Galaxy. Still, if you pressed Garber to explain how Beckham had been successful *after* signing his contract and arriving in Los Angeles—in other words, everything since his introduction on July 13, 2007—he had a hard time building his argument beyond attendance figures and jersey sales.

"It would be a shame after all of the success that this has been off the field that this team couldn't have gotten it together on the field, and ultimately this whole experience might not turn out to be as positive as it could have been," Garber finally allowed. "But it's part of the process that we've been going through for the last thirteen years. It's not easy. You've got to learn from your experiences, even if you make some mistakes. It's going to be part of what makes us better, and that's the reality of being in an emerging sport in this country. We all at some point might look back at it and say, 'Wow, wouldn't it have been cool if it was different?' But maybe we'll make decisions differently as a result of this experience, and that'll help us become what we want to be."

But the Galaxy wouldn't improve overnight, as it showed against Chicago that night. Eddie Lewis scored against the run of play to take a 1–1 tie into halftime, but the Galaxy defense crumbled during a two-minute stretch early in the second half. Reserve goalkeeper Josh Wicks, who seemed to cost the Galaxy a goal a game during his relief spell for the injured Steve Cronin, made a fatal mistake by coming off his line and allowing Blanco to score in the fifty-seventh minute. And two minutes later, Chris Rolfe put the game out of reach with his second goal, all that Chicago needed in a 3–1 victory. The final minutes provided a special kind of agony for the Galaxy as Donovan blasted a sitter over the crossbar and Beckham reached the limits of his patience in yet another ineffective performance. In the eighty-sixth minute, Beckham drove a corner kick onto the forehead of an unmarked Sean Franklin in the box, only for Franklin to nod the ball straight down at his feet. Exasperated, Beckham shook his head violently and threw his arms up in the air. "We're running out of games now," he mumbled afterward, adding later that his team had shown "no character" and "no fight."

Beckham rediscovered his smile the next day in time for a joint appearance with Victoria at Macy's in New York City to launch their new his-and-hers Signature fragrances in America. Hundreds of admirers crowded the department store, though you would have had a hard time finding anyone who could have named the result of the previous night's game or the Galaxy's place in the MLS standings. Maybe it was just as well. L.A. was now five points out of a playoff spot with four games to play, and Arena told the team it probably needed ten points (three wins and a tie) to have any chance of surviving into the postseason. Even worse, the Galaxy's next game was at Columbus, the best team in the league, on October 4.

In a sign of how woeful the Galaxy's goalkeeping had become, Arena started third-string keeper Josh Saunders in the most important game of the season, even though Saunders had never even played a minute in the league. Before a sold-out crowd dressed in black T-shirts for a promotional "Black Out," the Galaxy failed to manage even a single dangerous chance on goal. Donovan couldn't get any service. Beckham continued his run of poor form. And the Galaxy defense, despite playing better than it had in weeks, let its guard down in the last five minutes of the first half, long enough for Alejandro Moreno to head home the game's only goal. The Crew's 1–0 victory was especially satisfying for Moreno, an L.A. castoff, and for Columbus coach Sigi Schmid, whose firing by the Galaxy in 2004 had started the long downward spiral that now found the Galaxy at its lowest point in franchise history.

In a fifteen-game stretch—exactly half of the MLS regular season— David Beckham's Los Angeles Galaxy had won a grand total of once. With Toronto's victory that night, the Galaxy now had the lowest point total in the league. If you were on the ground with the team, it was hard to grasp how spectacular the failure had been in 2008, not least because the losses had become so commonplace, inducing a sort of stultifying numbness in anyone who bothered to watch game after game of terrible soccer. If the Galaxy were a racehorse, it would have been euthanized long before now. And yet you learned more about a person from how he responded to failure than to success. The Galaxy's epic misery had provided a unique laboratory, a chance to observe which players were truly serious when they talked about such rock-ribbed athletic values as "commitment" and "character" and "leadership."

Now we knew: David Beckham, circa 2008, was not one of them. In the face of more losing than he had ever endured in his career, Beckham's effort declined. His attentions wandered. His fire surfaced sporadically, but only then toward the game officials. His leadership, never robust to begin with, flickered and disappeared as he grew more distant from his teammates. He was hardly the only figure at fault, but he was the highest-compensated, and to absolve him from any responsibility—by blaming his skill-poor teammates or the Galaxy's front-office mess or the rules of MLS—was to ignore the evidence on and off the field. What's more, Beckham's first-half yellow card against Columbus, earned with a rash tackle from behind on Robbie Rogers, meant he had accumulated too many and would be suspended for his next MLS game. Although the Galaxy had three matches left, Beckham would miss the following week's game on international duty and the one after that serving his suspension.

The Galaxy was not yet mathematically eliminated from the playoffs, and L.A. extended its stay of execution on October 12 by beating Colorado 3–2 at home, Donovan coming on as a substitute the day after playing for the U.S. in a World Cup qualifier. The Galaxy still had a heartbeat, however faint, heading into a game it had to win on October 18 in Houston to stay alive. Beckham's England game had taken place three days earlier, and though he was suspended, Captain Galaxy could have traveled with the team to Texas in a show of leadership and support. That was what Peter Vagenas did, even though he couldn't play in the game due to injury.

Instead, Beckham stayed in England. On Thursday, he launched a new endorsement campaign for a food product. On Friday, he and Victoria went out to dinner in London with Geri Halliwell, the former Ginger Spice, and her husband.

On Saturday, as the Galaxy was losing 3–0 in Houston to sound the death knell of the most underachieving season in American soccer history, its captain, David Beckham, was hundreds of miles away in Los Angeles, having just arrived by plane from London. Why he couldn't have flown to Houston instead was a mystery.

CHAPTER 16

NEW BEGINNINGS?

On October 22, three days before the Galaxy's meaningless last game of the 2008 season, David Beckham was once again the first player to leave the field at the end of practice. A half-dozen journalists had gathered like cattle behind a yellow rope at the edge of the grass, and they now proceeded to lob questions at Beckham as he exited through a gate twenty yards away.

"David, the Milan deal! Do you have any comment on the Milan deal?"

Captain Galaxy did not respond, but something strange happened as soon as he reached the gate. Standing there was Ryan Maxfield, Beckham's personal assistant, essentially a glorified babysitter for the Beckhams' three sons. A parking lot and about 150 yards of public space separated Beckham from the HDC and the Galaxy locker room. Perhaps he feared the media would pursue him the whole way. Perhaps he was angry that news of his clandestine loan talks with the Italian giant AC Milan had leaked in the European media that day. But the moment he reached the gate, Beckham took off running, his soccer cleats *clack-clack-clack*ing on the asphalt like the clops of a Clydesdale.

It was, quite possibly, Beckham's most enthusiastic run in months.

Beckham *clack-clack*ed across the parking lot. His gofer ran in hot pursuit behind him, like a dog chasing a ball. And nobody else followed. The scene was more than a little undignified, the world's most famous athlete literally running away from a handful of media who had no desire to pursue him. It was like a bad *Benny Hill* sketch; the only things missing were a jaunty sound track and a bimbo with bad teeth.

The hacks might have chuckled, but the news was no laughing matter for the Galaxy, which had plenty to fear if Beckham was now signaling his intentions for a premature exit from MLS. For months team-mates and coaches had worried and wondered: What if Beckham woke up one morning and decided he wanted to go back to Europe? It was no coincidence that AC Milan, the team Beckham would have joined in 2007 had he not signed with Los Angeles, was his destination. What's more, while Beckham had trained with England's Arsenal during the previous MLS off-season, there were no concerns that he might want to leave the Galaxy at that point. Beckham had a house near London, he needed to stay in shape for national-team duty, and he never actually played for the Gunners during his stint there. This was different. Beckham did not own a house in Italy, and Milan officials were saying that Beckham would be suiting up in Serie A games for the famed Rossoneri.

Worst of all, the development completely blindsided Galaxy offi-cials. In a move that reeked of arrogance, Terry Byrne had initiated loan discussions with Milan on his own, neglecting to inform the team that owned Beckham's contract. "The first I heard about it was today," ad-mitted Galaxy coach Bruce Arena a few minutes after Beckham had fled from the media. That wasn't all that Arena and his staff didn't know. Dave Sarachan, Arena's top assistant, wore a look of stunned surprise on his face that week when he found out—from me—that Beckham had an opt-out clause in his contract that would allow him to walk away from the Galaxy as a free agent after the 2009 season (not after the 2011 sea-son, as Beckham, MLS, and the Galaxy had always claimed publicly). The new Galaxy coaches were learning what Landon Donovan had fig-ured out long ago: The aura of secrecy surrounding Beckham and 19 caused you not only to distrust Beckham and his handlers but to form your own conclusions about what might *really* be going on.

"The conspiracy theory is: How many weeks or months has this [loan] been in the works?" Sarachan said. "What's the true motivation behind this? Based on David's comments to Bruce and I, his main goal is to stay fit and play in a big club that keeps him on the front burner for England. But is there more to it? Are they going to buy him? It's all spec-ulation."

Sarachan didn't think Beckham had checked out on the Galaxy, but the coaches knew that their captain was deeply frustrated. After one late-season practice in which Beckham had struggled, Arena challenged him in a meeting in his office. "Do you think if you were at Manchester United you would have had a practice like that?" Arena asked.

"Maybe not," Beckham replied. "But when you have better players..."

Arena didn't want to hear Beckham's complaints, however. He had observed Beckham for weeks by now, and the coach was frank with his star. "Look, what do you want your legacy to be?" he asked. "We're here to get this right, and in order to get this right we need leadership. And in order to get the proper leadership, we need to make sure we hold everyone accountable." Arena said he wanted Beckham to be a more active captain, to put his arm around a rookie like Mike Muñoz when he screwed up, to communicate more openly with the Galaxy coaches. "You're the captain," Arena told Beckham. "We *want* to hear from you. We *want* you to come in." But there was more. Arena and Sarachan told Beckham he wasn't as fit as he needed to be, the result of his fatigue and too much travel, not all of it mandatory (the China trip in particular). Beckham needed to make a conscious decision to cut back.

"I think he's better than what he's shown," Sarachan said, "but all the travel plus the lack of fitness has caught up to him at this moment. I think he's frustrated by that, actually. You can't lie to yourself. I think he's a pretty honest guy when it comes to what got him where he is, other than just crossing and serving balls. He was a grafter, a worker. I think he realizes he's not at that level now, and the message from Bruce and I is, 'Look, let's get that part better. And by that, you, David, have to now back off some things.'" But it was one thing for Beckham to *say* he'd cut down on his travel and be a better captain. It was another to do those things. The coaches realized they were catching him at the low point of the Beckham Experiment, that his fortunes with the Galaxy could go nowhere but up—unless the Milan loan meant Beckham and 19 were now trying to dissolve the relationship completely.

There was another sore spot that the Galaxy coaches hadn't brought up yet with Beckham: his obviously tense relationship with Donovan. If the team was going to succeed, its two biggest stars couldn't continue acting as though they were countries that had suspended diplomatic relations. "Is the town big enough for both of them? Can they coexist?" Sarachan asked. "We'd heard all these things. I'm a big believer that I've got to see it for myself. And I think it's been a little edgy the last few weeks."

In fact, Donovan was angrier than ever with Beckham, and the latest media circus with Milan was the final straw.

Over a lunch of lamb pizza and a peach salad at Petros, a stylish Greek restaurant in Manhattan Beach, America's finest soccer player took a sip of Pinot Grigio and exhaled deeply. It was Thursday, twenty-four hours after the news of David Beckham's loan move to Milan had broken, and Landon Donovan was enjoying the Galaxy's day off from practice. Well, *enjoying* perhaps wasn't the right word, for Donovan was miserable. The Galaxy's awful season hadn't even ended yet, and now all the talk was about Beckham's possible departure. Donovan himself was convinced that Captain Galaxy had already vanished in spirit weeks earlier. "My sense is that David's clearly frustrated, that he's unhappy, and honestly that he thinks it's a joke," said Donovan, who was about to clinch the MLS goal-scoring title. "I also kind of feel taken for granted as a team. I don't see dedication or commitment to this team, and that's troubling."

The longer Donovan had been around Beckham, the more he asked himself: *Who is this guy?* Why is he so secretive, so unwilling to share the most basic of information? It was impossible to trust a teammate who was so guarded. Donovan had tried to have a conversation with Beckham the day before, but he'd gotten nowhere.

"So you're going to Milan?" Donovan said.

"We'll see," Beckham replied. "I've got to stay fit somehow during the off-season."

"It's a nice city, right?"

"Some people say it is, but I don't know."

And that was it. Their lockers were side by side, but they might as well have been a million miles apart.

No, Donovan decided, Beckham communicated far more clearly with his actions than with his words. Donovan still couldn't fathom why Beckham had stayed in England for nearly three days after his

national-team game the previous week, had refrained from even traveling to Houston to support his teammates in the most important game
of the year. It didn't matter if Beckham was suspended or not, Donovan
thought, didn't matter if he'd been given permission by the Galaxy. *He
was the captain of the team.* When Donovan had asked Bruce Arena
where Beckham was, the coach replied that he didn't know. Donovan
was amazed. How could the man in charge not know where Beckham
was? "What other team in the world is that allowed to happen on?"
Donovan asked. "It's ridiculous." If Beckham wasn't going to show up
for a team event until five days after his England game, Donovan
thought, he should be fined or suspended just like any other player who
pulled something like that.

"All that we care about at a minimum is that he committed himself
to us, to our team," Donovan said. "As time has gone on, that has not
proven to be the case in many ways—on the field, off the field. Does the
fact that he earns that much money come into it? Yeah. If someone's
paying you more than anybody in the league, more than *double* anybody
in the league, the least we expect is that you show up to every game
whether you're suspended or not. Show up and train hard. Show up and
play hard. Maybe he's not a leader, maybe he's not a captain, maybe he's
not good at those things. Fair enough. But at a minimum you should
show up and bust your ass every day. And that hasn't happened, and
that's why it's frustrating. And I don't think that's too much for us to expect. I really don't. Especially when he's brought all this on us."

Donovan had wanted the Beckham Experiment to work, had
wanted the Englishman's arrival to be mutually beneficial for everyone,
and there was no reason in his mind that it still couldn't be successful on
the field in 2009. But not if Beckham continued acting the way he had
during the last half of 2008. "When David first came, I believed David
was committed to what he was doing," Donovan said. "He cared. He
wanted to do well. He wanted the team and the league to do well. Somewhere along the way—and it coincides with Ruud being let go, clearly in
my mind—I think that's when in his head he just flipped a switch and
said, 'Uh-uh, I'm not doing it anymore.' And that's become very evident."

The analogy that Donovan used was to compare Beckham to an attractive girl you'd met as a teenager. For the first week you talked to her on the phone every night for three hours, and your initial impressions were that she was a perfect match. But anybody can seem amazing to you over a short period of time, Donovan thought. "Over time, the true colors come out," Donovan said, "and then you find out through good times and bad times what people are all about." Beckham was like the hot girl in high school that you couldn't stop thinking about for a week, only to learn she had some serious baggage that made a thriving long-term relationship impossible.

By now, in fact, Donovan no longer agreed with the "good teammate, bad captain" verdict that so many other Galaxy players had reached on Beckham. At the end of the 2008 season, Donovan was convinced that Beckham wasn't even a good teammate anymore. "He's not," Donovan said. "He's not shown that. I can't think of another guy where I'd say he wasn't a good teammate, he didn't give everything through all this, he didn't still care. But with [Beckham] I'm not so sure. I'd say no, he wasn't committed. And there's nobody else I could think of that I would say that about."

The most fascinating aspect of Donovan's verbal barrage against Beckham was the manner in which he delivered it. He sounded like a scientist revealing the findings of an experiment. There was no frothing-at-the-mouth anger, no violent finger-wagging, not even a raised voice. This was hardly an adrenaline-fueled postgame rant in the way of, say, Abel Xavier. On a gorgeous weekday afternoon in Manhattan Beach, Donovan was literally consuming wine and cheese as he spoke. ("Do you like lamb? You should try a bite. It's absolutely delicious.") At one point his wife, Bianca, called, and they had a short discussion about their dogs. The way Donovan saw it, he was just sharing his conclusions about a coworker, one who happened to be David Beckham. "If I'm being honest," he explained, "it's not perception without facts."

Here was another fact: Donovan didn't know what came next. He might be leaving the Galaxy after the season, perhaps for Bayern Munich, and who knows what might come of Beckham's loan to Milan? But he did know that things would have to change if both he and Beckham were back in 2009. "Let's say he does stay here three more years," Donovan said. "I'm not going to spend the next three years of my life, if

I'm here, doing it this way. This is fucking miserable. I don't want to have soccer be this way in my life." What could he do? "That's my issue too. I've got to confront it somehow, either confront him or do something about it, because otherwise this pattern's not changing. At some point he is who he is. Not that it's always bad, but you've got to deal with it the right way, and we haven't. If that's the way he's going to be, fine, then hold him accountable. Don't play him. Bench him. Just say: 'We're not going to play you, we don't think you're committed.'"

As angry as he sounded, though, Donovan had been just as upset at the end of 2007 with Alexi Lalas, and they had reached a détente in a long heart-to-heart after the season. Donovan still thought his relationship with Beckham could be saved, but only if Beckham returned to being the kind of teammate who at least *wanted* to play for the Galaxy on the day after an England game. Then again, it might have been a moot point anyway, given the Milan news. Donovan wasn't stupid. He knew how the soccer world worked, knew how Beckham and 19 Entertainment operated, too. "It could be that it's just a loan now," Donovan said, "but in two months he could play a few games and go, 'Shit, I want to stay here.'"

On a perfect fall afternoon in Manhattan Beach, Alexi Lalas was holding court over Newcastles, burgers, and fries at the Hangar, the famously seedy dive bar on Aviation Boulevard. His getup was classic Lalas: a pink bandanna wrapped around his head, a four-day-old red beard, a plain white V-neck T-shirt, and the same giant white sunglasses made famous in the iconic grunge-era photograph of Kurt Cobain. "It was just so *predictable* that these two big stars would fight," Lalas said when he learned of Donovan's strafing of Beckham. "How clichéd can you get? At the end of the day, they didn't respect each other, they didn't like each other, they didn't talk to each other. And they merely tolerated each other on the field."

Lalas shook his head and laughed. He was in his element again, the corporate nonsense of the AEG boardroom fading behind him in life's rearview mirror. The Ramones song "I Wanna Be Sedated" was playing on the old-fashioned jukebox. Released from the shackles of his old job,

Lalas felt liberated now, free to assume the role of the Beckham Experiment's voice of truth.

Beckham's fitness? "There's this whole eternal talking point about how he never wants to get out of shape and he's constantly worried about staying in shape," Lalas said. "It's all bullshit, okay? He's not in shape now, and he hasn't done the things he needs to do in order to get in shape."

Beckham's Milan loan? "It would not surprise me if this was the beginning of the extrication of David from the Galaxy. It would also be the best thing that could possibly happen to the Galaxy as a team. David's a great player, but it's gotten to the point right now where some things just don't work out. The Galaxy has gotten so far away from what it used to be in terms of being a soccer team that the only way for the balance to tip back is to make some massive and major change in terms of the team you have out there."

Beckham's handlers? "Look, I regret some things, and I thoroughly regret letting the Galaxy be co-opted and letting outside influences infiltrate and spread like a disease. I certainly sounded the alarm, but what I should have done is said, 'This doesn't happen, and if it does happen I'm outta here.' And I didn't have the balls to do that."

Lalas did nothing if not practice what he preached. If soccer was going to make it in America, he felt, the sport needed entertainers, figures who could generate headlines on and off the field. And if that meant issuing wildly extreme viewpoints and taking on the Establishment's sacred cows—hello, David Beckham!—then so be it.

Besides, Lalas was not merely spewing venom at Beckham. As the man who'd once been in charge of the Galaxy's business operations, Lalas knew better than anyone that Beckham had been a tremendously successful signing for the bottom lines of the Galaxy and of Major League Soccer. Only Beckham could have brought so much attention to American soccer, Lalas argued, and in that regard his impact would be a positive one lasting well beyond his time in MLS. But at the same time, Lalas felt that far too many people—Beckham's handlers most of all—were allowing Beckham to act like an overgrown child, allowing him to shirk his own responsibility for the Galaxy's debacle in 2008. And Lalas was going to make sure that didn't happen.

"David Beckham is thirty-three years old," Lalas said. "He has a wife. He has a bunch of kids. He's not a child. He's a man. He, his people, and people all over the world have held him up as this pillar of professionalism, as this leader, as this man of impeccable character and personality, so much so that he has been the captain of England and the captain—after he demanded to be—of the Los Angeles Galaxy. So I'm not going to sit here and coddle him. As we all share in this responsibility for what has happened, and as he looks to take that next leap and go over to AC Milan, just remember to take a look in the mirror and recognize that as the captain, as the leader, as David Beckham, you share a huge responsibility. And I don't see any of that. You can't just wash your hands of this."

Lalas was rolling now. Few topics got him going like the question of whether Beckham himself was responsible for the actions of his advisers after they took over the Galaxy and installed their own handpicked coach. Could Beckham plausibly claim deniability over what his handlers had wrought? Not a chance, Lalas argued. "You can't have it both ways," Lalas said. "Either you knew what was going on the entire time, and therefore shame on you because you're a narcissistic, manipulative person, or you've lived in a bubble and you're completely naïve and childish, and you've confirmed the worst of what people think about you in that you have absolutely no clue what's going on. That's the person we want to lead the Galaxy? Shame on me and shame on all of us for letting that happen."

Not everyone with the Galaxy was furious with Beckham. Alan Gordon just wanted to know what was going on. While the players were stretching in the locker room before practice one morning that week, the ESPN news crawl flashed by on the television in front of them: REPORTS: DAVID BECKHAM TO GO ON LOAN TO AC MILAN.

In typical fashion, Gordon didn't hold back. "So are you going to Milan or what?" he blurted to Beckham. "What's the deal?"

"Nothing's finalized," Beckham replied. "But I'd like to stay fit for England."

Gordon had zero interest in participating in the tension-filled intrigue surrounding, say, Beckham and Donovan. "That's so far above my head," he said. "I'm just trying to make this team, so I don't give a shit. I don't care who's fighting with who as long as I'm on the team and have a salary."

In fact, Gordon's staying power was remarkable. Arena had become the fourth Galaxy coach to not just keep Gordon on the roster but to put him on the field as well. One reason was his play: Despite his raw skills, Gordon's five goals and seven assists in 2008 were impressive, especially for a player who often came off the bench. Another reason was his bargain salary: $72,504 was peanuts for a No. 3 forward who could hold his own in MLS.

Amid the growing uncertainty over which Galaxy players might not return in 2009—perhaps not even Beckham or Donovan—one of the few who appeared likely to come back was Gordon. "I want you here next year," Arena told him that week. Still, Gordon knew nothing was ever certain in MLS, especially when other teams saw his bargain value and contacted the Galaxy all the time about potential trades for him.

Even though Gordon was one of Beckham's closest friends on the team, Gordon was also a powerful symbol—a sort of anti-Beckham, if you will, when it came to MLS. Alan Gordon represented all the American players who were the league's backbone, who competed for the love of the game, who kept MLS climbing slowly upward without the glitz or the hype associated with David Beckham. Like so many other MLS players, Gordon had been willing to put up with a $30,870 salary for four long years, with the insecurity of a non-guaranteed contract, with risky cortisone shots in his foot, with having to take a second job as a youth coach and borrow $1,800 from his girlfriend just to move into a new apartment. Yet Gordon always gave his maximum effort, even if it was rarely aesthetically dazzling, and by the start of the 2009 season (after Seattle's selection of Peter Vagenas in the expansion draft) he would be the longest-tenured player on the Galaxy roster.

For all the abuse that Gordon took from Galaxy fans for his sometimes artless displays on the field, they had no idea how much value he brought to the locker room. But even some of the supporters' opinions were changing as the season ended and they considered Gordon's overall production. Five goals and seven assists for a player earning just

$72,500 was nothing to lampoon. Consider the post by a Galaxy fan on a Bigsoccer.com thread titled *Does Alan Gordon Get a Bad Rap?*: "The Flash represents for all those fools that don't have the natural skills but give the max and try hard anyway. People say he sucks . . . people say the same thing about MLS, but he and the MLS press on, unperturbed by the negativity. The Flash is a symbol of all that is good in U.S. soccer."

Nearly three full days passed after David Beckham's bizarre parking-lot sprint from reporters before he finally addressed the public about the loan to Milan. Beckham and 19 Entertainment were upset that AC Milan vice president Adriano Galliani had leaked the news to the European press, but in truth they had no one to blame but themselves. Terry Byrne certainly could have waited until after the MLS season to ask Galliani if Milan would be open to a loan—Byrne was a fool if he thought a European club director would keep a lid on such information with the media. As usual, 19 wanted to control the public message as much as possible, and so, instead of making Beckham available to CNN or the *Los Angeles Times* for his first public comments, his handlers taped their own "interview" with Beckham on Friday and posted it online that night.

On the plus side, the video allowed 19 to define the content of the tone-setting first news reports without subjecting Beckham to pesky questions from actual journalists. But there was a downside, too. Much like the "town meetings" of George W. Bush to which only Bush supporters were invited, the 19-produced video created the impression that Beckham not only had something to hide but that a slick PR machine was controlling everything, from the questions to the answers. What's more, Beckham's dyspeptic demeanor made him look like the dead-eyed (and potentially sedated) subject of a hostage video. Judging from his monotone voice, you half expected him to say: "My captors are treating me well."

Of all the softball questions he was fed by 19, the most important was whether the loan meant he was leaving MLS and the Galaxy. Beckham was unequivocal. "No, it doesn't mean that I'm leaving the States," he said. "I'm still very committed to my role, obviously, as a Galaxy player. I came to the Galaxy to actually win trophies, so I want to do that, and also I'm very committed to my role as the MLS ambassador as well." Beckham made the exact same promise the next morning when he addressed his Galaxy teammates at the HDC. Remarkably, it was the first time that Captain Galaxy had stood up and addressed a team meeting since the start of L.A.'s free fall more than four months earlier.

Only then did Beckham emerge from the Galaxy's locker room into the tunnel of the HDC, where some sixty print and television reporters were waiting for him. In different circumstances, the scene might have been pleasant. Beckham's two younger sons, Romeo and Cruz, were knocking around a soccer ball on the concrete surface in their Manchester United uniforms. But Beckham himself wore a sour expression, his arms folded, his gray T-shirt combining with the gray cinder-block backdrop to create the impression that he was facing a firing squad. The first question was straightforward enough: Would this be his last game with the Galaxy? "No, it won't be," Beckham said. "I've made that clear. I've said that my commitment is still to the Galaxy, and that's not changed."

Beckham was so adamant about being committed to the Galaxy that it didn't seem worthwhile to question him any further on the point, but it did make sense to ask why his loan to Milan would be good for the Galaxy. So I did. "You've talked about how important the preseason is for any team, you're the captain of this team, it's at its lowest point in the history of the club, you'd miss the preseason if things work out this way—"

Beckham interrupted. He faced me, a look of surprise on his face. "It's at the lowest point right now?" he asked.

"Yeah," I replied.

It was a revealing moment, one of Beckham's few unscripted actions the entire week, and it showed several things. For starters, Beckham did care what people thought of him. But if he was unaware of his team's historically dire state, he really did live in a bubble. The Galaxy had now missed the playoffs three years in a row after qualifying every season during its first ten years of existence. It was about to finish tied for the lowest point total of any team in Major League Soccer's 2008 season. In a sporting sense, the Galaxy had turned into the laughingstock of American soccer.

I continued the question. "—and potentially risk an injury like you had at the end of your Madrid stay. I can understand how this move is good for you, but how could it be good for the Galaxy?" Beckham never tried to answer the question—he hit the same talking points about not wanting to take off four months—and was generally snippy with other reporters too. "You always ask negative questions," he said to one who asked if Beckham thought he was in Serie A form. It was an entirely legitimate question considering Beckham's swoon during the second half of 2008. After producing five goals and six assists in the Galaxy's first fifteen games, Beckham had added zero goals and just four assists in the final fifteen games. At the end of the season, he would deservedly be left off the list of MLS's Best XI. Donovan, the only Galaxy player who made the MLS team, also won L.A.'s MVP, Humanitarian, and Golden Boot awards. (Beckham, for his part, was shut out.)

At least Beckham was honest enough to admit that he hadn't been in top form. "It's been on and off," Beckham said of his performance during the second half of the season. "You know, I think I've had good games, I've had bad games. We've scored a lot of goals, we've conceded a lot of goals." He sounded like a man who was ready for the MLS season to be over, ready to experience top-level soccer again in Milan and come back rejuvenated to the Galaxy in 2009. "I've not enjoyed not having success with the Galaxy," Beckham said, "but I've enjoyed having success with the sport in this country so far. But the other thing that I will enjoy more is winning trophies with the Galaxy. That's gone this season. And next season we have to put that right, and hopefully we'll win something."

An unusual blanket of fog surrounded the Home Depot Center on the morning of the Galaxy's final game of the 2008 season. It was an apt metaphor for a franchise that had lost its way, enveloped in a cloud of confusion and uncertainty and clashing egos after the arrival of David Beckham. Aside from the fog, though, the not-so-grand finale was par for the course in 2008. The Galaxy's offense produced two more goals, including Landon Donovan's career-high twentieth of the season. The defense was terrible, squandering an early lead and causing the home fans to boo on Fan Appreciation Day. And in the end, the Galaxy didn't win, managing nothing more than a 2–2 tie against another poor team that had failed to make the playoffs.

Yet no matter how badly the Galaxy had played in 2008, there was another constant that was true again that day. The stadium was sold out, the Galaxy punched the cash register, and whenever Beckham was around you could hear the same girlish squeals of delight. In the sixty-fifth minute, a strange thing happened: The Galaxy won three corner kicks in a row. Each time, Beckham ran over to take the kick. Each time, the squeals resumed and the camera flashes fired and the rhythmic claps commenced.

Each time, the message of the adoring crowd was clear: *You're a star, you're a star, you're a star.*

CHAPTER 17

COMMITMENT ISSUES

I n July 2008, on the day before 46,754 fans watched him play against the New York Red Bulls at Giants Stadium, David Beckham unwittingly revealed his new, less ambitious goals for the Beckham Experiment. Of all those spectators, I asked Beckham, did he think more of them were coming to see him because of his celebrity or because of his soccer? "I don't care," Beckham replied, "as long as they're here and as long as they're watching the game, whether it's because I'm a celebrity or whether it's because they want to watch the Galaxy play or whether they just want to see a soccer game." On the surface, it seemed like a reasonable answer. In some ways, butts in seats was the name of the game for Major League Soccer, and drawing nearly 50,000 fans was far more preferable to Beckham than the usual 13,500 that showed up for Red Bulls games.

But if they were only there for Beckham's celebrity, how much did it really help MLS and American soccer in the long run? If Beckham's primary goal was to raise the level of the sport and create new fans in the United States, shouldn't he have wanted the spectators to be there for the soccer—and not just for his celebrity? Shouldn't he have hoped that the crowds for New York and other MLS teams wouldn't shrink back to their usual niche-sport size the week after his once-a-year visit? Where was the sports legacy in that?

By the start of 2009, it was fair to ask: Did America care about David Beckham? The answer depended on which Beckham you were talking about. Ever since his Simon Fuller–choreographed arrival in July 2007, Beckham and his wife had been successful A-list celebrities, fixtures in the Hollywood media. Fuller had made a science of packaging pop stars, and his formula had worked to perfection with Beckham the celebrity, catapulting the world's most famous athlete to even higher levels of recognition. Indeed, Beckham was rated the seventh-most-popular athlete among U.S. teenagers (ahead of Kevin Garnett, Tom Brady, and Derek Jeter) in a summer 2008 Tru*Scores survey, a sort of Q rating for athletes. The reason: While Beckham was far down the list when it came to teenage boys, he had by far the highest score among teenage *girls*. Likewise, Beckham was named "Choice Male Athlete" at the 2008 Teen Choice Awards, beating out Tiger Woods, Eli Manning, Kobe Bryant, and LeBron James. The award was meaningless, of course, except as a way to measure Beckham's popularity among young Americans, which was undeniable.

But did any of it have to do with the sport of soccer? The vast majority of the Americans who had embraced Beckham the Celebrity didn't know (or didn't care) that the Galaxy had tied for the worst record in MLS in 2008. That was probably good for Beckham in some ways, insulating him from the Galaxy's ineptitude, but it was also evidence that his celebrity wasn't converting large numbers of mainstream Yanks into MLS fans. Beckham was still a significant attendance draw in 2008—the Galaxy averaged 28,132 fans per game on the road, nearly 10,000 more than any other MLS team—and the league's average attendance increased slightly (by 6.9 percent to 16,459) in the two years since his arrival. But TV ratings are always the best measure of national impact, and Beckham did nothing to improve ESPN2's minuscule ratings for MLS games in 2008, drawing the same 0.2 rating for his Galaxy games that the network got for its non-Beckham MLS broadcasts. In 2007, Beckham's games had at least drawn a 0.3 rating compared to the 0.2 that ESPN2 got for non-Beckham games. So low was the viewership that ESPN yanked MLS's Thursday-night slot for the 2009 season and would be showing games on a variety of days instead.

From a business perspective, Beckham had been an unqualified success for the Galaxy and MLS. By the spring of 2009, 350,000 official Beckham Galaxy jerseys had been sold. The Galaxy's average attendance at the HDC in 2008 was 26,009, up 24.9 percent from 2006, even though the team had raised average ticket prices from $21.50 to $32. What's more, Beckham's arrival had increased the Galaxy's sponsorship revenue by $6 million in 2007 alone, and the number of people worldwide who were now aware of Major League Soccer and the Los Angeles Galaxy had multiplied dramatically. "The signing of David Beckham remains one of the most important things this league has ever done," MLS commissioner Don Garber argued in late 2008. "We are far more recognized, far more credible, and far more popular than we ever were."

Maybe so, but it was also true that Beckham's main accomplishment in MLS had been signing with the league, and that he had achieved next to nothing concrete for the Galaxy since his arrival in July 2007 other than simply showing up. Beckham had not come close to having "a greater impact on soccer in America than any athlete has ever had on a sport globally"—the proclamation that Tim Leiweke had made upon his signing in 2007, a claim that now seemed laughable after Beckham's injury-plagued 2007, his loss-filled 2008, and a grand total of zero playoff appearances by the dreadful Beckham-era Galaxy. Astonishingly, the Galaxy's winning percentage in Beckham's first two seasons was better in the twenty-two games Beckham had *missed* (.477) than in the thirty-two games he had played (.406).

When I asked Beckham at the end of the 2008 season to look back on his first two years with the Galaxy, the only success he could point to had taken place away from the field. "I've enjoyed the experience of obviously being in the MLS and being the ambassador of the MLS," Beckham said. "I've enjoyed that part. I've enjoyed seeing the success off the pitch with the game, with the attendance, with the new buyers coming into the league and the new teams starting up and the new stadiums coming into the league as well. The frustrating part has obviously been the Galaxy's performances and the Galaxy's success, because we haven't had any. But it's something that we need to work on. I think everybody knows that behind the scenes. I think now we've got a manager obviously with Bruce and his staff behind him that obviously knows the league, and we need some stability in this team now. If we get that stability and we get the team right, then hopefully the success will come." Despite Beckham's constant talk of the Galaxy needing stability, the question as he left for Milan was simple: Would he practice what he preached?

By now, though, Beckham was acutely aware that his credibility as a soccer player was nearing an all-time low in relation to his fame as a celebrity. The Beckham sweet spot was dangerously out of whack. That would have been a concern even if Beckham had won championships with the Galaxy, considering the challenges of drawing attention to soccer in America, but L.A.'s spectacular failures and Beckham's own middling play had created the need for Beckham to reestablish his bona fides as a sportsman and keep himself in contention for a spot on England's 2010 World Cup team. The loan to AC Milan—and the potential for a full-fledged transfer—addressed those needs, but it was also a repudiation of Simon Fuller's original strategy for the Beckham Experiment. Fuller may have known how to package celebrities, but he had wildly overestimated his acumen in the world of sports. "Shoot for the stars, and if you don't hit them it was fun trying," Fuller had said in 2007 on the eve of Beckham's arrival. But the reality had been clear for months: Beckham wasn't having any fun.

No matter what would happen in 2009 and beyond, the lessons from the first two years of the Beckham Experiment were numerous. For all of its advances since 1996, Major League Soccer didn't appear ready yet for a player of Beckham's stature. The same cost-saving rules that had kept the league afloat created too great a disparity between the haves and the have-nots, between the players earning $12,900 and Beckham's $50 million annual income. The impact was obvious on and off the field. "We created this SuperClub, and yet in MLS we're not allowed to have the mechanisms that fuel and facilitate a SuperClub around the world," said Alexi Lalas, who had landed a job with ESPN for the 2009 season. "It would be wonderful to see what the Galaxy could do if all the restraints were taken away. Unfortunately, it might be good for the Galaxy, but it might not be good for the league or the sport."

By the end of 2008, moreover, Tim Leiweke had concluded that handing the keys of your sports franchise to the star athlete and his advisers was a recipe for disaster. "We're the owners, and we're gonna act like it," Leiweke promised, but learning that lesson had been painful, not just for the Galaxy but for MLS. "This is history that's being written as we're going," said Garber. "This was the first time we had a huge megastar come into the league, and managing that process is difficult. How do we go about hiring the next high-profile star from another country? How do we package our relationship with them? How do we involve their managers and their close associates? This is the first time we've had it, and we've got to adapt and figure out ways not to let this situation happen again."

It was tempting to play the what-if game. What if Beckham hadn't been injured in 2007 at the height of his popularity in America? What if the Galaxy front office had put together a better team around Beckham and Landon Donovan? What if the Galaxy had won big instead of turning into a fiasco on the field? In the end, that was the biggest lesson of the first two years of the Beckham Experiment: Its success or failure had to be measured in wins and losses. We love sports because we don't know what will happen. The results aren't preordained or controlled. They can't be managed like the Galaxy's business side or Hollywood's celebrity star-making machine. As Sir Alex Ferguson liked to say: *You can't escape the field*. "David can sell as many T-shirts as he wants, but at the end of the day we're all judged by what happens on the field," said Chris Klein. "So I'd say to this point the Beckham Experiment is failing."

By hiring Bruce Arena to overhaul the Galaxy, though, Leiweke was convinced that he had given the Beckham Experiment a chance to do more than just make money for everyone involved. "I've always said the success of David Beckham will depend on what happens not just off the pitch but on the pitch," argued Leiweke in late 2008. "If we don't win, this will not be a success story. I think we're in the middle of this book, maybe not quite to the middle yet, and this has not been a success. We need to win. But there's a long way to go before we finish the story."

Or was there?

From the moment David Beckham donned the famous red and black stripes of AC Milan in January 2009, he looked like a completely different player from the one who'd gone 70 percent, sullen and out of shape, during the last half of the Galaxy's 2008 season. This Beckham was fully fit, buzzing up and down the right flank like the Goldenballs of old. This Beckham saved his emotional outbursts for his teammates, not just the referees, jumping on the back of teenage phenom Alexandre Pato after feeding him a perfect pass for a goal. This Beckham cracked Milan's starting lineup from the start, defying expectations, and produced two goals and two assists in his first five games for the Rossoneri—one of the strikes coming on a trademark bending free kick that turned the clock back by a decade.

It was only the latest unexpected career renaissance for the thirty-three-year-old Beckham, and on February 4, after a friendly in Scotland against Glasgow Rangers, Beckham made his desire public for the first time: He wanted to stay in Milan indefinitely. "Playing for Milan has been an incredible experience for me, better than I thought it would be," he told reporters. "I've been welcomed into the team incredibly well, I've been made to feel at home, and it has made me want to stay. Confidence-wise and physical-wise, this has been one of the best things to happen to me."

Beckham's change of heart contradicted everything he had told his Galaxy teammates and the media the previous October about his commitment to Los Angeles and Major League Soccer, but those statements were ancient history in the era of the twenty-four-hour news cycle. Beckham's priorities were clear: The England coaching staff had told him he needed to be playing at a higher level in Europe to be considered for the national team and the chance to play in the 2010 World Cup. Appealing to patriotism was a staple of the Beckham/19 Entertainment playbook, but it wasn't the only reason for his desire to shut down the Beckham Experiment. The Beckham sweet spot was also dangerously unbalanced, and he needed to restore his soccer credibility to revive the Beckham Brand. (Pepsi, one of Beckham's most lucrative endorsements, had ended the partnership in December 2008.)

Yet one stumbling block remained: AC Milan had to reach an agreement with the Galaxy and MLS on a transfer fee to buy out the last guaranteed year of Beckham's MLS contract (which had an opt-out clause allowing Beckham to walk away from the final two years as a free agent after the 2009 season). Thus began a month-long global saga in which executives for Milan, MLS, and Los Angeles postured in the media while Beckham issued increasingly strident avowals reiterating his wish to stay in Milan, saying it would be "good news" if he could depart a league that was "five, ten, fifteen years" from being on a level anywhere near that of Europe. Once Beckham announced he wanted to stay in Milan, the European media and AC Milan vice president Adriano Galliani treated the move as inevitable, but those who jumped to conclusions didn't know the hardball tactics of Tim Leiweke or, for that matter, the vast disparity between Beckham's singular value to the Galaxy (in ticket sales, sponsorships, and merchandising) and his value to Milan on the international transfer market. The Galaxy wanted in excess of $10 million, but Milan's initial offer for Beckham was a paltry $3 million, Leiweke said, "a ridiculous offer to which I replied no in a few seconds."

By the end of the episode, nobody's credibility was left unscathed. Beckham had turned his back on his promises to the Galaxy. Leiweke and MLS commissioner Don Garber had announced negotiations were over, case closed, only to reopen talks with Milan. And Galliani had proclaimed that Milan would not increase its $3 million bid, only to do exactly that. Finally, on March 8, one day before Beckham was required to return to the Galaxy, the parties reached a deal. Beckham would extend his loan with AC Milan until the end of the 2008–09 Serie A season, then rejoin the Galaxy halfway through the MLS regular season, making his debut on July 16 at Giants Stadium against the New York Red Bulls.

Beckham would finish the 2009 season with the Galaxy, but what happened next remained to be seen. In a major change to his old deal, Beckham could no longer opt out of the final two years of his MLS contract for free; instead, he and/or Milan would have to pay a "significant" buyout, Garber said. For his part, Beckham was clear that he planned on rejoining AC Milan in January 2010 if he had any chance of competing in the 2010 World Cup. "I need to play my football in Europe to give myself a chance of being involved in that World Cup," Beckham told ESPN. "That will happen up till then, and afterward then we'll see." Sources close to Beckham said the most likely scenario involved working out a deal that would allow Beckham to return to the Galaxy after the 2010 World Cup and finish out his playing days in America.

Ultimately, the Beckham Experiment was more tarnished than ever, but it remained on life support because each side made concessions to get what it wanted. Beckham had to give up some of his own salary, agree to new buyout conditions, and commit himself to a punishing schedule with three teams (Milan, the Galaxy, and England), but he got to continue with Milan and increase his chances of playing in the World

Cup. Milan had to pay the Galaxy more than it wanted for Beckham's 2009 loan, but keeping Beckham for the rest of the season would help the team qualify for the Champions League and enhance its own bottom line through jersey sales. As for the Galaxy, it had to play the first half of the '09 season without its top drawing card, but in return it received a multimillion-dollar payment from Milan and Beckham, the chance for another payday to buy Beckham out of his contract after 2009, a lucrative exhibition game against AC Milan on July 19 (in Beckham's return to the HDC), and at least a half-season for Beckham to achieve some success on the field with the Galaxy. After the deal was announced, Leiweke sounded less like a sports executive than a Mafia don. "After some conversations between us and David and his folks, David began to understand that he didn't want to leave the league either," Leiweke told the *Los Angeles Times*.

Maybe, maybe not. Alexi Lalas couldn't help but muster a wry laugh as he followed the circus from his home in Southern California. He thought Beckham had done everything possible to show that he wanted out of MLS, and Lalas was convinced that Galaxy fans—true Galaxy fans—would greet him with boos and whistles at the HDC in July. "Galaxy fans want to feel that their players want to be here, and David has gone out of his way to make very, very clear that he *doesn't* want to be here," Lalas said. "I don't think it's too much to ask from your players that they actually want to play for the club."

Indeed, plenty of questions remained. Would Beckham be counting down the days until he could say good-bye to the Galaxy? Would he simply go through the motions on the field? Would he be booed by the home fans upon his return? "I'm sure I will now after Alexi's comments," Beckham cracked to ESPN, revealing only a hint of the antipathy that had developed between them. "Maybe he'll be one of them in the stands doing it." Most important, considering the Galaxy was clearly his No. 3 priority behind England and AC Milan, did Beckham even care about American soccer and the once-lofty goals of the Beckham Experiment anymore? It was as if Beckham felt the more he *said* he was dedicated, the more he could magically make it so, his actions and previous statements to the contrary. In a ten-minute interview with ESPN, Beckham mentioned no fewer than twelve times that he was "committed" to the Galaxy and MLS, even though he was speaking in an AC Milan warm-up from a training field 6,000 miles from Los Angeles on the eve of the new MLS season.

"I'm committed to the Galaxy and my teammates there," Beckham said, "but at the moment I need to play my football here." It was the ultimate example of self-serving doublespeak. In yet another unwittingly revealing statement, Beckham had joined John Kerry ("I actually did vote for the $87 billion before I voted against it") in the Twisted Logic Hall of Fame.

Two hundred miles to the north, in a well-appointed apartment in Munich, Landon Donovan was on the phone with Galaxy coach Bruce Arena. Donovan's own two-month off-season loan to Bayern Munich was coming to an end, and while Donovan had enjoyed some good moments in Bavaria, there hadn't been enough of them for Germany's most storied team to meet MLS's eight-figure transfer-fee demand and make Donovan's European dream a reality. Donovan was coming home to the Galaxy for the 2009 season, and now Arena was on the line with a proposition. "I'm leaning," Arena told him, "toward making you the captain."

Donovan felt a sudden surge of . . . what, exactly? Pride? Relief? Responsibility? Maybe it was all three, he thought. Aside from his wife, nobody, not even Arena, knew how much he had gone through as the Galaxy had lost its way during the Beckham Era. Two seasons after being forced to give up the captaincy to Beckham, one season after watching Captain Galaxy shirk the leadership role that Beckham's own handlers had sought, Donovan had the armband back. Arena made the news public upon Donovan's return to California, and Tim Leiweke added that the Galaxy was now Donovan's team, its long-term future centered around the twenty-six-year-old American star. Even when Beckham returned in July, he would not regain the captaincy.

"It's a big responsibility, but it's something I want," Donovan said. "The reality is that I will play and act a certain way regardless of whether I have the armband or not. But having the armband gives me a little more power to push across things to the team. Last year, too often I took a backseat in hopes that David would do those things instead of just saying things that I needed to say or doing things that needed to be done."

Donovan wasn't sure if he wanted to try his hand in Europe again someday, but he knew that he cared about the Galaxy, knew the road back from MLS laughingstock to the top of the standings would not be easy or immediate. Now it was his job to make sure his teammates—*all* his teammates—were as fully invested in the Galaxy as he was. When Beckham rejoined the team in July, he would encounter a new captain who planned on finally confronting Beckham about the Englishman's commitment issues. All Donovan had ever wanted from Beckham was his unwavering dedication to the Galaxy, and he had been furious with Beckham over the way he distanced himself from the team during the second half of 2008. "Last year I just held things in and didn't let David know how I felt," Donovan said. "There needs to be some clarity. Not that it has to be a bad conversation. I just want to be up-front with David about all this. Whatever he takes from it is up to him, but I feel it's important that things are said and are out in the open."

No matter how many times Beckham paid lip service to his commitment, Donovan felt, his actions continued to speak otherwise. How could Beckham talk about the Galaxy needing stability to move forward and then create so much *in*stability? From a personal perspective, Donovan argued, he felt bad for Beckham since he so clearly wanted to be with Milan full-time instead of having to return to Los Angeles. But from the Galaxy's point of view, Donovan thought another year of the will-he-or-won't-he Beckham soap opera was the last thing the team needed. "I think it's really sad," Donovan said, "because we're trying to build a team here that can compete, and we're kind of getting held back by this situation. We want to keep adding pieces and getting better and have some kind of resolution to all this, and now it seems like it's just going to linger for another year. From that standpoint, it's very disappointing."

And yet, Donovan felt, there was still a faint glimmer of hope in the Beckham Experiment. Though Donovan saw little chance that Beckham would return to the Galaxy after 2009, the new Galaxy captain decided there was no purpose in anyone counting down the days until Beckham's departure. "Whether David likes it or not, whether the situation is ideal or not, the fact is he's going to be back in July, and he's still a damn good player," Donovan said. "Even if he only plays six or seven games, he might be able to help us."

Maybe, maybe not. Whenever anyone asked Beckham if he had made a difference in American soccer, he was quick to mention the jersey sales, the attendance increases, and the unprecedented global attention that his presence had brought to the Los Angeles Galaxy and Major League Soccer. All true. From a financial perspective, the Beckham Experiment had been a runaway success, and the agreement that brought Beckham back to the Galaxy in 2009 (albeit against his wishes) was one more example. Once again, the Galaxy had pulled off a shrewd business deal. Once again, Beckham's fame and celebrity had generated mountains of international media coverage. And once again, it was hard to envision how the move would pay off for the Galaxy on the field itself.

Three seasons into Beckham's American adventure, the same question remained: Would it ever be about the soccer?

AFTERWORD TO THE PAPERBACK EDITION

The Los Angeles Galaxy played a game on July 11, 2009—a 1–0 win against archrival Chivas USA—but that was hardly the most compelling Hollywood showdown of the day. A 5,000-word first excerpt of this book had appeared in *Sports Illustrated* on July 1, ten days before David Beckham was set to return from Europe and rejoin the Galaxy, and it aired some of Landon Donovan's most explosive criticisms: that Beckham was a poor captain, that he wasn't fully committed to the Galaxy, and that he had become a bad teammate during the second half of the 2008 season.

Donovan's broadside set off a global media firestorm unlike anything Major League Soccer had seen since Beckham joined the league. Never before in Beckham's career had he been so harshly judged in public by another player, much less a current teammate. What's more, Donovan's words suddenly carried more weight than they would have only a few months before: He was coming off a sterling performance at the Confederations Cup in South Africa, where he led the United States to an upset of world number-one Spain (its first loss in thirty-five games) and a hard-fought 3–2 defeat to Brazil in the final. For all those reasons, Donovan's diatribe grabbed headlines not just in the U.S. and in England but everywhere from Spain to Singapore to Australia. Suddenly MLS had an epic internecine feud that rivaled the famous bust-up between Los Angeles Lakers teammates Kobe Bryant and Shaquille O'Neal. Would the result of this one be the same? Would Beckham or Donovan have to leave the Galaxy? Those were the questions hanging in the air that day.

The drama reached a climax just a few hours after Beckham landed in Los Angeles late on July 10. The next day, Beckham appeared at a community event promoting new soccer fields in El Segundo, California, with his former Real Madrid teammate Zinédine Zidane—a not-so-subtle reminder to the media of Beckham's standing in the soccer world. Then Beckham spoke to reporters for the first time since Donovan's comments had been published. "It's unprofessional, in my eyes," Beckham said. "In every soccer player's eyes throughout the world, it would be unprofessional to speak out about a teammate, especially in the press and not to your face. But I'm going to turn it on a positive spin because that's what this needs. But in seventeen years I have played with the biggest teams in the world and the biggest players, and not once have I been criticized for my professionalism. It's important to get this cleared up, and I will be speaking to Landon either this evening or over the next couple of days."

Beckham didn't suit up that night, but he did walk into the Galaxy locker room before the game and encounter Donovan. It was the first time the players had seen each other in eight months. They exchanged brief hellos, and Donovan felt a palpable awkwardness. "Obviously, it was uncomfortable for both of us," Donovan would say.

In the days since Donovan's comments had gone public, the American star had sent Beckham several text messages without ever receiving a response. Donovan had also sat down for interviews with ESPN and the *Los Angeles Times,* in which he apologized for voicing his opinions to a reporter before speaking directly to Beckham, but Donovan pointedly hadn't backed down from what he had said in the book.

Donovan felt badly about the timing of the excerpt's release, but he also thought his comments wouldn't be viewed as so controversial once people had read the entire book, which was set for publication later that week. "I don't think we should ever apologize for the way we feel," Donovan would explain. "However, I got caught up in the way I felt about it, as opposed to trying to figure out where those feelings were coming from. If I had taken the time during that year to really think about what was going on, to understand it from David's perspective, I wouldn't have said those things. I would have had a different outlook on all of it. But at the time I got caught up in all the emotions of it. . . . And some of the things I said I didn't even really mean."

Such as? "When I say he should have come in and done something monetarily for the guys, I don't really believe that. That's not his job. I just had these expectations of him that were unfair. I realized that he's a person just like everyone else."

A few minutes after he had showered and finished his postgame interviews, Donovan was sitting at his locker when Galaxy coach Bruce Arena came by. "Let's get this done," Arena told him. There would be no wasted time. The coach had already pulled Beckham into his office, surprising Donovan, who thought Arena would wait until at least the next day before bringing the two players together. Donovan followed Arena into his office, an austere, windowless space in the warren of rooms inside the Home Depot Center. Arena took a seat behind his desk. Beckham and Donovan sat on the other side. And then, for the next fifteen minutes, the healing process began.

"I did most of the talking," Donovan said. "In the simplest form, I apologized to David and he accepted it. It was pretty basic. There wasn't a whole lot that Bruce had to do. It felt good just to talk about it. I learned a lot, actually, from how David dealt with my apology, how he dealt with the whole situation, because if I put myself in his shoes I would have been really pissed off. He might have been mad, but he was a man and he accepted my apology. And he didn't hold it against me. Anytime before this year I wouldn't have been the same way. I probably wouldn't have accepted it, and I would have held a grudge."

When the meeting was over, Donovan felt as though a weight had been lifted from his shoulders. The relationship could be saved. "I would describe it as real from that point forward," Donovan would say. "We could talk openly and honestly. We could still argue and disagree on things, just like anyone else on the team, but when you have that basis of trust and understanding, then there aren't any issues." They would never be best friends. But the town would be big enough for the two of them after all.

In fact, the circumstances of Beckham's return set him up for another surprising comeback. Few athletes in modern sports had engineered remarkable comebacks more than once in their careers, and Beckham was one of them. A year after his red card at the 1998 World Cup made Beckham the most hated man in England, he recaptured his fans by helping lead Manchester United to an unprecedented Treble.

And after he'd been banished from Real Madrid and England in early 2007, Beckham somehow rallied to rejoin England and guide Madrid to the Spanish league title.

Now Beckham was at his lowest point in America, the subject of deserved criticism from his most important teammate for a lack of commitment, and this part-time Galaxy player had no choice but to respond in the only way that would earn back the respect of American soccer fans, who were savvier than he may have believed.

Just win, baby.

It certainly helped that Arena had put together a competitive Galaxy team in 2009, one that didn't need Beckham as a savior. L.A. was 5–3–9 when Beckham arrived, having won three straight games. Arena had brought in eighteen new players, including a defense anchored by useful veteran pickups (goalkeeper Donovan Ricketts and defender Gregg Berhalter) and smart draft picks (rookie defenders Omar Gonzalez and A. J. DeLaGarza). Beckham's absence during the season's first half forced the shorthanded Galaxy into what Arena called "survival mode." It wasn't always entertaining soccer—L.A. ground out eight ties in one nine-game stretch—but that foundation set the stage for a second-half surge once the Galaxy was at full strength.

During Beckham's first six weeks back with the team, though, he stood out less for his game-breaking passes than for his temper's short fuse. In Beckham's first home game at the HDC—a friendly on July 19 against AC Milan—the L.A. Riot Squad fan section hung a banner that read GO HOME FRAUD and booed Beckham, its own player, every time he touched the ball. As the teams left the field at halftime, Beckham charged toward the Riot Squad shouting epithets, attempted to climb a signboard, and pointed a finger at the jeering fans. When Beckham challenged one to come down on the field, Josh Paige, a twenty-eight-year-old video-game technician, jumped from eight feet onto the grass, where he was immediately nabbed by security guards and frog-marched out of the stadium.

"When David Beckham calls you out, you get on the field," Paige told the *New York Times*. "In hindsight, I wish I didn't stoop to his level.

I wish I was the bigger man." For his part, Beckham claimed, implausibly, that he was only inviting the fan to come shake his hand. The MLS league office didn't buy it, handing Beckham a $1,000 fine. In the Galaxy's next game at Kansas City, Beckham had another incident with a heckler, in which the Englishman exchanged angry words with the man and attempted to shake his hand before a throw-in during the middle of the game.

It was strange behavior by Beckham, who had kept his cool while enduring far worse treatment from fans in England after his '98 World Cup red card. Most observers expected that Beckham would embark on a charm offensive upon returning to America, using his charisma to win back the Galaxy fans who were upset that he had skipped nearly two-thirds of the MLS season. Instead, Beckham went the other way. He refused to apologize to Galaxy fans, calling the L.A. Riot Squad "a disgrace." He started wearing short-sleeved jerseys for the first time, showing off his hard-man tattoos. He got in the faces of his opponents after hard challenges like a man possessed.

Say hello to David Beckham, heel. The apotheosis of Beckham the Villain came against Seattle on August 15, when he drew his first MLS red card in the seventeenth minute on a reckless studs-up challenge against Peter Vagenas, his friend and former Galaxy teammate. Playing down a man, L.A. fell 2–0 at home and lost the suspended Beckham for the next game as well. It was an odd time for Galaxy fans, whose team was on a roll—the Seattle game was L.A.'s only league loss in a ten-game stretch—even though its most famous player was struggling on the field. In the Galaxy's first six league games following Beckham's return, he provided zero goals and just one assist despite playing in the central midfield.

If there was one moment that turned around Beckham's MLS season, it came on August 29 against Chivas USA. In the eightieth minute of a scoreless game on national television, the ball bounced toward Beckham after a throw-in near the Chivas penalty box. Beckham raced toward the ball and struck it with a piece of world-class skill, bouncing his shot off the ground, off the Chivas goalpost, and into the net. The sold-out crowd roared, including the L.A. Riot Squad, as the Galaxy finished off the 1–0 victory. Winning solves a lot of problems, and L.A.

won consistently down the stretch, beating San Jose 2–0 in the regular-season finale to go to 12–6–12 and earn the Western Conference's top seed in the MLS playoffs.

By any measure it was a remarkable turnaround, not just for the Galaxy (which had tied for the league's worst record in 2008) but for Beckham himself. Under Arena, the Beckham experiment was finally about the soccer, and it became clearer than ever that Beckham had a special connection on the field with Donovan, who was enjoying perhaps his finest year as a professional. Donovan's twelve goals and six assists helped earn him his first MLS MVP award, and it was a Beckham–Donovan connection that made the difference in the first round of the playoffs against Chivas. With the teams deadlocked on a 2–2 aggregate late in the second leg, Beckham unleashed a jaw-dropping forty-yard diagonal rainbow—the kind of pass that only Beckham would even try—that hit Donovan in mid-stride. The American passed to teammate Mike Magee, who drew the penalty that Donovan would convert for the decisive goal.

There was more of the same in the one-game Western Conference final against Houston the following week. The Galaxy and Dynamo were scoreless until extra-time, when Berhalter bundled in the game's first goal off a scramble in the box following a Beckham free kick. Donovan sealed the 2–0 victory with a penalty kick, and the lasting image from the night was Donovan and Beckham celebrating together, arms around each other's shoulders, gleefully commemorating the Galaxy's first trip to MLS's championship game since 2005. The controversy from July was a distant memory. "To their credit, they've dealt with it in a professional way," said teammate Chris Klein, who was close to both Beckham and Donovan. "The way they've played on the field takes care of a lot of other issues that could be hanging out there. They've both been fantastic."

The fourteenth MLS Cup final—the Galaxy versus surprise finalist Real Salt Lake—was set for November 22 in Seattle, where the first-year Sounders had been the other big success story in MLS, averaging more than 30,000 fans a game and turning Seattle into Soccer City, USA. Two days before the game, Donovan retreated to a quiet downtown hotel room and pondered how far he and Beckham had come since the book's release in July.

"There's mutual respect finally, which helps," Donovan said. "This would make a great movie. In my opinion [the lessons] would be much more useful for people who followed this than if David had come in his first year and we'd won the last three MLS championships. As everybody knows, life doesn't happen that way always. This is more a symbol of what life is. You go through hard times, we all have issues, but at the end if your intentions are good, if you try to be better people, then good things can happen. It's an incredible story."

Donovan had always been more reflective than most professional athletes, but now the Galaxy captain was entering territory that was new even for him. "The key element in all this was communicating," he explained. "Once you let people know how things are affecting you, without sounding too Dr. Phil, it's therapy. There's such a taboo on psychiatrists and therapy in sports because it's a macho world, but those things are a big part of making a team cohesive. I'm a huge believer in therapy. What person doesn't benefit from talking about their problems and dissecting them? Heaven forbid when Joe Blow who works at the office has an issue. Nobody makes fun of him for being depressed. But in the sports world it's kind of unacceptable to have any kind of personality issues. That's funny to me. Hopefully over time it will change."

It had been a transformative year for Donovan, and not just on the soccer field. In July came the announcement that he and his wife, Bianca, had separated. By now, lawyers were arranging their divorce, and yet Donovan emphasized their split was amicable. ("I wouldn't be anywhere close to where I am today without her.") Meanwhile, after years of silence, Donovan had reconnected with his father, Tim, who'd sent him a picture of the 1980 U.S. Olympic hockey team on the day the U.S. had upset Spain at the Confederations Cup. Tim Donovan would be in Seattle attending the final. "My family are my roots," said Landon. "I had kind of drifted from the important things in my life: my close friends, my family. Getting back to them grounds me. I need that."

At one point Arena opened the room's door to crack that Donovan was speaking only for a new book chapter, not an entirely new book.

Donovan laughed. Arena had earned every bit of his MLS Coach of the Year award, not just for turning around the Galaxy on the field, but for the way he had handled the Beckham–Donovan crisis in July. Lesser coaches would have let the team be ripped apart. The way Arena saw things, 80 percent of coaching was psychological. There was only so much you could do tactically on a basketball court or a football field or a soccer field. Coaching, Arena felt, was more about man management and maximizing your talent.

Besides, Arena argued, Beckham and Donovan weren't chronic malcontents. "It wasn't like we had two bad people we were dealing with," Arena said. "I could throw out a bunch of names of NBA or NFL players where if I was in that situation I don't think anyone could solve those problems with the egos and the quality of the characters of some of those players. But these two guys are good guys, and whatever happened, happened."

Yet there would be one more plot twist in what many had expected to be the Galaxy's coronation atop MLS. Heavily favored L.A. went up 1–0 in the first half against Salt Lake in the final, Donovan taking a pass from Beckham on the break and delivering an inch-perfect cross to Magee for the lead. But then, before 46,011 fans at Seattle's Qwest Field, the game slowed from its frenetic pace, and RSL's Robbie Findley scored an opportunistic equalizer midway through the second half. After 120 minutes of deadlocked soccer, it was on to penalties. Beckham, who hadn't taken a penalty since missing one in the 2004 European Championship for England, confidently converted for the Galaxy in round one, and the teams were even at 2–2 after three rounds when Donovan stepped to the penalty spot.

Donovan's career conversion rate for spot kicks was remarkable: 91 percent in MLS, the best in league history and far above the all-time league average of 76 percent. Only once had he ever failed to connect on a penalty for the U.S. national team. His only important penalty failure that anyone could remember had come in the 2007 Superliga final against Pachuca. Now Donovan faced RSL goalie Nick Rimando, went through his usual pre-kick ritual, and advanced toward the ball. Later, Donovan would wonder if fatigue had set in or his technique had failed him. Whatever the reason, he launched his kick high over the crossbar, bringing back memories of Roberto Baggio's ill-fated penalty in the 1994 World Cup final.

Salt Lake won the championship in the seventh round, after Rimando had saved Edson Buddle's spot kick, but all anyone could talk about afterward was Donovan's miss. Beckham was the first person to approach him on the field and offer a pat on the back. "I know he had compassion because he's been in that situation," Donovan said. "He said a lot to me throughout that night. It's a crappy feeling, but it's good to know that your teammates care about you."

The 2009 Galaxy season didn't have a storybook ending, didn't provide the money-shot image of Donovan raising the championship trophy and riding around the stadium on Beckham's shoulders. But it did restore Beckham's credibility in America as an athlete, not just some British pretty boy who appears in celebrity magazines. That was no small achievement. If Beckham had been unaware of the magnitude of the challenges facing him when he arrived in Los Angeles in 2007, he now knew for sure that making soccer matter in the U.S. on a daily basis was hard work, a process that would take years, perhaps decades. While there would be no lightning in a bottle, there would be victories along the way. The Galaxy's resurgence was the major one, but there were others too. Television ratings in the 2009 postseason were up: the Western Conference final drew a 0.5 rating on ESPN2, the channel's highest ever for a playoff game, while the MLS Cup final got a 0.9 on ESPN, an 18 percent improvement over the previous year on ABC.

Yet no single development was more surprising than the change in the relationship between Beckham and Donovan. By the end of the season, Donovan's criticisms of Beckham were viewed as a catalyst for the positive changes inside the team. "It was the ultimate form of public therapy," said Alexi Lalas. "It forced the Galaxy and the individual players to look at their relationships and communicate." Maintaining relationships in the small world of American soccer was important, not least because you never knew when you might work with someone again. As fate would have it, ESPN's analysts for the 2010 World Cup would include Lalas and Ruud Gullit, the same men who had clashed so bitterly while running the Galaxy until losing their jobs in August 2008. And, sure enough, the U.S. and Donovan had drawn England and Beckham for their first game in South Africa. It was a dream matchup, the kind that was almost guaranteed to draw the highest television ratings in the history of U.S. soccer.

And then, for Beckham, it all fell apart.

The injury didn't look like much. In the waning moments of a run-of-the-mill Serie A victory for AC Milan on March 14, 2010, Beckham pulled up lame over the ball, even though there were no defenders close to him. Non-contact injuries are almost always serious, however, and as Beckham was stretchered off the field in tears, it became clear that he had suffered major damage. Within an hour came the verdict: He had ruptured his left Achilles tendon. Beckham would not be able to compete in the 2010 World Cup, which would have been his fourth, an unprecedented feat for an England player.

It was a crushing blow for Beckham, who had put himself through a punishing schedule by playing for thirteen of the previous fifteen months, shuttling between three teams (Milan, England, and the Galaxy) in an attempt to satisfy his paymasters while fulfilling the mandate of England coach Fabio Capello that he play at the highest level in order to be considered for the World Cup team. If you stripped away the glitz of the Beckham Brand, Beckham himself was a player's player, and his dream of taking the field in South Africa was always genuine, so much so that he was willing to subject himself to weeks in Milan away from his family, to dip into his own pocket for his loan deal, to throw his thirty-four-year-old body headlong into demands that, ultimately, it could not withstand.

Beckham probably would not have started for England at the World Cup. But he almost certainly would have been a regular late-game substitute, a wily veteran who could still change a game with a few well-placed crosses into the box or a swerving free kick still considered among the world's best. By all accounts, Beckham was also a useful presence in the England locker room, no small attribute on a team racked by leadership issues. It was impossible to escape the talk of Beckham's ankle in London on the day after his injury. THE END OF THE WORLD blared one tabloid headline.

But it wasn't just news in England. In Los Angeles, Donovan had returned that day from his successful ten-week loan to Everton in the English Premier League. That night he called Galaxy coach Bruce Arena to ask about the next day's practice. As soon as Arena spoke, Donovan could tell something was wrong.

"Did you hear about David?" Arena asked. Donovan hadn't. As soon as the coach informed him, Donovan's heart sank. "It's just sad for David," Donovan said. "We know everything he's done and all the work he's put in and all the sacrifices he's made to even give himself a chance. And literally in one second that's all out the window now."

The day after his injury, Beckham had surgery in Finland to repair his ankle; his surgeon said that Beckham could return as soon as September to the Galaxy if everything went well with his rehabilitation. While the Galaxy supported Beckham publicly, it was also another case in which he had put the team toward the bottom of his priority list, another case in which a serious injury suffered in Europe would have a significant impact on the Galaxy's season. It was no coincidence that the Galaxy had not been profitable in 2009, due partly to Beckham's lengthy absence. (By the time Beckham was set to finish his five-year MLS contract at the end of 2011, he would likely have played only two full seasons, 2008 and 2011.) The Galaxy knew it would miss Beckham on the field as well in 2010. "The immediate future is that we're not as good a team without him," said Donovan. "We're missing what I would say is our most talented football player and somebody who gives us a dimension that nobody in the world can give you. From Bruce's standpoint, you've got a guy that's a Designated Player and counts a lot against your salary cap that you can't use. But the overwhelming feeling is just being sad for him."

When Beckham and Donovan exchanged text messages now, it was to congratulate each other, communicate about the Galaxy, or exchange good-natured trash talk about the U.S. and England national teams. Both men had worked to rebuild the relationship. The Beckham experiment was finally about the soccer, but the story of Beckham and Donovan had become about much more than that. It was a textbook case of conflict resolution. "To me it's not only a sporting issue, it's a lesson in life," said Arena. "It's really interesting. In all of this stuff it's about people and how they work together, whether it's on a soccer field or in a workplace.

"They got their workplace right."

ACKNOWLEDGMENTS

There are many people to thank. One is Mary Choteborsky, my editor at Crown, who supported this project with the same conviction and intensity that she displays on the soccer field. Her encouragement was unwavering, even when a certain player's injuries forced me to spend a year longer than planned on the reporting trail. Another is Chris Parris-Lamb, a dynamite agent whose enthusiasm for ideas, sports, and good writing is contagious. Special thanks also go to Terry McDonell, the editor of the Sports Illustrated Group, who generously granted me a leave of absence from *SI* to move to South Africa for seven months and write this book.

This project would not have been possible without the participation of the Los Angeles Galaxy. None of us knew how the Beckham Experiment would fare, but several members of the Galaxy organization agreed to participate and, to their credit, continued despite diminishing returns on the field. I especially appreciated the candor and insight of Landon Donovan, Alexi Lalas, Alan Gordon, Chris Klein, Greg Vanney, Tim Leiweke, Frank Yallop, Peter Vagenas, Edson Buddle, Kyle Martino, Gavin Glinton, Kyle Veris, Chris Albright, Joe Cannon, and Dave Sarachan. I would also like to thank Galaxy press officers Justin Pearson, Patrick Donnelly, and Jaime Cárdenas, as well as Michael Roth and Glenn Lehrman.

From the beginning, it was important to me that this book remained an independent account, neither "authorized" nor "unauthorized," a fair-minded chronicle of the Beckham Experiment's successes and failures that wasn't subject to the approval of David Beckham's management team. In exchange for one-on-one access to Beckham, many media outlets are willing to give Beckham's handlers approval over everything from interview questions to the images used to the story itself. In my own private interviews with Beckham over the years, *Sports Illustrated* has never agreed to such constraints. I have always had a solid working relationship with Beckham, have interviewed him more than any other American journalist, and material from those interviews appears throughout this book. Our arrangement for *The Beckham Experiment* was straightforward: Although Beckham would not do one-on-one interviews specifically for the book, he was available to the media before and after games—twice a week, in other words, or far more accessible than at any point in his European career. I know it wasn't always fun for him, but that access was appreciated.

This is my first book, and it would not exist were it not for the people who helped me make a career out of writing: Bambi Wulf, Gloria Emerson, Bill Colson, Peter Carry, Martin A. Dale, David Remnick, Landon Y. Jones, Gene Miller, Carlos Forment, Judy Barnes, Jane McCue, Jack Liles, Nora Pinkston, and Judy Dunseth. I am also indebted to the writers, editors, and photographers of *Sports Illustrated*, past and present, especially Jon Wertheim, Alex Wolff, Steve Rushin, Scott Price, Gabriele Marcotti, George Dohrmann, Simon Bruty, Seth Davis, Luke Winn, Hank Hersch, Aimee Crawford, Mark Mravic, Greg Kelly, Craig Neff, Mike Bevans, Rob Fleder, Chris Hunt, B. J. Schecter, Jonah Freedman, Gabe Miller, Mark Bechtel, Chris Stone, Dick Friedman, Sandy Rosenbush, and Albert Lin. This book is also dedicated to the memory of two soccer fans, Sandra Magalhaes and Mike Penner. My deepest appreciation also goes to David Hirshey and David Gernert.

My parents, Helen and David Wahl, gave me a love for sports and the freedom to pursue whatever I wished, and my brother, Eric Wahl, has always been one of my staunchest supporters.

My wife, Céline Gounder, is an everlasting source of inspiration and strength whose determination to save lives in Africa and elsewhere blows me away. (At least one of us has a serious job.) It wasn't easy to live in Baltimore and have your husband covering a team in Los Angeles. She understood.

Finally, a warm three-part handshake to the staff of the Lulu coffee shop at Johannesburg's Melrose Arch: Gift, Noble, Kelvin, Muzi, Zoro, Mpho, Harrison, Shark, Vuyisile, and Professor. After all that coffee, the book got done. See you at the World Cup.

INDEX

ABOUT THE AUTHOR

In thirteen years at *Sports Illustrated*, senior writer GRANT WAHL has written thirty-three cover stories and more than two hundred articles while covering five World Cups, three Olympics, and twelve NCAA basketball tournaments. Wahl's writing for *SI* includes coverage of college basketball and soccer, investigative reporting, and features on a variety of topics.

Wahl began his career as an intern with the *Miami Herald* in 1996. He first won critical acclaim for his work (with L. Jon Wertheim) on the 1998 *SI* cover story "Where's Daddy?," which documented the staggering number of illegitimate children born to professional athletes. Wahl has also won four Magazine Story of the Year awards given by the U.S. Basketball Writers Association. *The Beckham Experiment* is his first book.

Wahl grew up in Mission, Kansas, and attended Princeton University, where he graduated *magna cum laude* in politics in 1996. When he isn't traveling for *SI*, Wahl spends his time cooking, running, watching indie movies, and touring the world's food capitals with his wife, Céline. They live in Baltimore.